13

THE CULTURAL LIFE OF THE AUTOMOBILE

LLILAS Translations from Latin America Series

THE CULTURAL LIFE OF THE
Automobile
ROADS TO MODERNITY

GUILLERMO GIUCCI

Translated by Anne Mayagoitia and Debra Nagao

UNIVERSITY OF TEXAS PRESS, AUSTIN

TERESA LOZANO LONG INSTITUTE OF LATIN AMERICAN STUDIES

This translation was made possible by a generous subsidy from the Cultural Department of the Brazilian Ministry of Foreign Relations.

Originally published in Portuguese in 2004 as *A vida cultural do automóvel: Percursos da modernidade cinética*. Rio de Janeiro: Civilização Brasileira.

Published in Spanish in 2007 as *La vida cultural del automóvil: Rutas de la modernidad cinética*. Buenos Aires: Universidad Nacional de Quilmes.

LIBRARY OF CONGRESS CATALOGING-IN-PUBLICATION DATA

Giucci, Guillermo, 1954–
    [Vida cultural del automóvil. English]
    The cultural life of the automobile : roads to modernity / Guillermo Giucci.
        p.   cm. — (LLILAS translations from Latin America series)
    Includes bibliographical references and index.
    ISBN 978-0-292-72872-1 (cloth : alk. paper)
    ISBN 978-0-292-73784-6 (pbk. : alk. paper)
    ISBN 978-0-292-74359-5 (e-book)
    1. Automobiles—Social aspects. 2. Automobiles—History. 3. Automobiles—Social aspects—United States. 4. Automobiles—United States—History. I. Title.
    HE5611.G58 2012
    388.3'42—dc23   2011046437

For Gabriel and Leonardo Jaguaribe Giucci, the intrepid ones from Gargonza

CONTENTS

ACKNOWLEDGMENTS   ix

PREFACE   xi

1. Henry Ford: From Popular Inventor to Legend   1

2. Fordism and Cultural Circulation   20

3. The Transnational Object   51

4. Contradictions of Mobility   107

5. Mechanical Actors   141

Final Remarks: Kinetic Modernity and the Automobile   189

NOTES   195

BIBLIOGRAPHY   209

ILLUSTRATION CREDITS   223

INDEX   225

ACKNOWLEDGMENTS

My thanks to Maria Conceição Monteiro, Adrián Gorelik, Álvaro Casal Tatlock, Anahí Ballent, Barry Katz, Beatriz Jaguaribe, Claudio Lomnitz, Darío Henao Restreppo, Efraín Kristal, Enrique Rodríguez Larreta, Fernando Colla, Fernando Rabossi, Gonzalo Aguilar, Graciela Silvestri, Héctor Domínguez Ruvalcaba, Jeffrey Schnapp, João Cezar de Castro Rocha, Jorge Myers, Jorge Schwartz, Karl Erik Schollhammer, Maite Zubiaurre, Mary Pratt, Mauricio Tenorio Trillo, Pablo Rocca, Remo Ceserani, Sylvia Saítta, and Virginia Hagerty.

PREFACE

*The twentieth century has seen the birth of a vast array of machines—
computers, remote-guided airplanes, thermonuclear weapons—in which the
latent identity of the machine is ambiguous. An understanding of this identity may be achieved by studying the automobile.*   J. G. BALLARD

THE AUTOMOBILE was born in Europe at the end of the nineteenth
century and not long afterward wended its way through the entire world,
completely took over cities, and became a feature of daily life. Today a
restless civilization travels on a network of roads, streets, avenues, and
highways, its trademark, the individual on the go. In this book I examine the rise of automobility as a decisive element of kinetic modernity
between 1900 and 1940.

I define "kinetic modernity" as the part of modernity that is particularly linked to the idea of movement. *Kinetic* comes from the Greek and
means "of or resulting from motion." This adjective is used in physics to
refer to movement, as in the case of "kinetic energy." The dates 1900 to
1940 are not meant to indicate a beginning and an ending, but rather an
"emergence." This era is known as the Second Industrial Revolution, when
electric and combustion engines replaced human and animal muscle
power to a great extent.

Four technologies dominated history in the past century: automobiles, flying machines, electronic communication, and biotechnologies.[1]
The motor vehicle system is illustrative of the idea that technology greatly
influenced social change. The effects of the motor vehicle system on the
following list are truly impressive. It includes population distribution,
business, industry, government, health, death, family, leisure time, sexuality, mores, urban and rural life, values, education, housing, language, and
the perception of time and space. However, the results of technology are
not homogeneous, as there are contradictory consequences in different
groups and historical moments. Claude Fischer questions the cumulative
effect of technology.[2] He argues that when there were only a few television
sets, friends and neighbors got together to watch the programs. Following

the massification of TV, the tendency changed to individuals watching programs on their own.

What can be observed with telephone and video games is also applicable to the automobile. As long as there was only one vehicle in the family, it affected decision making and promoted travel as a family; the advent of a second car implied enough independence to fragment the family's cohesiveness. We see here a valuable mobile object interjected into preestablished social conditions that makes possible, limits, or determines the possibilities of its consumption and use.[3]

Could we possibly imagine the twentieth and twenty-first centuries without the automobile? We do not need to go to extremes, as in the case of the anecdote by a French journalist who reported that collectors of cars from the 1950s met every Friday in the Place de la Concorde in Paris. They were members of the Cruising Automobiles of the Fifties Club and attempted to go back in time through esoteric experience. But the medium was not a person or a time machine, but rather American cars from that decade—Cadillacs, Buicks, Chevrolets. One of those collectors, Albert, drove an ordinary car during the week, but when he drove his Chevrolet Bel Air, he dressed as a Teddy Boy and his wife sat in the backseat with their son. He looked over his Bel Air every night, and before taking it out of the garage he gave it a few pats on the side and spoke to it.[4] Although examples such as this are interesting, the importance of the automobile stems from its *centrality* in the transformation of urban life.

The intensity of the phenomenon—the boom of the automobile as a manufacturing project—attracts our attention. An enormous number of businesses attempted to build cars at the beginning of the twentieth century in France, Germany, England, Italy, and the United States. The assembly line changed the panorama of individual pioneers and artisans. In 1921 more than half the automobiles in the world were coming out of the Ford factories, and the number of manufacturers dropped significantly as Fordism took over the North American market and established affiliates in other parts of the world. Fordism meant mass production, classified work, consolidation of the assembly line, standardized parts, vertically integrated production, and automated factories.

The automobile produced transformations of capital and therefore became seen and heard in the different means of communication. There were no constraints on it, except perhaps the initial difficulty artists had in depicting technological topics. No prohibition excluded the automobile from social discourse, which was often accompanied by the representation of the ego in day-to-day life. It was the opposite of a forbidden word.

And as is the case with all broad-ranging technical artifacts, the automobile motivated ambiguous reactions. Rural people called it a "devil's car," and criticism increased in the urban milieu but tended to be in the field of automobility. Not even religion escaped its influence.

The reconstruction of the material culture of the era being studied is usually one way to avoid historical anachronism. We forget that the "intelligent" automobile was for many years an unsafe collection of parts and mechanisms. No key—the vehicle started with a crank and later on by pressing a button—no turn indicators or rearview mirror, no hydraulic drive, no air conditioning, no heater or radio, all of which played a major role in transforming a car for transportation into a car to be lived in. With brakes and tires entrusted at the outset to bicycle manufacturers, automobiles were driven on streets shared with pedestrians, animals, carriages, and trolley cars. Until the mid-1920s, manufacturers had no enclosed test tracks. No one at the time knew about spending hours and hours inside a car; nothing was known about huge traffic jams that create gridlock. Decades would pass before drivers might be held up at gunpoint while stopped at a red light or a recent immigrant to an industrialized nation might buy a super car as soon as he could and send its picture back to his family and close friends to show he had "arrived."

Despite its experimental character, the automobile arrived as the manifestation of a new phase of technical progress. The spectacle was nothing short of amazing: the automobile was destined to become something situated beyond religion, ideology, sexual identity, social class, economic model, and the nation-state. It is easy to make the claim that vehicle production maintained a fundamental link to the nation, that its importance was more than sectoral, and that an entire system of interests and services revolved around it. What is more, seen in detail, there were moments and years that seemed to threaten the consolidation of the automobile. Between 1929 and 1931, the start of the Great Depression, the production of cars—even then the most important sector of American industry, the most powerful economy on the planet—plummeted in the United States.[5] But just as in the view of British historian Eric Hobsbawm, the period from 1914 to 1945 was an uninterrupted period of war, and from the perspective of the cultural life of the automobile, such setbacks were just parentheses in the history of burgeoning automobility throughout the entire twentieth century.

Automobilization, however, became an essential adjunct to modern individualism, and the automobile is its chief material exponent: a cult object. It is the most sacred thing in the modern era, affirms Peter

Sloterdijk, to the extent that it is impossible to conceive of the modern era without thinking about movement.[6] That numinous machine would become the nucleus of a "universal kinetic religion" and the "rolling sacrament" that unifies body and speed. Whoever drives a car, according to Sloterdijk, "feels how his small ego expands into a superior being who has the expressways for a homeland and understands he was called to be something greater than half an animal-like pedestrian."[7]

According to Sloterdijk, modernity as a process is characterized by a kinetic element whose common denominator is the concept of mobilization (in a broader sense than the military meaning). The dream of this kinetic modernity would be to function as an escalator, as a pure being that generates movement. It stops at nothing, and its imperative is permanent expansion. But that impulse is threatened by unforeseen effects that transcend controlled projects. At times movement is transformed into immobility. The enormous summer traffic jams at sundown on the European autobahns confirm for Sloterdijk the demise of an illusion and the loss of the hope of salvation through acceleration.

Just as there is a perverse evolution in the imperative of a kinetic utopia, the object on wheels becomes a protagonist that renders the expectations of mere functionality useless.[8] Utility is an essential aspect of the automobile, but by no means is it the only one. Its attributes of automobilization, mobility, and visibility protect it from neutrality—the public thoroughfare is still one of the best ways of advertising its distinctiveness. There is, in addition, a historical relationship between technology and violence that is prolonged in the automobile, a motorized vehicle of fundamental importance for capitalism as well as for Fascism, Nazism, and Communism.[9]

An indicator of the legitimation of the automobile is its formulation of its own history, which, based on distinct periods of automotive evolution, was disseminated a half century after the car's invention as "formative period," "growth period," and "mature period." We have valuable books at our fingertips that review the origins and development of automobility based on personal experience. They are like appendixes to a history that developed outside textbooks. Books were not needed in order to dignify the car. At any rate, when an object becomes extremely popular, its inventor or major manufacturer considers himself important enough to will his memoirs to the world. Such memoirs usually start with the narration of traditional ways of life in small towns, where everything was changed by a new technology. Jules Verne was ahead of his time in *Paris in the Twentieth Century* with his images of vehicles moved by an invisible force along the boulevards; inventors transformed this vision into reality. One can assert about these first successful builders of automobiles what Villiers de l'Isle Adam wrote about Thomas Edison: they were living myths. Henry Ford was certainly a living myth. The "Sage of Dearborn," a millionaire prophet of epigrammatic phrases and incomprehensible parables was chosen in 1999 by *Fortune* magazine as the Businessman of the Century. The precursors of manufacturing and marketing of automobiles—Benz and Daimler in Germany, Panhard and Peugeot in France—glimpsed the transnational scope of the phenomenon only with difficulty. These European manufacturers were not able to foresee that the United States would take over the lead in a short time; that later on Japan would be the major worldwide producer and the representative of a new labor organization known as "Toyotaism"; and that in the twenty-first century China would become the giant of automobility. We have here a clear example of displacement of the demands for mobilization beyond its European platform, which has led to countless economic and social conflicts.

It is said that Daimler visualized a world market that would never be greater than one million vehicles and that shortly afterward William Durant and Henry Ford estimated a million cars per year would be produced. Before his death in 1929, Karl Benz showed his pride in the worldwide victory of automobility. One of the most gratifying experiences in his life was testifying that the idea he had once been ready to sacrifice everything for had conquered the planet.[10] For Benz the automobile dominated "the entire world," an idea reinforced by Alfred P. Sloan when he stated the history of General Motors "covered the twentieth century and many parts of the Earth, wherever there was a road to travel."[11]

Canals and railroads were crucial to the progress of movement and communication in the nineteenth century. During the first half of the twentieth century, the civilizing metaphor extended to the road and highway networks. Norbert Elias uses the example of roads and highways to illustrate the process of human training in the most advanced societies.[12] For Elias, traffic on the main streets of a large city requires modeling that is vastly different from the psychic apparatus. Automobiles speed from one place to another, pedestrians and cyclists try to dodge their way through the multitude of cars, and there are traffic police at all important intersections attempting to regulate traffic. According to Elias such external regulation is basically focused on molding human behavior to the needs of the social framework.

Wherever the automobile goes, uniformity tends to go right along with it. As merchandise it contributed to an increase of locally available goods, but as a trend in motorization it meant a decrease in contrasts throughout the world.[13] The automobile crossed borders, hierarchically arranged environments, changed the rhythm of day-to-day life, cut through social classes, and became an object of collective desire. This does not mean that its presence necessarily promoted equality or that there were the same possibilities for all. We know that it was received in varied ways depending on the different senses of cultural logic. The automobile could as easily compel the feeling of belonging to an imaginary collectivity as foster individual differences, thereby reaffirming the economic gaps in society.

The extraordinary vitality of the automobile sprang from its rather quick passage to being perceived as a must in the modern world in many key areas—time use, general usefulness, work, freedom, independence, prestige. It was popularly acclaimed although it was often inaccessible to the general public. As a matter of fact, except in the United States, it did not gain prominence in industrialized societies until after World War II.

The discrepancy between the center of production and the periphery of appropriation continues to be a valid thesis regarding those first decades of the twentieth century. Pauline Garvey states that, in the case of Norway until the 1950s, since there was no domestic motor vehicle industry, the car had no ties to the development of trade and the strength of proletarian labor; instead it was perceived as an expression of state control and a symbol of luxury and individual privilege.[14] This observation is also applicable to Latin America, where, at most, assembly plants were set up. Nevertheless, thinking of the mobility of goods means that the relational and contextual categories are strengthened and traditional distinctions between the internal and the external are weakened.

In the National Historical Museum of Rio de Janeiro I once found a perfectly restored 1908 German Protos that had been used by the Baron of Rio Branco. The feeling of experiencing the social life of a thing was intense. A motorized vehicle had arrived from far away and evoked several stories, at the beginning, of a baronial nature and, later on, of a popular nature, before being abandoned as useless. The stimulating work of Igor Kopytoff about the cultural biography of things and the process of mercantilization fits into this line of research.[15]

Kopytoff proposes, rightly, that in situations of cultural contact, the importance of the adoption of alien objects is not that they are adopted, but rather the way they are redefined culturally and put to use. In order to illustrate his argument he uses the biography of an automobile in Africa: how it was purchased; the buyer-seller relationship; the way the automobile was used; the identities of its frequent passengers; the garages where it was repaired; the passing of the car from one person to another over the years; and, finally, the ultimate disposal of its parts. All these details reveal "an entirely different biography from that of a middle-class American, or Navajo, or French peasant car."[16]

I start from the assumption that the exaltation of the produced machine passed into a second plane. We know our technology is not represented by the turbine, factory smokestacks, or the aerodynamic profile of trains, but rather by machines of reproduction lacking visual linkage, such as television sets and computers.[17] The automotive sector no longer symbolizes the promise of rapid expansion or anticipation of the future. Nevertheless, this "industry of industries" will continue to a great extent to dictate the worldwide rhythm of economic growth.[18]

It has been pointed out that anthropology and sociology have overlooked the fundamental importance of automobility, compared with other examples of material culture such as food, clothing, and housing. Daniel Miller emphasizes the need to analyze the "humanity of the automobile" and proposes conducting ethnographic studies of greater empathy, with the object examined in different cultural contexts.[19] Such studies should include the "externalities"—external costs, added effects, patterns of work and of entertainment—and the "entailments"—ways of reconciling state and market intervention—with a more personalized relationship between automobiles and those who drive them.

For English sociologist John Urry the automobile is the most important example of putative globalization and global technology, as it is primarily rooted in and defined by an automobility that blends flexibility and coercion.[20] There is freedom of the road, but that flexibility is possible only within the framework of automobility itself. According to Urry, seven combined components generate the specific character of dominion exercised by automobility throughout the planet: production of the object by industrial sectors that are of great importance to capitalism; an industry that has generated key concepts (Fordism and post-Fordism) used to understand the progress of and changes in the economy; the main individual consumer item that provides status for its owner; a complex machine made up of several interdependent parts; a very important topic of environmental discussion; the predominant global form of mobility, which subordinates other public mobilities; the dominant culture that organizes and legitimizes different forms of sociability; and a discussion of what constitutes the good life and provides powerful images and literary and artistic symbols.[21] Of the seven components I have mentioned, I emphasize the discourses of culture, basically, the representation of the automobile in literary production. Questions abound. What is the relationship between tradition and mobility? How do we narrate speed? Is progress inevitably linked to accidents? Is there a need for a new vocabulary? Does the automobile incite eroticism and love? What connections are there among advertising, style, and consumption? Are we heading toward the end of nature? These are topics—tradition, speed, accidents, vocabulary, love, advertising, and nature—that in a context of profound socioeconomic transformations find innovative answers in the cultural production of the era.

It would be difficult to find Baudelaire's vast "skies that make one dream of eternity" in that cultural production or those beautiful books that, according to Proust, are written in a sort of foreign language. Although authors such as Proust, Huxley, and Céline dedicated countless pages to the topic of the automobile, there is a wealth of bibliographic, iconographic, and musical treasure in less prestigious genealogies. The automobile demanded an outstanding place in articles, stories, novels, newspapers, periodicals, advertisements, photographs, films, paintings, and songs.[22] A considerable part of that material came from writers, journalists, and artists relatively well known in their local milieu and historical context, but they tended to disappear once the relevant problems they addressed in their time were assimilated. In this book I pay special attention to the primary South American sources during the first half of the twentieth century, which remain largely unexplored.

The texts that acknowledge the importance of the automobile enrich the literature of our kinetic modernity. But the cultural fine points are markedly different. The juxtaposition of automobiles and sexuality can be found in stories by authors as distinct as Liu Na'ou, Bartolomé Galíndez, and Lima Barreto, as well as in newspaper articles by Miguel Ángel Asturias and the poems of E. E. Cummings. Automobiles as indicators of modernity and associated with conspicuous consumption, speed, and eroticism; linked to change, anguish, and death. There is, however, a differential component concerning the landscapes: the emotion, the use of time, the feeling of responsibility, the idea of rights and duties. The ways of socialization also vary in those stories. No matter how many times the product is mentioned, no matter how broad the analogies, there are still specifics derived from cultural appropriation.

Such is the presence and profusion of images about the automobile that it has become second nature. It is difficult to appreciate what has become naturalized: it seems part of daily life, just like electric lights and water faucets. Objects such as those draw attention only when they are not in proper working order. With its characteristic freedom in the face of empirical evidence, and unconcerned with sociological methods, artistic production was particularly sensitive to the experiences of motorization. Between art and movement there was a fertile interaction, calling attention to the technology of transportation, an aspect of the growing mechanization of daily life, which got its start with only the train and the bicycle; then came the automobile, the electric trolley car, the motorcycle, and the airplane. Among them all, the automobile was the unchallenged champion and provided an infinite range of representations. Even public figures were created, such as Maria-Gasolina in Brazil, a woman who dates only men who have cars, because they are seen to have a certain social status and wealth, and Zé-Povo, who denounced urban abuse and accidents in newspapers and magazines.

Between 1900 and 1940 the automobile had not yet become a product used by the masses. Precisely because it was an item that was hard to purchase and had lasting public visibility, its cultural meaning was made even stronger. It was impossible to ignore. It was subject matter of comments, jokes, and rumors, a focus of curiosity, an element of ostentation, and a differentiator. People who have no opinions, prejudices, or stereotypes about the automobile are rare. Starting with the totemic object of modernity, a group of reminiscences and places in common was built up, a sort of "world memory," singular and collective at the same time.[23]

We are, paradoxically, facing a limited, open history. We cohabit with automobility, although not with its first problems and answers. The automobile is our past, present, and future all rolled into one. It did not disappear; on the contrary, its presence increased enormously all through the twentieth century, and it remains vigorous in the early years of the third millennium. Studying the cultural life of the automobile from the vantage point of kinetic modernity means explaining its dispersal and updating that heterogeneous worldwide archive, often less documentary than brilliantly imaginative.

THE CULTURAL LIFE OF THE AUTOMOBILE

1. HENRY FORD

From Popular Inventor to Legend

The Sage of Dearborn

French novelist and symbolist poet Villiers de l'Isle-Adam died penniless in 1889, when the automobile was still in its infancy. This devout Catholic wrote nothing about this new vehicle. But his sensitivity to fantastic thought of the era, combined with theories derived from modern science, led him to examine a foremost figure of the twentieth century: the popular inventor. In *L'Ève future* (Tomorrow's eve) Villiers de l'Isle-Adam took as a theme the mythical dimension of the inventor, in particular that of the popular American inventor. Thomas Edison deserved to be the hero of this book, as he developed many devices as strange as they were ingenious, among others, the telephone, the phonograph, the microphone, and the incandescent light bulb, all of which spread worldwide. Edison's glorious nicknames—Magician of the Century, Wizard of Menlo Park, Father of the Phonograph—attest to the attraction and enthusiasm of his contemporaries for this figure's "sort of mysterious quality." Edison, then slightly under forty years of age, already belonged to fantastic literature, according to Villiers: he was a modern legend. His work, his character, his language, and his theories transcended reality. For that reason, the French author had to project a mythological figure in his novel, developing the "Wizard of Menlo Park," more than a flesh-and-blood engineer.

Thomas Alva Edison (1847–1931), the leading individual to apply electricity to domestic life, was recognized in his day as a servant of humanity. Famous and a millionaire, he made it possible for technology to become part of day-to-day life. As the newspaper *Jornal do Brasil* (October 18, 1931) expressed it at his death: Edison, with his 1,093 patented inventions, was the inventor of modernity.[1]

Just as the Wizard of Menlo Park was the first incarnation of the great myth of the popular inventor, the second was Henry Ford (1863–1947), the Sage of Dearborn. The photographs that show Edison and Ford proudly together are an unmistakable demonstration of the power of the image of the American inventor.

Let us consider myths and legends as structures of meaning, far above individuals and collectively important.[2] It is impossible to separate Henry Ford the man from Henry Ford the figure. They are condemned to remain together, generating one contradiction after another. There are several well-known portraits: the defender of the masses, the superman, the hero of a Greek tragedy, the conservative, the revolutionary, the anti-Semitic dictator. Not always rationalizable ends are projected onto the figure of the popular hero. Idols who were constantly being renewed in kinetic modernity were in themselves an expression of mobility and tended to partially counteract the blurring of a symbolic repertoire loaded with sacred meaning.[3] But Henry Ford's place in posterity is guaranteed, for he was the superhero of mobility. With the arrival of the Sage of Dearborn, kinetic modernity rejoiced: the movement's definitive impetus had arrived as a promise.

Many think, mistakenly, that Ford invented the automobile; in reality, he popularized it. His was a humble beginning as the son of Irish farmers who had immigrated to the United States. He was self-taught and the very symbol of a self-made man who appeared at the right time to offer the "car for the masses." Clearly, mere psychological motives are not enough to explain his success. Lévi-Strauss reminds us that the creative effort determines cultural mutations that are important only if there is a sufficiently large audience to confirm the initiatives of the creator. Ford was a mixture of businessman and social engineer and disseminated the idea of high efficiency at low cost. He was the popular aspiration of mobility whose image served as a mirror for the American masses and then for the world. The Model T, in particular, displaced the identification of the automobile as a symbol of economic status and transformed the assembly line into a manifestation of the exemplary progress of the American nation, not to mention the whole of civilization. Automobile, market, consumption, and citizenship can be identified as interchangeable elements.

The automobile, as an object of consumption by the family, announced the progressive mechanization of daily life. The Ford Motor Company was the primary force responsible for the worldwide circulation of the mechanical lizard. When leading business and finance magazine *Fortune* chose Henry Ford as the Businessman of the Century in 1999, the editors were not just awarding a prize to the individual who, in his time, was the richest man in the world. Ford earned the distinction for having popularized the automobile and having created a mass market for it while at the same time providing the means to supply the market. The prize was for the intensification and efficiency of the movement, the lowered costs and the shorter working day, the increased wages, and industrial standardization.

Stemming from the Ford factory work model, the word *Fordism* was coined to designate the production of cheap goods coming off an assembly line. Henry Ford introduced the Model T in 1908, promising an automobile for the masses. After a year of production there were 10,000 Model Ts on the road in the United States. By 1927, when manufacture of the Model T ceased, Ford had sold more than 15 million all over the world. It had four cylinders, a semiautomatic transmission, flexible suspension, an electric magneto, and was, in its time, the most modern and sturdiest of cars. What made the Model T an automobile that marked an era was the interchangeability of its parts, from axles to gearboxes.

On January 1, 1910, Ford inaugurated the gigantic Highland Park factory in Detroit. When the assembly line was installed in 1913 the modern automobile industry came into being. Within only a few years Ford was producing almost half the automobiles in the world. Siegfried Giedion points out that Henry Ford's contribution was that he recognized the democratic possibilities in a vehicle that had theretofore been classified as a privilege to own. Europeans saw the idea of transforming a complicated mechanism such as the automobile from a luxury item into an ordinary object to be used by all as unthinkable, as was putting the price within the reach of the average man.[4]

The first assembly line did not involve the entire car, only the magneto. Even though it was a very limited improvement, it was a milestone just the same. According to Witold Rybczynski, it was one of the examples that defined an era, such as the first book printed with movable type by Johannes Gutenberg in the fifteenth century or James Watt's steam engine, built with a high-pressure condenser and patented in 1769—the era of the printing press, the era of steam, and, starting in 1913, the era of modern assembly line manufacturing.[5]

The assembly line as other than a novelty had never been used on such a scale. The model was based on the "process chain," used by Singer for sewing machines and by Colt for firearms. Ford, however, innovated in a different way: the assembly line never stopped. The conveyor belt moved without ceasing, and the workers had to adapt to its speed. I believe there is no more eloquent image of the triumph of movement than that of an object moving on a constantly moving belt while semistatic workers are converted into automated agents of mobility.

Ford did not contribute any crucial technological progress to the automobile itself. David Harvey points out that he rationalized old technologies and a planned, detailed division of labor that permitted enormous benefits in terms of productivity.[6] What was special was the explicit acknowledgment that mass production meant mass consumption and a new system of reproduction of the labor force—in short, a new kind of democratic, rationalized, populist society.

Up to that time, the automobile had been considered a whim of the rich. Could it also be cheap, useful, and well built? It was not enough to put the product on the market. Mass demand had to be stimulated, which would increase production and reduce costs, lead to higher wages, shorten the workday, constantly improve the same product (the idea of a new model each year had not yet arrived), and visibly advertise the advantages of the product, the opening of the factory to visitors, and the export of the Model T to other countries.

While the Ford Motor Company would make use of existing technological developments, it would also introduce a number of changes in the mass-production process and in disseminating techniques that would have profound impact. Under "Mass Production" in the 1926 *Encyclopædia Britannica,* Ford gave this definition: "Mass production is not merely quantity, for this may be had with none of the requisites of mass production. Nor is it merely machine production, which also may exist without any resemblance to mass production. Mass production is the focusing upon a manufacturing project of the principles of power, accuracy, economy, system, continuity, and speed."[7]

The Ford Model T embodied those principles. Underlying the production system were speed, uniformity, simplicity, and interchangeability. However, there were substantial differences between Fordism and Taylorism. In the long run, Ford did not attempt to improve the efficiency of his workers by a time and movement study, as Taylor advocated. Ford put machines to work. While Taylor sought ways to review the production process, Ford's engineers mechanized the processes and hired workers to feed and tend the machines.[8]

No other person in the history of the United States has been able to reduce complexity to the lowest common denominator as effectively as the hero of mobility, Henry Ford. In a society that valued movement and individual success to the utmost, his triumph was unquestionable: he was as famous, as quoted, and as discussed as several of the presidents of the United States. He was perceived as a revolutionary of technology and as an innovator who transformed the era but nonetheless managed to keep his powerful corporation in the family, as someone who did not abandon his simple character, his rural temperament, in spite of all the luxuries he could afford. Keith Sward refers to a "process of beatification" and to elevation to "national sainthood," but he also makes it clear that Ford was crafty, at times heartless, and a creator of illusions.[9]

During the 1920s, the Ford Motor Company received more publicity than any other commercial institution. Its director seemed to be a miraculous magnet. Whatever he did, whatever he said, his thoughts, his belongings, all was newsworthy. His unfathomable parables, his activity in the aviation sector, his trips to the countryside, his interest in antiques, his old-fashioned style of dancing and preference for violinists, his opinions on health, diet, longevity, and reincarnation were constant topics of conversation. The public seemed to have an insatiable appetite for news about Henry Ford, which the *Detroit Saturday Night* called "Ford-osis":

> It's on the brain and in the blood of the American people. They gobble the Ford stuff, and never stop to reason whether they like it, or whether it has any real merit in it. . . . You may hear him confess that he doesn't know who this fellow Benedict Arnold was, and still you would like to get his personal viewpoints on facts of American history. . . . Some of his words and acts, if spoken and done by any other man, would strike you as being more or less silly. Yet, under the spell of Ford-osis, you would hail them as matters of boundless consequence, and you would be the first to snatch from the fingers of a screaming newsboy the edition that breaks this news to the world.[10]

His physical appearance was appropriate to symbolize the new type of tycoon: average height; slender; upright; darting, lively eyes. He rode his bicycle, ran, and often challenged newsmen to a 100-yard dash. He was an untiring worker. John Reed was amazed at his vitality: "A slight, boyish figure, with thin, long, sure hands, incessantly moving; clean-shaven—the fine skin of his thin face browned golden by the sun; the mouth and nose of a simple-minded saint; brilliant, candid, green eyes, and a lofty forehead rising to shining gray hair like the gray hair of youth; the lower part of his face extraordinarily serene and naive, the upper part immensely alive and keen. He spoke swiftly, easily, without raising his voice, without hesitating, and his vocabulary consisted chiefly of words of one syllable."[11]

Ford himself contributed profusely to the cult of his personality. He enjoyed the publicity, collected references to himself, and openly vaunted his success. The Sage of Dearborn received thousands of letters every day. Even his critics acknowledged that no political candidate in the history of the United States had attracted so much attention nationwide and that, perhaps, he could have been president had he wanted it.[12] All of this despite his enormous ignorance of American history, as would be proved during a lawsuit in 1916. Most people did not seem to care that Ford was not on speaking terms with American history. His famous remark to Charles Wheeler—"History is more or less bunk"—indicates precisely the weak link between history and technology. Political history is seen as irrelevant to day-to-day life, while technology is a decisive element of change and progress. In an interview with Wheeler, Ford noted that the world's problem was that people lived in books and tradition. The Fordists wanted to escape from the past and tend to the now: the history of the present had to be made. The ones who started the war in Europe knew everything about the past, but they had started the worst war of all time.[13] To prove that history was made in the present, thousands of Model Ts rolled off the assembly line every day.

Henry Ford became the symbol of the new era and a representative of the Second Industrial Revolution. For some he was a prophet and for others he was a dictator, confirming that celebrities are not always viewed the same way. In any case, the sacred formula of Fordism was behind his reputation: mass production, lower consumer prices, higher wages for the workers, and an abundance of material goods. Could this model be applied to society as a whole? Ford strove vigorously in that direction while the books about his life and way of working multiplied.

We will see later that there were also some very critical appraisals of Ford and his work methods. But the tendency to motorization was on the upsurge, and not even Ford's manias, including his rejection of the idea of introducing a new model every year, managed to stop the self-propelled character of kinetic modernity.

In both Germany and the Soviet Union, Ford and Fordism became a part of the mobilizing project. Germany emerged from World War I defeated and demoralized, and the incipient Weimar Republic was searching for new models of industrial and technological development. For Thomas Hughes, the German fascination with the New World in the 1920s is comparable only to the American fascination with Japan in the 1970s.[14] Many in the Weimar Republic, who identified scientific administration (Taylorism) and mass production (Fordism) with "Americanism," felt the American model of technological civilization was to be imitated. But there were also powerful anti-Fordist lines of thought that became confused with anti-Americanism, with the assembly line at the center of much of the criticism of Americanization.

The Soviet Union emerged from World War I and the Russian Revolution with a firm commitment to transforming itself into a world power, even though it was still in the throes of underdevelopment. It set itself to overcoming its "backwardness."[15] Richard Stites reports that Ford's book, *My Life and Work*, published in 1922, had four Soviet editions by 1925.[16] Lavishly favorable prefaces introduced the book, recommended as indispensable reading matter for party members, economists, Taylorists, engineers, managers, and technical students. If Lenin was the Russian God, observed an American business reporter in 1930, Ford was Saint Peter.[17]

The dissemination of the Ford name went hand in hand with the diffusion of the Model T and the Fordson tractor throughout the world. By the end of the 1920s Ford had become part of Peruvian indigenist poetry, in which the poetic word was at the service of the people's revolution. "Poema keswa para la fiesta del Inti" (Keswa poem for the Inti festival), by César Alfredo Miró Quesada, was written as a political-social indigenist poem—far, far away from Detroit and the assembly line. Nevertheless, next to the proletarian rural worker with large eyes, a caudillo in his *chonta*, who is making the revolution appears the "Keswa Indian, a farmer / with the morning peeking over his shoulder, / turning over the furrows without Henry Ford." There are only two references to symbolic characters in the poem: Karl Marx and Henry Ford. Next to Karl Marx, Henry Ford and his tractors represent the future.

Also very far from Detroit—in Buenos Aires—a declared Communist sympathizer was praising Henry Ford (surely with a bit of irony) as an expression of adventure and the dynamic life. He was Raúl González Tuñón, who, in "Las cinco partes de la aventura" (The five parts of adventure), says he has seen Ford's portrait and has heard about him, and he puts him in the same class as Napoleon, Disraeli, Trotsky, Basil Zaharoff, and John Pierpont Morgan. All of these men deserve eternity, because they represent audacity, intelligence, strength, and, above all, adventure. González Tuñón declares his love for communism and some genial capitalists, along with the city's subway network, cranes, and Ford engines:

That humble, smiling man, a multimillionaire from the country of Lindbergh, Chaplin, and Edison, has been concerned about movement in the life of man. Money does not sully him, does not weigh him down, because he is a man of quality. With five dollars you can buy a pair of shoes just like his.

I would like to be Henry Ford's friend. We would talk about shortening the workweek, about workshops sparking in the constant fervor of the open hearth furnaces.

I admire him. You are sure that as a great industrialist, he could be a wonderful athlete, a great poet, a formidable warrior, and a saint. Isn't that right?

Speed, steel, grace, flight, movement!

And since things are organized the way they are in the world, since this does not change, I also admire Al Capone, because he is a great thief, because he is the Henry Ford of the thieves outside the law.[18]

In different parts of the world the defenders and detractors of the intensification of mobility appear. They speak good or ill of it, but, just the same, they speak.

Biography of the Universal Automobile: *My Life and Work*

For modern literature, 1922 is considered the *annus mirabilis*. All of the following were published that year: *Ulysses,* by James Joyce; *The Waste-land,* by T. S. Eliot; *Siddhartha,* by Hermann Hesse; *The Hairy Ape,* by Eugene O'Neill; *The Forsyth Saga,* by John Galsworthy; *Babbitt,* by Sinclair Lewis; *Paulicéia desvairada,* by Mário de Andrade; *Trilce,* by César Vallejo; *Desolación,* by Gabriela Mistral; *Veinte poemas para ser leídos en el tranvía,* by Oliverio Girondo; *Andamios interiores,* by Manuel Maples Arce. That same year Henry Ford's *My Life and Work* was published.

Written by ghostwriter Samuel Crowther, the book faithfully reflects Ford's ideas. It is a visionary text, optimistic, targeted at an average reader. The limits of the Ford assembly line, consumers' demand for variety, workers' monotony in the workplace, and forms of state intervention—none of these were common when this book was published. Yet it was destined to accompany the circulation of automobiles throughout the world. In various countries, especially among the entrepreneurial groups, *My Life and Work* became a mandatory reference work. In November 1923 *Mein Leben und Werk* was published in Germany, one year before the Ford factory in Cologne was inaugurated. In 1924 *Mi vida y mi obra* was published in Spain. The book was published in 1926 in Brazil as *Minha vida e minha obra,* by the Companhia Editora Nacional, translated by Monteiro Lobato.

My Life and Work is a manual of advice expressed as formulas for the success of businessmen and companies. Its basic premise is that, despite inflamed speeches about progress in the United States, the history of abundance has barely commenced. It is a proud bet on the present and the future as well as on the industry's opportunities. Ford had discarded the apocalyptic visions of a world composed of machines and mechanized beings. For him, nothing was better than the knowledge and use of machines in order to enjoy nature, trees and birds, flowers and fields.

Ford never limited himself to simply advising industrialists: he was a prophet with a formula. Not all the powerful shared his viewpoint. For example, Alfred P. Sloan, the chief executive of General Motors from 1923 to 1946 and considered one of the greatest entrepreneurs in history, was far from presenting himself as savior of the world. When he published *My Years with General Motors* in 1964, Fordism had been replaced by "Sloanism." The scope of Fordism could then be seen in relative terms.

According to Sloan, the year 1908 was marked by two events of lasting significance in the progress of automotive history: William C. Durant formed the General Motors Company, precursor of today's corporation; and Henry Ford announced the Model T. Each of these events represented more than a company and its car; they represented different points of view and different philosophies. History was to assign these philosophies to leading roles in the automotive industry in successive periods. Henry Ford's came first and lasted for nineteen years—the lifetime of the Model T—bringing him immortal fame.[19] In various places in his book, Sloan refers to the decline of the unchanging car model (Model T), pointing out the triumph of the "A Car for Every Purse and Purpose" campaign carried out by General Motors. *My Years with General Motors* can be read partly as a history of the decay of the Ford Company and the triumph of General Motors. The old pioneer had probably not managed to overcome the change, but the legend persisted, cultivated by sentimentalists, that he had left a great car, an expression of the concept of basic cheap transport: "The fact is that he left behind a car that no longer offered the best buy, not even as raw, basic transport. . . . And so, for engineering and marketing reasons, the Model T fell. . . . Mr. Ford regained sales leadership again in 1929, 1930, and 1935, but, speaking in generalities, he had lost the lead to General Motors. Mr. Ford, who had had so many brilliant insights in the earlier years, seemed never to understand how completely the market had changed from the one in which he made his name and to which he was accustomed."[20]

There were four important transformations: installment selling; the used-car trade-in; the closed-car body; and the annual model.[21] These meant consumer facilities and preference for quality merchandise. Ford perceived these changes in the automotive industry with a certain amount of disdain. For many years he had rejected the idea of producing varied cars for a market segmented in tastes and economic levels, resisted the idea of distinguishing products from one another. He finally had to accept the changes in order to be competitive. His face-off with the organized creation of dissatisfaction and artificial obsolescence was grounded in the desire to modify the world through Fordism. It was not just a matter of business; it was a wide-ranging social project: "Power and machinery, money and goods, are useful only as they set us free to live. They are but means to an end. For instance, I do not consider the machines which bear my name simply as machines. If that was all there was to it I would do something else. I take them as concrete evidence of the working out of a theory of business which I hope is something more than a theory of business—a theory that looks toward making this world a better place in which to live."[22]

The heart of that world needy for practical ideas was the United States, but the goal of abundance and consumerism was worldwide. With Ford the idea of automated work became almost ridiculous, as Chaplin would show in *Modern Times*. The philosophical reflection of the nineteenth century—work as a humanizing phenomenon and source of recognition—was converted into an instinctive driving force that could not be stopped: "the natural thing to do is work." A notion of work appeared that not only differentiated us from animals and humanized us, but it also forced us to work in an intelligent, planned, and untiring way until we died. Thousands of years had to pass before this notion could be imposed, that prosperity and happiness could be obtained through mechanized human effort. If the evils of humanity persist, Ford argued, it is because we keep on trying to escape from the "natural" law of work. Living is developing this biological driving force that goes beyond the category of workaholic, because the realization of the being lies in work. "Work is our sanity, our self-respect, our salvation. So far from being a curse, work is the greatest blessing."[23] It would have been difficult for Max Weber to find a more perfect example of the Protestant work ethic at the beginning of the twentieth century. In the capitalist idea of salvation through work, the kinetic vocation and the spirit of mobilization of industrial production were vigorously expressed.

Ford valued manual work, even farming, striving to provide adequate tools to minimize the loss of time and expenditure of effort. It was impossible to think of work separate from technology, which also contributed to hominization and deserved a preeminent place in the production system. Mechanical work appeared to be superior to the contemplative life, although Ford emphasized the role of pioneerism to the detriment of repetition. In such modern legitimation of the active life, work had a humanizing character that led to freedom: of movement, of course, predominantly oriented in the direction of material values. Ford liked differentiating himself from everything, from repetition, from radicals, from reactionaries. He had confidence in himself and did not expect protection from the government; he distrusted laws that did not produce anything constructive. His society was simple: it depended on agriculture, manufacturing, and transportation, but it could not be organized in a way that contradicted human nature, ignoring the right to the fruits of labor (Ford mentions the Soviet Union as a negative example).

The passion for experimentation and pragmatism implied a mistrust of nonutilitarian knowledge and determined the educational ideal. His education basically consisted of playing with tools. We can imagine him: the boy in the field, always looking for machines and artifacts, avid to discover mechanical objects. He "educated" himself with them, testing, perfecting, and repairing them. He benefited from a few books, such as *The World of Science*, but books were not of much help when compared with hands-on learning. In that sense, Ford was similar to the German Karl Benz, who sketched smoke-belching trains as a child and in high school preferred physics and chemistry. They shared a taste for watches. We know that taking machinery apart and putting it back together is one of a mechanic's favorite pastimes and that objects often serve to test the limits of forms. This rivalry with limits is one of the characteristics of technical imagination, whether in the building of automats, telephones, or automobiles. For the German inventor, who developed his personality in the practical struggle with problems and perceived his training as an ongoing activity, the highest goal was knowledge derived from experience, never knowledge learned from books.

When the Henry Ford Trade School was founded in 1916 to maximize the educational possibilities of the child and at the same time start his industrial training on a constructive basis, it had three guiding principles. First, the boy would be kept as such, not prematurely transformed into a worker; second, academic training would always be accompanied by industrial training; third, the boy would be given a feeling of pride and responsibility in his work, for he would be taught in accordance with articles of acknowledged industrial value.

The basic primer was the Ford factory itself. Theory and practice were combined in the classes of arithmetic, physics, and chemistry, with the industrial plant providing a state-of-the-art laboratory. Henry Ford felt the factory offered more resources for a practical education than most universities. But the most interesting thing, from the perspective of kinetic modernity, was the geographical viewpoint. The boy was taught to observe the world or, better yet, to follow the circulation of Ford automobiles throughout the world: "Cities are no longer black specks on maps and continents are not just pages of a book. The shop shipments to Singapore, the shop receipts of material from Africa and South America are shown to him, and the world becomes an inhabited planet instead of a coloured globe on the teacher's desk."[24]

Ford's insistence on the value of a practical education was not disassociated from thinking. "Thinking" here means something very different from mentally practicing what we are going to say or cogitating with the purpose of learning. It means discipline in life and mental activity directed at the achievement of goals. To be sure, it stems from the principle that man thinks better when his knowledge of the past does not get in his way. Once again, the planetary image imposes itself as a test of education, understanding by "world" the amplified model of American utilitarianism: "One good way to hinder progress is to fill a man's head with all the learning of the past; it makes him feel that because his head is full, there is nothing more to learn. Merely gathering knowledge may become the most useless work a man can do. What can you do to help and heal the world? That is the educational test."[25] The success of capitalism corroborates, according to Ford, this marketing system's solid economic and moral foundations, even though much could be improved. Even human inequality is naturalized: "There can be no greater absurdity and no greater disservice to humanity in general than to insist that all men are equal. Most certainly all men are not equal and any democratic conception which strives to make men equal is only an effort to block progress. Men cannot be of equal service."[26] The efficiency of the system is constantly pursued, simplifying mechanisms, improving the product, increasing production. The function of business is to produce for consumption, which implies the quality of the article must be high and the price low, serving both the consumer and the manufacturer. Consequently, Ford rejects the idea of the monopoly and exaggerated earnings, less oriented to things than to profits. One cannot work to put money in one's pocket; rather, one must render services, for wealth is a result of the service and the common good. Time and again he insists on this point to differentiate him and his model from speculation and from speculators.

Nothing seems more terrible to Ford than a life without difficulties. In his model of civilization there is no place for idleness, joblessness, and laziness. He is much closer to the active Robinson Crusoe than to the lazy Macunaíma. Objects should not be more complex than necessary. Clothes, food, and furniture should be much simpler and even more aesthetic. That way there would be easier access to material goods, relieved of useless adornment that only serves to make the product more expensive.

The notion of the strict utility of the object is the basis of the eventual failure of the Ford Model T: increasingly accessible to the buyer, but always painted black, too small inside for sexual maneuvers, and running on the public thoroughfares like so many hearses. Ford kept in mind the value of use—utility with respect to satisfying needs—and the value of change—the market value of a product—but not the logic of ambivalence or the difference of the sign, typical of consumer society, which produces an object less to address a lack than to produce something different.[27]

Thorstein Veblen's *The Theory of the Leisure Class* had been published years before, in 1899. There are members of the leisure class, Veblen says, who associate expenditure with status and prestige. Ford was not aware of Veblen's book, but he would not have been worried about conspicuous consumption: he was interested in the purchasing power of the masses. The company's advertising aimed to point out the "real" qualities of the product: utility, durability, design, quality of the materials, low price. There was no mystification of the object. From the first ad it could be seen that the purpose was to build and sell an automobile especially designed for daily use and abuse in business and in the family that would go fast enough to satisfy an average buyer without reaching dangerous speeds that were universally condemned. It was a machine that could be admired by men, women, and children thanks to "its compactness, its simplicity, its safety, its all-around convenience, and—last but not least—its exceedingly reasonable price, which places it within the reach of many thousands who could not think of paying the comparatively fabulous prices asked for most machines."

Just as there is a principle that says the object must fulfill a utilitarian function, anything else being a complicator of the price, Ford defined "service" as the maximum advantage offered to the consumer with a minimum amount of gain for the producer. A well-managed business cannot fail to generate earnings, the reward for good service. Service is uppermost; earnings follow.

Ford was not concerned with the possiblity of saturation. He would roll over in his grave if he learned that at the beginning of the third millennium fifty million cars per year are being produced; even so, factories in the United States, Europe, and Japan have unused capacity, because the market in several regions of the world is saturated. In his day Ford answered his critics by saying that abundance was something to be desired. Why worry about a vision of a splendid world where everyone owns what he wants? On the contrary, his effort was focused on accelerating prolif-eration, and he lamented the slow pace of the universal dissemination of goods. Planning the relationship between production and distribution in industry and agriculture would be enough to abolish poverty. Charity and philanthropy were to be avoided. Nor was it a matter of economizing, of saving money instead of making it circulate and increase, for that would be wasting one's life.

The history of the Ford Motor Company backs up the formulas of its founder. On May 31, 1921, car number 5,000,000 rolled off the company's assembly line. Ford placed this Model T in his museum next to his very first automotive project, the gasoline buggy built thirty years before. In appearance, construction, and materials, the differences were enormous, but the basic structure of both vehicles was relatively similar. The Ford Company, the assembly line, and the Model T could all be seen in the buggy.

The modern era is understood to be about industrial development, where the individual and society converge in images of the mechanized world. Memory singles out certain objects that are the starting points of the new era of mobility. We visualize Henry Ford receiving a watch as a boy. We see the same boy still a farm kid, the budding engineer barely twelve years of age, experiencing his greatest revelation on finding him-self with a machine on the outskirts of Detroit. The modern era seems to consist of technical objects. Emotion, sensitivity, and memory seem to be equally mechanical. The encounter on the clay-surfaced country road with a self-propelled vehicle was the *biggest event* of his childhood. Every-thing seems to take on meaning in retrospect and everything is remem-bered with unusual sharpness:

> I remember that engine as though I had seen it only yesterday, for it
> was the first vehicle other than horse-drawn that I had ever seen. It was
> intended primarily for driving threshing machines and sawmills and
> was simply a portable engine and boiler mounted on wheels with a water
> tank and coal cart trailing behind. I had seen plenty of these engines
> hauled around by horses, but this one had a chain that made a connection
> between the engine and the rear wheels of the wagon-like frame on which
> the boiler was mounted. The engine was placed over the boiler and one
> man standing on the platform behind the boiler shoveled coal, managed

the throttle, and did the steering. . . . It was that engine which took me into automotive transportation.[28]

This starting point must be understood as an inflection of modern subjectivity in the broadest sense of what Lewis Mumford calls "assimilation of machinery." Ford fervently sums up the powerful trends of an era that he did not create but helped develop with his dedication and zeal. He became in that way one of the most efficient spokesmen for the meaning of movement and mechanical acceleration. The mechanization of daily life, which Ford discovered metonymically in a chance childhood episode and which was reinforced by the successful trajectory of his automobile company, is one aspect of a broad mobilizing process with global dimensions.

The transnational trend of kinetic modernity is expressed in the project of the automobile that would become universal. This should not be confused with Renato Ortiz's world car: the Ford Fiesta assembled in Spain, its windows brought from Canada, its carburetor from Italy, its radiator from Austria, the cylinders and the battery from England, the pistons from Germany, the gearbox from France.[29] Nevertheless, both models, the Model T and the Ford Fiesta, are examples of kinetic utopia. What Marx and Engels had detected midway through the nineteenth century—that the bourgeoisie, impelled by the need for fresh markets, would invade the world and would impose a cosmopolitan character on production and consumerism in all countries—became a stark reality with the exportation of automobiles.

Ford was betting on the domestic market; he even had a strong desire to consolidate the nation's autonomy in relation to raw materials. But as a good capitalist, Ford thought in an irresistibly transnational way. However, he failed to value cultural exchange and interaction as signs of modernity. Ford was not attracted by "impurity." On the contrary, his universalism was little more than the application of the Fordism formula to the entire world, little more than his own values converted into a model of conduct. This explains the moral value associated with the cleanliness of the workers and the machinery in his factories. Hygiene appears, symptomatically, to have been related to intelligence; the cleanliness of the machine was an indication of the intelligence of the operator. Without personal hygiene and clean machines, no morality was possible.

The goal of manufacturing the universal car dictated the work rules, demanded a lower price for the article, and determined the human and mechanical layout of the factory. There could be no lost time. In reality, nothing could be lost. The word *waste* evoked terrible images, and there was a lot of Taylorism in that particular phobia. Organization of the factory was methodical so as to minimize lost time and misused space. Useless luxury had to be eliminated; even experimentation had to be justified as productive. One minute lost, one square foot too much space, one absent-minded worker, and that minor form of waste meant an unnecessary increase in the final cost of the universal automobile.

The American car has always been known for its size. Several factors permitted that "national" style: government policies that protected domestic markets by making importation difficult; gasoline prices lower than in other countries; the vast size of the nation. A comparative study of workers' incomes shows that it was easier for an American to buy a car than it was for a European.[30] The pleasure of traveling, the sense of privacy, and the feeling of power were common to all automobile owners at the beginning of the century, but the standard mean in the United States, the Ford Model T, was not a large car: one of its nicknames was "sardine box." Its great success came from interchangeable parts, trustworthiness and durability, low cost, and the broad network of dealers and repair shops. Karl Benz spoke ironically on this point, arguing that a business that depended on a broad network of stations with replaceable parts to keep itself running did not appear to him to be an ideal of the automotive industry. However, Benz could not fail to recognize that Henry Ford, thanks to his organizational talent, made the most of the automotive business as no one else in the world could have done.

The universal car project was Henry Ford's trademark. He announced it with pride: "I will build a motor car for the great multitude. It will be large enough for the family but small enough for the individual to run and care for. It will be constructed of the best materials, by the best men to be hired, after the simplest designs that modern engineering can devise. But it will be so low in price that no man making a good salary will be unable to own one—and enjoy with his family the blessing of hours of pleasure in God's great open spaces." It would be the Model T, known by nicknames as varied as "Tin Lizzie," "Henry," "Flivver," "Can Opener," "Sardine Box," "Road Louse," and the like.

This project of the universal car, a necessity in the modern world according to its manufacturer, determined the factory layout: "We put more machinery per square foot of floor space than any other factory in the world—every foot of space not used carries an overhead expense. We want none of that waste. Yet there is all the room needed—no man has too much room and no man has too little room. Dividing and subdividing

operations, keeping the work in motion—those are the keynotes of production."[31] He completed this idea further on with significant details:

> Our machines are placed very close together—every foot of floor space
> in the factory carries, of course, the same overhead charge. The con-
> sumer must pay the extra overhead and the extra transportation involved
> in having machines even six inches farther apart than they have to be.
> We measure on each job the exact amount of room that a man needs;
> he must not be cramped—that would be waste. But if he and machine
> occupy more space than is required, that also is waste. This brings our
> machines closer together than in probably any other factory in the world.
> To a stranger they may seem piled right on top of one another, but they
> are scientifically arranged, not only in the sequence of operations, but
> to give every man and every machine every square inch that he requires
> and, if possible, not a square inch, and certainly not a square foot, more
> than he requires.[32]

The same reasoning of constant improvement and the need for constant
sales of the article at low price underlie aspects as varied as advertising,
discipline, hygiene, individual responsibility, salaries, opposition to spe-
cialization, and marketing. Up to that time there had been no demand for
automobiles. They were considered luxury goods and were not thought of
as important elements in industry. Much attention was placed on financing, little on service. While the article would generate earnings, producers
were indifferent to improvements in manufacturing methods. Money was
more important than consumers: once an automobile was sold, the business could toast its success.

Ford, on the other hand, never valued the motor vehicle industry as
a means of obtaining money from the privileged classes. He also refused
to consider the idea that a business would sell a defective article at a high
price and later persuade the consumer to purchase a newer one. Ideally, the
Model T would last forever. And there would be a constant need for new
cars. But in the United States in the 1920s the used-car market expanded,
offering cars at much lower prices to meet the need for basic transportation.
As the cost of the Model T depended on volume sales, the company could
not sell fewer cars or reduce its prices without affecting profits. Henry Ford
did not become aware of this change in the sales system in time: meeting
the needs of basic transportation did not require new cars.[33]

The attributes of the Model T, the "Universal Car," were carefully accentuated: one low-cost model with the advantages of high-quality steel (vana-

dium), simplicity in operation (the masses were not mechanics), sufficient horsepower, low gasoline consumption, absolute reliability, light weight, ease of control ("anybody can drive a Ford"). One ad referred to "Ford, the universal car" and pointed out its advantages: a new carburetor system; hot plate–style vaporizer; easier lubrication; reliable brakes; less need to grind valves; better ignition; increased acceleration; and fuel economy.

Globalization of an object demands other factors: higher wages; curiosity about and interest in the product; more dignity for workers; and identification of the industry with progress. *My Life and Work* summarizes all these factors. Better pay for the workers, in order to stave off job desertion and make possible the purchase of more Ford automobiles, became a powerful selling point for Ford. It was the opposite of charity or paternalism; it was simply considered good business. "It pays," Ford declared.

Curiosity about the new is not restricted to the automobile. It is known that consumption is largely based on novelty and difference. But among all the technical products, none attracted more interest from the public than the automobile. News stories of the era show people spontaneously gathering to observe the first vehicles putt-putting noisily about town. Ford also remembers the curiosity of the crowds and what a bother they were: "My 'gasoline buggy' was the first and for a long time the only automobile in Detroit. It was considered to be something of a nuisance, for it made a racket and it scared horses. Also it blocked traffic. For if I stopped my machine anywhere in town a crowd was around it before I could start up again. If I left it alone even for a minute some inquisitive person always tried to run it. Finally, I had to carry a chain and chain it to a lamp post whenever I left it anywhere."[34]

The progress of industry means a step forward for civilization. Jobs are not lost from the evolution of the industrial process; on the contrary, there are more job possibilities:

> The stage-coach drivers lost their jobs with the coming of the railways. Should we have prohibited the railways and kept the stage-coach drivers? Were there more men working with the stage-coaches than are working on the railways? Should we have prevented the taxicab because its coming took the bread out of the mouths of the horse-cab drivers? How does the number of taxicabs compare with the number of horse-cabs when the latter were in their prime? . . . No, every time you can so arrange that one man will do the work of two, you so add to the wealth of the country that there will be a new and better job for the man who is displaced.[35]

Civilization was in play: the production of material goods, the circulation of things, the functionality of the system. All implied a struggle against lost time, against the lack of planning, and against the monotony of poverty. Ford called it "learning to live." However, a persistent ambivalence threatened the staunchest efforts to propel the society of mobility forward. It was impossible to imagine the magnitude of the future "external costs" of the automobile—environmental damage, traffic jams, accidents, criminal behavior—but Ford's efforts to demonstrate the usefulness of the motor car for the "good life," curiously, suggested doubts about its value.

With demands as exuberant as a natural setting full of birds and flowers, the confidence Ford showed in the future of production returned as a curse. The natural world surrounding the great entrepreneur became zoo-like. Ford, the man who "put America on wheels," imported birds of various species (yellow woodpeckers, green canaries, royal chaffinches, jays, linnets, larks, calanders). He needed them for their beauty and as a delight for the eye, as civilization moved on to living in an extensive human park, marked by constant ambivalence. This is evident for the contradictory evaluation of the civilizing role of the industrial city. For Ford, had it not been for the cities, the rural areas would not have seen improved living conditions. Crowding in cities necessitated better hygiene, electric lighting, and social organization, all products of the urban experience. But Ford also thought that all social problems originated and were concentrated in big cities. While the small communities lived in harmony with the seasons, far from extreme poverty and extreme wealth, there was something in a city of a million inhabitants that was ferocious and threatening. "Thirty miles away, happy and contented villages read of the ravings of the city! A great city is really a helpless mass. . . . City conditions of work and living are so artificial that instincts sometimes rebel against their unnaturalness."[36]

Ambiguities such as these reaffirm the Henry Ford who detested the "impure," and they express the impossiblity of reconciliation with the derivations of kinetic modernity. The enormous process of producing the material goods that Ford helped to perfect produced, logically, unforeseen effects. The effort to comply with the promise of the utopia of movement was titanic, but while the founder of Fordism appealed, senselessly, to the metaphors of the organic community and nature, the automobile spread throughout the world. Kinetic modernity was on the way to becoming a triumphant, proliferating way of life, continually threatened by elephantiasis.

2. FORDISM AND CULTURAL CIRCULATION

Tourists and Artists in the Industrial New World

The effects of automobilism were undeniable: not even the southern states could sleep peacefully, points out C. P. Russell in "The Pneumatic Hegira," published in *The Outlook* in December 1925: "Southern States, long negligent of their roads, have been stimulated into transforming rough or sandy rural thoroughfares into straight and stately hard-surfaced boulevards, with a consequent fillip to internal intercourse. Old-fashioned Southern villages have been awakened out of their sleep, with an ensuing desire to paint up and brush up. And for the first time in history the common, ordinary 'fo'kes' of the North and South are meeting one another on a really large scale, mostly by means of the National chariot—the Ford car."[1]

Automobilism linked the lives of people and stimulated the reorganization of the social web. Although the twentieth century had not yet been divided into "Fordism" and "post-Fordism," the tendency of classifying the multiple temporalities according to the common denominator of movement and the production line could be seen.

The automobile was at the heart of this; the Model T was the reference point of an era. "The ordinary farmer was a small repressed Babbitt, who dreamed of a radio, a Ford, and a tiled bath," writes Ronald de Carvalho in *Itinerário*. While Paul Morand affirmed that in the United States "one goes to school in a Ford," Mayakovsky picks out the Ford as the expression of the throbbing American culture, and Vachel Lindsay calls it the "country of Fords rolling from north to south, from east to west." Surely, the 1928 presidential campaign slogan of Republican candidate Herbert Hoover— "a chicken in every pot and a car in every garage"—was inspired by Ford's assembly line.

The Ford Motor Company soon outgrew the image of an automobile factory and went on to represent a model society. Assembly-line production and low prices were the tools motorization needed to consolidate its evolution. Highland Park and River Rouge were Henry Ford's two main industrial complexes. Both followed the custom, common in the early years of the twentieth century in the United States, of opening their doors so visitors could observe the factory in full production. These two industrial complexes transformed the workplace into tourism destinations par excellence: a team of employees guided hundreds of visitors daily in each factory.

The Highland Park factory, a masonry structure with broad windows, was the most advanced metalworking establishment in the world, wrote H. L. Arnold and F. L. Faurote in *Ford Methods and the Ford Shops*. German engineer Otto Moog affirmed that no symphony, no *Eroica*, compared in depth, content, and power with the music that greeted visitors when they went through the factory. Beethoven dethroned by the infernal racket of machines! Visitors found the dynamics of the machinery and the rational distribution of space tremendously fascinating. Electricity powered the metamorphosis of raw materials into automobiles, relegating to the background the working conditions of the many sweaty workers who appeared to be robots dotted about the geometric industrial landscape.

When the human consequences of mechanization are acknowledged, the panorama changes. The workers did not even have time to observe the visitors and were punished if they let a single drop of oil fall to the floor.

The construction of the River Rouge factory between the two World Wars was considered a national achievement. Laurence Goldstein writes that this plant that included all the aspects of the manufacturing process, from the blast furnaces and the foundry to the assembly line, symbolizes the self-sufficiency and the astonishing magnitude of the North American free-enterprise system and, by extension, of the American Dream itself.[2] In 1927 River Rouge had 75,000 workers, 5,000 of whom had been hired just to keep the industrial complex impeccably clean. The 93 structures designed by architect Albert Kahn represented the new industrial era; their glass walls and bright interiors flooded with natural light contained 90 miles of railroad, 27 miles of conveyor belts, and 53,000 machine tools. It was a "total institution" that was functional, highly mechanized, economically efficient, and completely devoid of ornamentation and that provoked a sort of stupor in architect Le Corbusier. He watched the cars being assembled on the line—6,000 automobiles per day, one car every 45 seconds—and confirmed what seemed impossible: that the system *never* failed. Shiny, impeccable, without an oil or grease stain, without a fingerprint on the bright finish, a car was born and disappeared as in a mythological epic. For Le Corbusier this represented the perfect convergence of all acts and all thoughts, a goal of unity that ought to serve as an example to modern architecture. As a matter of fact, River Rouge was a geometrical, concentrated industrial complex, feeding the world with its efficient, resistant, inexpensive automobiles. It was also a carefully constructed image of the model factory that renounced the vagaries of style and was impressive because of its size and production.

Ford expanded nationally and internationally. While the tree trunk was in Detroit, the branches spread globally. In 1914 there were branches in Canada, Australia, France, and England. After that Ford moved into Germany, Denmark, Spain, the Soviet Union, and Italy. From the port of Trieste Fords were shipped to the Balkans, Turkey, Cyprus, Egypt, and the Middle East. Allan Nevins and Frank E. Hill report that the foreign operations were generally characterized by a vigorous entry of the Model T at the beginning of the 1920s, followed by a surge of interest in Chevrolet that diminished Ford's sales, and, finally, a severe reduction in the supply of vehicles because of the depression starting in 1930.[3]

Frank E. Hill and Mira Wilkins researched the history of this expansion in detail.[4] Ford dealers sold their product wherever it was possible, from Salisbury in Rhodesia to Tianjin (Tientsin) in China. Latin America was a difficult market; political instability and the economy of each country made business a hard task, and there were few roads for cars to travel on. Those that did exist were for animal-drawn conveyances, not for automobiles. But orders came in nonetheless, especially from Argentina and Brazil, as there was an emerging bourgeois class ready to buy the costly product, despite the lack of local infrastructure.

World War I made exports of the European models difficult and bolstered sales of the American models to Latin America. Ford started business in Argentina. Then came Brazil, Uruguay, Chile, Mexico, Venezuela, Peru, and Central America. The plants in Argentina and Brazil, buildings three or four stories high, were miniature copies of the Ford complex in Highland Park. In 1926 more Model Ts were sold in Latin America and the Far East than in Europe. Since Latin America did not have its own automotive industry, Ford did not have to face local competition or discriminatory governmental policies that favored domestic manufacturing. Such conditions, according to Wilkins and Hill, differed from those of industrial Europe, where there was traditional pride in national products and processes. In Europe it was difficult to compete with government-imposed protective tariffs that favored national industry (Fiat, Citroën, Peugeot, and Renault). Nonetheless, Ford was proud of the worldwide prestige of its products.

These two factors—the popular car and the model company converted into a powerful emblem of progress during the first half of the twentieth century—help explain the spread of the Ford name and of Fordism throughout the world. There are certainly other factors—economic, political, social, and technological—that must be considered, but the myth of the popular car and the model company in an era when heavy industry was still perceived as synonymous with progress is an indispensable element in understanding the *cultural* scope of the phenomenon. According to Germán Arciniegas, in order to build his empire Ford had gathered a team of bright men and in only a few months "had begun to build a factory as large as the tombs of all the pharaohs to fill the world with windows such that the sun, from Oceania to the heart of New York City, would be reflected only from Ford windshields."[5]

A visit to the Ford assembly plant in São Paulo, Brazil, was one of the favorite weekend outings of local residents. The assembly line had become a special tourist attraction. On May 12, 1920, the *Jornal do Brasil* ("Ford *Bigode* Is a Hit in São Paulo") reported that the Brazilian with enough money to buy an automobile no longer had to buy it abroad. He had only to wait for a Ford Model T Moustache to roll hot off the assembly line the American company had set up in downtown São Paulo in 1919. The factory was only an assembly plant, as all the parts were imported from the United States, and Ford needed the labor of only twelve workers to place each part in its proper place. The spectacle delighted the inhabitants of Paulicéia, who avidly sought new things: "The Paulistanos, who love novelties and automobiles especially, made the assembly plant a tourist attraction of the city. On weekends hundreds of people can be seen trying to understand how a pile of parts can become a car."

Mário de Andrade refers explicitly to the impact of the assembly line on São Paulo and compares the assembly of a Ford automobile to writing poetry. On reviewing *Poesias*, by Manuel Bandeira, he mentions the qualities and defects of the verses of the author from Recife. Unlike later work by Bandeira, which has emotional power, fine irony, sincerity of daily life, and vital contemplation, "Cinza das horas" expresses the search for a style of one's own. Bandeira seeks inspiration in the books of other poets. He mentions that someone needs gas. How does a poet arise? He is usually born like a Ford car. This affirmation is based on the image of "literary Fordism" and translates into a surprising reflection on the beginning of modern poetry:

> In the last automobile show, the Ford Company organized an advertising gimmick with a terrific result: assembling an automobile in public. Each worker did only one task. This one adjusted the springs. That one installed

a wheel. Another one calibrated the headlights. And so forth. The car gradually began to come to life. Each one had exactly one minute of work. If he
took a little more time, the whole assembly would be ruined. The people
were enthralled. And at the end, victory! In half an hour a Ford rolled out,
alive and shiny bright! The people thought it was going to wind up in Rio
Prato, eating up thick clouds of Pauline dust, in the midst of a drought. . . .
Poets usually are born like a Ford. Each book, each poet from the past that
they read is a worker who adjusts a wheel for them, or the carburetor, or
the springs. At the end another friend puts in the gasoline. Then the poet
rolls off the assembly line—beep-beep!—and writes poems. Many of the
poets I know were short on gasoline for the rest of their lives. Poor things![6]

Monteiro Lobato was a Brazilian businessman and writer and an enthusiastic admirer of American industrial civilization. He admired Henry
Ford, whom he defined as the best model of an organic idealist. "Whoever read and understood Henry Ford is invincible," he once wrote. As a
businessman he tried to apply Ford's methods to his workers in Brazil. He
also published articles in the newspaper O Jornal that were translated into
English by Aubrey Stuart under the title "How Henry Ford Is Regarded in
Brazil."[7] In 1926, when a review of the book in which Ford recounted his
life and work appeared in the Revista do Brasil, the tone of the review was
one of admiration:

Ever since Watt's invention, over a century ago, man has been in the
machine age and societies have been immersed in the increasingly complex machine-ism of modern industry. But up to now it had not been possible for the men who were truly representative of this age of social evolution to emerge. The industrial order of the nineteenth century in Europe
was represented by small or mediocre types of men. The character of the
great banker was more vigorously defined as a faithful representative of
the subordination of labor to money, or of industry to the bank. Now,
however, the United States reacted and following the millionaires whose
wealth came from railroads, the meatpacking industry, steel, and the oil
and gas industries, in the first quarter of the twentieth century the true
figure of the modern industrialist appeared. Ford, the biggest producer of
wealth, the man whose capital annually produced more gold than anyone
else, embodied that vehemently notable reaction.[8]

Ford was a man of action. He did not cultivate literary artifice, he
believed in the goodness of man, he generated wealth, and he applied his

ideas to benefit society. Monteiro Lobato even excuses his anti-Semitism, arguing that Ford had carefully studied the participation of the Jews in the American economy. In contrast to writers and philosophers who vehemently denounced the machine and the dangers of mechanization, the American industrialist emerges in the writing of Monteiro Lobato as the representative icon of modern heroism. The future belongs to machines and work: humanity triumphs by organizing industry. Ford represented that new state of things that sought to suppress both poverty and privilege. "Based on the principles of Henry Ford," writes Lobato in his preface to the Brazilian translation of *My Life and Work,* "industry ceases to be the Moloch that devours millions of creatures to benefit a small group of the wealthy; it becomes transformed into an inexhaustible source of wealth. The fearful antagonism between capital and labor that threatens to subvert the world is done away with. Production readjusts itself to consumption and, as a result of more equitable distribution, the monstrous cancer of human misery disappears."[9]

Monteiro Lobato and his family moved to the United States in mid-1927 as he had been named Brazilian commercial attaché in New York. He went in search of American efficiency. For some time he had been contrasting the United States and Brazil, which he called a "country of tortoises." He arrived to find a country in full effervescence but also an imaginary territory that had exerted its allure over him long before he could experience it personally. In an era in which many Latin American intellectuals dreamed in French and venerated Paris, Monteiro Lobato, a nationalist, planned to found his Tupi Publishing Company in New York, but he never managed to carry out this project.[10]

The United States dazzled him. Whom did he meet on the dock in Hoboken? None other than the general agent of the Ford Motor Company, who handed him his business card and told him he had orders from Henry Ford to greet him and do everything possible to help him. Two weeks later Monteiro Lobato reported that he was "Americanized," having acquired a car, a radio, and a beautiful apartment. The contrast with Brazil was radical: "I imagined it would be large, but it is larger! It is immense, it is infinite, it is a new world. I am enthralled with America! The country I dreamed about. Efficiency! Galloping speed! Future! No one walking backwards! What infinite stupidity to ruin an entire life there! . . . The Brazilian's illusion is a serious case. The world is already in the era of radio, and Brazil continues to carve stones. It is a nation of troglodytes. Brazil sleeps. You can hear it snoring from here. It sleeps and is completely blind."[11] But he also stated in his letters that the sleeping giant must be awakened and provided with iron and oil. Curiously, Fordism nurtured nationalism, providing images of grandeur for Brazil.

Monteiro Lobato spent four years and a few months in the United States. He lost everything he had when the stock market crashed, although economic collapse did not seem to affect his enthusiasm for the country, as portrayed in his book *América*. Short on funds, he traveled little. But there were two places he could not miss: the Ford Motor Company and General Motors. He did not manage to meet Henry Ford, who was in Scotland when he visited the plant. As compensation, he had lunch with Ford's son Edsel at the round table in the company's boardroom. With all that he had seen, he said, he could write a book larger than the *Encyclopaedia Britannica*.[12]

As the years went by, dependence on American technology intensified. In order to understand the new production methods one had to travel to Motor City: the Detroit plant offered the possibility of short apprenticeships to anyone interested. In Latin America there were few American representatives, their stay there was short, and they were not high up on the administrative ladder. Henry Ford himself never traveled to South America, not even to supervise the Fordlândia project in the Amazon jungle. On the other hand, South American executives visited Detroit often. The idea was that they could learn much more from these expeditions to Detroit than from the visits of North American representatives to South America.[13]

Let us remember that in the first phase of the automobile not only was mechanical training a must, but so were driving lessons. Ford agents, in order to sell their product in Latin America, often had to teach the customer to drive. "Selling service above all else" was the fundamental slogan. When he returned to Caracas after perfecting his knowledge of the Ford factory in Detroit, Édgar Anzola drove a Model T on the rutted roads made for animal-drawn conveyances to Los Teques, Barquisimeto, San Felipe, Maracaibo, and San Cristóbal. In each place he had to be willing to teach the buyers, or their chauffeurs, the basic principles of mechanics and driving.

Besides selling cars and offering training and professional information, the Ford agent functioned as an intermediary between two worlds. He was the mediator of motorization in towns that did not know the meaning of the assembly line. The case of a Dane, Kristian Orberg, who headed the assembly plant in São Paulo in 1921, is revealing on this point. Orberg traveled throughout Brazil as a publicity agent for Ford. Not only did he sell cars, he pushed for better roads, and he recruited and trained new dealers, as well as ironworkers, dentists, doctors, and anyone else who could be useful to the business.

The Ford plant in River Rouge was the showcase of the new world. For a clergyman named William Stidger, it was a matter of the "miracle" of production.[14] David Nye says that the Reverend Stidger, on describing the open-hearth steel ovens, presented the factory in terms of the sublime in nature: "We looked through blue glasses and saw typhoons of flame leaping white against the brick walls, Niagaras of tumbling, turbulent, tumultuous, white waters of flame and fire, awe-inspiring, soul-subduing romance! Romance! Romance of Power! . . . Power! Power! Power! That is the source of the romance of the River Rouge plant."[15]

Every visitor was impressed by the mechanized geometrical architecture. André Citroën visited it in 1923. Between 1922 and 1923 an engineer, John H. Van Deventer, wrote thirteen articles about River Rouge that provide a detailed technical description of the factory. Years later, in 1927, Ray L. Faurote wrote ten articles about what he had seen. In 1929 a German, Clärenore Stinnes, on her trip by car across several continents, visited the Ford factory in Detroit and was impressed by the assembly line. A car could be assembled in eight and a half minutes, which meant 8,000 cars a day. Stinnes was particularly attracted to Henry Ford's eyes, which gleamed with satisfaction while he guided a select group of visitors through all the rooms of the factory.

While the foundry was the most impressive unit of the River Rouge plant, the machinery and the layout of the workshops surprised even specialists.[16] Both Van Deventer and Faurote mentioned that the workshops could appear crowded and congested for one who was accustomed to traditional workshops, but they were efficient work sites in a plant where the work moved and the workers stayed in one place. For Van Deventer, who described the total effect on the observer of the flow of manufacturing, the visitor perceived the units "not only in their impressive individual and astounding collective magnitude, but he also [saw] each unit as the part of a huge machine—he [saw] each unit as a carefully designed gear which meshes with other gears and operates in synchronism with them, the whole forming one huge, perfectly-timed, smoothly operating industrial machine of almost unbelievable efficiency."[17]

A visit to the River Rouge plant was like a pilgrimage: hundreds of tourists passed through there every day: caravans of people came and went, attracted by a sort of modern miracle. And by 1927 Ford had managed to centralize the various phases of automobile production into a unique, gigantic place. A Uruguayan tourist, José María Delgado, visited the Ford plant in Detroit toward the end of the 1920s and believed he was in another world. Despite the declared death of time and space by the futurists, it is worthwhile insisting on the "distance" separating the editor of the magazine *Pegaso*, whose literary work abounds in epic poems and in Pindaric odes in celebration of athletic events, from the automated factory in River Rouge and from the assembly line. Nonetheless, this author, born in the interior of Uruguay, who rendered homage to metal, is an example of the triumph of kinetic modernity.

Delgado likened the automobile factory to a marvelous mosque and referred to his visit as a sort of pilgrimage to a secular shrine. This was a new type of miracle, which had lost its mystical form and mysterious intangibility. It was not the spiritual temple of silence and concentration but "something prodigious, active, energetic, moved by wheels and pulleys, red from hearths with the power of the sun, where iron and steel become as easy to tame as water, vibrating with hammers and pylons, and all the voices of the modern mechanical epic poem."[18] The impact on entering the workshop has something of the supernatural. This ritual crossing invokes the image of a magician's show and of transformism, where the mechanical skeleton is fitted with sparkplugs and wheels, its cables are connected, and its radiator is attached, the hood is fastened down, and a perfect, working automobile rolls out. It only needs to be adjusted and taken to the boxcars that disperse machines such as this one throughout the world. A perfect piece of machinery, exact, and made to work by a legion of artisans who transform "errant entrails" and an "army of organs" into a mechanical body full of life.

The process of mechanical creation on an assembly line is described as an interminable technical miracle. The feeling of magical metamorphosis characteristic of kinetic modernity predominates, and, consequently, Delgado describes entrance into the workshop as if he were narrating entrance into an authentic science fiction landscape: "Thousands of frenzied machines, all moved by electricity, greeted us in a wondrous symphony; convoys of wagons and trucks constantly passed by on either side of us and above our heads, at each blow of the enormous drop forges, soon-to-be-used wheels and crankshafts jumped, magically; marvelous looms transformed rustic yarn into noble weavings; the ovens where metal boiled, looked at us through windows of mica with a volcanic incandescence, and on numerous aerial cables, endless in theory, went wheels, cylinders, axles, radiators, marching along as though they knew where they were going."[19] The factory is a place of dreams, where fantasy can become reality.

We are not just seeing the image of a factory, if by that we mean an establishment fitted with machinery, tools, and the facilities necessary for the manufacture of certain objects, the obtaining of certain products or industrial transformation into a source of energy. We are facing a mass-production system inconceivable in Latin America. The Ford factory in River Rouge was the most advanced example of automobile production in the world. When it was visited by Delgado, the traditional Ford Model T that had been produced until 1927 was no longer in production; it had been replaced by the newer Model A, an automobile, according to its admirers, that combined mass-production methods with art.

In contrast to the image of the unceasing movement of industrialism and the noisy work of man-machines, Charles Sheeler's photographs and paintings present the technological experience from an aesthetic indus-trial perspective. Sheeler experienced a sort of conversion to industrial-ism when he was in charge of photographically documenting the new Ford plant in River Rouge. The advertising campaign was supposed to transmit the image of the Ford factory as an enchanted place and to promote the aes-thetic dimension of industry. Symptomatically, Sheeler did not photograph the facilities of the industrial complex that directly produced the automo-biles, but the foundry where the raw material was converted into steel. His photos and paintings offer architectural compositions of the foundry as an idealized, grandiose landscape. Barbara Haskell notes that, together with the identification of factory and religious expression, Sheeler offered silent, calm compositions of industrialism that transmit the experience of the technological sublime.[20] The temporality of the human presence and the brutal reality of the assembly line give way to a secularized spiritualism where the universal values of harmony, purity, and order prevail.

From the beginning Ford employed photographers to document the con-struction of the River Rouge industrial complex. But Sheeler's photographs have another objective: the combination of art and industry. More than a documentary, they celebrate an American monument to mass production. Besides being a well-known artist, Sheeler was a spokesman for photogra-phy as art. He had demonstrated this with his paintings and photographs of the majestic skyscrapers of New York and with his ten-minute silent film, *Manhatta* (1921). In River Rouge he used well-defined, sharp lines, geomet-ric shapes and surprising angles, a mixture of realism and abstraction. He took his photographs from walkways, ledges, railways, and ground level, concentrating on the architecture and the machinery associated with the initial phases of automobile production—on structures, not on people.[21]

Another fascinating example of displacement and artistic representation is Diego Rivera and Frida Kahlo's trip to Detroit in 1932. Rivera was chosen to paint a mural about modern industry in the Detroit Institute of Arts. Edsel Ford, president of the Ford Motor Company and a patron of the arts, was behind the invitation. The automobile and the Ford Motor Company were to be honored, using Detroit industry as a theme. Rivera and Kahlo visited the River Rouge industrial complex. The Mexican muralist's ambition—to paint the history of a new race in the steel age—was not simple. Communist Diego Rivera, collector of pre-Columbian art, working in the United States for capitalist clients, was enthusiastic about the industrialism of Detroit, despite not knowing how to drive a car and having painted Emiliano Zapata in Cubist style.

While Rivera worked on the mural, Kahlo had an unfortunate miscarriage. *Henry Ford Hospital*, dated July 1932, is her first self-portrait to highlight the dramatic element of emotion. Realism abounds in the figures in the painting: while the female nude evokes a long tradition of the seductive woman lying on a bed or a sofa, the event is dramatized here from a bloody perspective. An enormous blood-stained bed floats in the air holding a deformed nude body, the tear indicative of sadness, the swollen belly from which disconcerting images emerge and are intertwined. We see a human fetus, a snail, a salmon-colored torso on a pedestal that appears to have been X-rayed, a violet orchid, a human bone model (possibly of the hip), and a strange machine (clearly part of a sterilizer). All proportion is consciously deformed, and the realist register is subordinated to the dramatization of the subject. The parallel between Mexican ex-votos and this small oil painting on copper has been pointed out.[22]

In any case, the background—the industrial complex of River Rouge, its coke ovens, conveyor belts, smokestacks, and water towers—could not be less Mexican. While still in Detroit Frida continued working on the theme of the contrast between the natural and the artificial. *Self-portrait on the Border between Mexico and the United States* (1932) juxtaposes two worlds. Mexico is agrarian and mythical; the United States is electric and metallic. Mexico is fed by roots, the United States, by cables. The Mexican landscape is contrasted with the industrial scene of Detroit: sun and moon versus the smoke of the chimneys; pyramids versus skyscrapers; pre-Columbian sculptures versus metal tubing; flowers versus motors; the organic cycle of life and death versus artificial existence. Frida is standing on a pedestal in the middle of the painting, wearing an elegant pink dress and lace gloves, a cigarette in one hand and a small Mexican flag in the other. Two apparently irreconcilable worlds that, in fact, were much more interconnected than her artistic representation suggests.

While Frida Kahlo expressed her ambiguous relationship with the United States, Diego Rivera finished the mural, *Detroit Industry*, or *Man and Machine*. Unlike Sheeler, Rivera concentrated his attention on the vitality, movement, and energy of the industrial process. He highlighted the workers who labored at the plant, their outward appearance, their concentrated effort, and the harsh working conditions. Showing scant interest in the automobile he piled up machines, workers, and tourists. The dramatic element of manufacturing fades when the machine is completed: the finished product hides the complexity and difficulty of the process.[23]

The inauguration of the murals in March 1933 unleashed unmistakable signs of disapproval. Here was the representation of the birth and development of the technological era, with its machines, war planes, and, especially, the different stages of production of the Ford V-8. The workers were confined in a metallic space. The machine ruled, the operator being mechanically subordinated to the frenetic functioning of the industrial society. Understandably, such a representation of the "spirit of Detroit" provoked uneasiness. Nevertheless, Edsel Ford and George Pierrot defended Rivera's work and his attempt to create a new aesthetic for the steel age. Quick explanations of the meaning of the painting were needed in order to assuage the controversy.

While painting the murals, Rivera relied on several artistic models. Andrea Kettenmann and Linda Downs point out some of them: the compression of space and the simultaneous nature of the events and the fragmentation of the forms into a basic geometric element were derived from Cubism's methods of composition; the massive creations of pre-Columbian sculpture serve as a reference for the representation of the machinery; the composition of the murals relies on the sculpture of the tympanums of medieval churches; the use of portraits of contemporaries and the technique of painting al fresco come from Italian painting of the Renaissance.[24] Everything worked together in the Detroit murals to transmit the aesthetic of the steel era. They were murals to be discussed and questioned, but not to be annihilated like Rivera's mural *Man at the Crossroads*, commissioned by the Rockefeller family for Rockefeller Center in New York and destroyed when it was almost finished. Rivera would take vengeance for the destruction of his work by repainting it the following year in the Palace of Fine Arts in Mexico City under the title *Man as Controller of the Universe*, or *Man in the Time Machine*.

In 1978 an exhibition, *The Rouge: The Image of Industry in the Art of Charles Sheeler and Diego Rivera*, was held to commemorate the Ford Motor Company's seventy-fifth anniversary. The differences between these artists are noteworthy. Sheeler's photographs and paintings depict the architecture and the machinery in a classic style, practically without human presence, while the severe beauty of industrial power is expressed through smokestacks, coke ovens, conveyor belts, boilers, and sheet metal presses. Rivera's al fresco painting shows some common trends of this industrial aesthetic—a tendency toward pure and abstract industrial forms—but the Mexican artist emphasizes the human impact, placing the labor force as a literal and figurative mode in the foreground, with conveyor belts and assembly lines interwoven around, above, and behind them.[25]

The Factory Panopticon

What calls one's attention at first sight of the panopticon—an architectural space created by Englishman Jeremy Bentham for prison design at the end of the eighteenth century, the shape of which allowed for complete observation of the prisoners—is its static nature. The principle of mobility seems to have found a terrible enemy. In fact the prisoners are isolated in individual cells and cannot even establish contact with other prisoners, while the watchful eye of the guard hides in the shadows: it sees without being seen. From the point of view of the evolution of kinetic modernity "scientific" institutions that punish by depriving prisoners of freedom of movement are important. Unlike exile, chains, or death from starvation, this model consists of constant, cruel surveillance of individuals deprived of their freedom, alone and segregated, without the right to any privacy from the terrible watchtower.

The panopticon is both an applied utopian model and a model of surveillance through architecture that can be adapted to any type of establishment. Michel Foucault understood it that way when he said the prison project had extended to the rest of society's institutions such as hospitals, asylums, schools, and factories. According to his definition, the panopticon meant spatial units could be organized in such a way that they allowed continuous surveillance and immediate recognition, inducing in the prisoner a permanent, conscious state of visibility that ensured the automatic exercise of power. While visibility ensures order, it is apparent that this phenomenon is widespread. In other words: total mobilization. Because the goal of the panopticon scheme is to become an operational principle, it is possible to identify it with the very essence of modern subjectivity. What is important is a strengthening of social forces: increase production, develop the economy, disseminate instruction, raise the level of public morals, cause growth, and multiply.[26]

It is known that Foucault conceived the image of total visibility of bodies when he was studying the origins of clinical medicine. He could have obtained a similar result by examining the development of automatization in Henry Ford's factories, for they were effectively transformed into a space where the individual in the production line could be controlled. Taylor and Ford were obsessed with the problem of time lost during production. The image is surprising: semi-immobility of the workers on the assembly line stimulates a brutal intensification of planetary movement. The enormous resistance of the workers, who often failed to show up or simply abandoned the job, indicates that motorization demands much more than the mixture of idealism and utilitarianism to achieve its objectives.

Ford fostered the creation of a totalitarian ministate to achieve his goals. The Sociology Department took charge of obtaining information about the employees' private lives, sending inspectors to their homes to ask about their marriage and financial situations. This interference in their private lives implied control over the use of alcoholic beverages and gambling, as well as mandatory English classes for immigrants.

A young Ukrainian immigrant named Charles Madison arrived in Detroit with his family at the beginning of the century. Over the years he worked in Dodge, Studebaker, and Ford factories. His account of his experience in the Ford Motor Company illustrates the daily terror imposed on the workers by foremen and administrators. The "five dollars a day" advertisement attracted thousands of candidates to Highland Park: endless lines of aspirants tussled with each other for a chance to get in while the police had to control the disorder. It was not difficult for Charles to get a job, since he had experience with the lathe. But on his first day he found himself facing an inspector—an efficiency expert—who timed his work to find out how many parts he could assemble in eight hours of work. The young man, who worked quickly, understood it would be very difficult to achieve the expected quota, even though everything worked without a hitch and he took no breaks. For the utopia of movement to become a reality, the agent has to become inhuman.

Expelled from Paradise, he becomes a self-propelled machine that inhabits an environment occupied by other machines. The machines invade everything. Repetition and exact measurements are characteristics of that new work space. Madison's vision of work in the Ford factory in Highland Park is terrifying: "No allowance was made for lunch, toilet time, or tool sharpening. I refused to disallow necessary delays, although I managed to keep the machine going while munching my sandwich. When I failed to produce the assigned quota of finished parts, the foreman scolded me. The next day another efficiency timekeeper with a stopwatch was assigned to observe my work. After an hour of making notes as I worked he told the foreman I was too slow in placing the part in the machine and was making no effort to speed up."[27]

The young man's arguments that it was humanly impossible to meet the job's requirements were fruitless. He continued working hard without ever reaching the required quota. He put up with a job he considered inhumane solely for the five dollars a day, the promise of money being more powerful than the will to leave the factory and never come back. He had to resign himself and forget about self: the goal of planetary mobilization exacted its price. Hence his astonishment and anger when he received his first pay and discovered he was being paid 25 cents an hour—two dollars a day—certainly not the five that had been promised. When he protested, the foreman told him they would start to pay the five dollars a day when he had worked in the factory for six consecutive months and had proved his ability to maintain the required quota. Madison not only asked to be fired immediately, but he remembered his experience in the Ford factory as a hell on earth that transformed human beings into controlled robots. His resentment against the company that exploited employees in a much crueler way than the other automobile companies, dominating their lives and depriving them of individuality, is a warning that the kinetic imperative has a tragic human cost.

Like all processes that forecast the future as a redemption of the present, the compromise with modernity is composed of illusions and broken promises. The result is often a nightmare. It was hard to imagine that the Sociology Department would be replaced by an even more severe organ of control: the Ford Service Department, headed by a former prizefighter, Harry Bennett. This man who, just as Charles Sorenson, enjoyed Ford's complete confidence, imposed an inescapable system based on fear during working hours, modeled on the social organization of the army. At the end of the 1920s even the *New York Times* referred to the Ford Motor Company as the most outstanding example in the world of industrial dictatorship and characterized its president as "an industrial fascist—the Mussolini of Detroit."[28]

Detroit became a city of hate and fear, and nowhere was this more visible than in Ford's River Rouge factory. The working conditions were horrifying. The lunch period was fifteen minutes long, and that included using the bathroom. No one escaped surveillance; a group of foremen demanded strict compliance with the rules, which prohibited leaning on the machine or sitting down, singing, whistling, or smoking. When the end of the Model T came in May 1927, after the production of fifteen million flivvers, it meant the end of an era. The mass-production system had to be made more flexible as it was necessary to face the challenge of a yearly model change imposed by General Motors. The Ford Motor Company was forced to struggle against what its director and prophet of the practical new world had always denounced as waste: style and comfort. The perception of the car as an object to be used until it wore out had gone out of fashion, and the loss of first place in the American automotive industry was intolerable. In order to compensate for the loss, ever-greater demands were constantly imposed on executives and workers.

The combination of Fordism and Americanism was commonplace when Antonio Gramsci asked himself at the start of the 1930s what had caused the European reaction against Americanism. However, the notion that Americanism demanded a "rational demographic composition" as a preexisting condition was a novel idea. Unlike in Europe, where wealth enabled certain social classes to survive without participating in the production process, in the United States such parasitic classes did not exist. That explained, according to Gramsci, the intellectual and moral resistance in Europe to the introduction of Fordism: the anachronistic social demographic structure in Europe contradicted a highly modern form of production.

The problems that arose in the United States because of Fordist industrialization revealed to Gramsci that the old economic individualism model had given way to a more planned economy. Any progressive movement initiated by a given social group generates resistance by subordinate groups that must be manipulated and rationalized according to the new objectives. But the United States did not have significant historical and cultural traditions that could impede economic development. This is, for Gramsci, one of the main reasons, more important than so-called natural wealth, underlying the formidable accumulation of capital. It is also a warning of the power of movement in modern culture. Once the task of rationalization of production and work has been simplified, the entire country can be oriented toward production, and the hegemonic approach starts in the factories. In order to be exercised, such hegemony needs a minimum number of professional intermediaries in politics and ideology. In America, Gramsci concludes, rationalization determined a need to create a new type of human being, in keeping with the new forms of work and production. If the fundamental question of hegemony had not yet appeared, it was because psychological and physical adaptation to the new industrial structure, stimulated through high salaries, was still in its infancy.

Gramsci related the new work methods to styles of living, thinking, and experiencing life. The rationalization of work implied prohibitionism and sexual puritanism. Industrialists had to guarantee the upright moral standards of their employees, even by sending inspectors to survey the intimate life of their workers. Nervous energy could not be wasted on a disorderly, exciting search for occasional sexual satisfaction. Monogamy and stability, a wife, and high moral standards yielded better results. That led to a great collective effort to rapidly create a new model of worker and a new man: Taylorism and Fordism worked together to reward the domesticated gorilla, to praise the human being who had been converted into an automated production machine.

While Gramsci's philosophy of praxis mainly concerned itself with the influence of technology and capitalist production on the workers, literature broadened the topic of the mechanized society and expanded the prison metaphor. It had to do with a prophesied totalitarian state, where authoritarianism suppressed the individual's concept of self: Yevgeni Zamiatin's *We* and George Orwell's *1984* are two examples of an abundant literary production that fictionalized technological society as a monstrous panopticon.

Two extraordinary novels, both published in 1932—*Voyage au bout de la nuit* (Journey to the end of the night), by Louis-Ferdinand Céline, and *Brave New World*, by Aldous Huxley—provided gloomy versions of Fordist mechanization. The vision of a member of a tour group is inevitably external. From "inside" the factory, from the experience of the worker, the perspective changes radically, as happens in Céline's description in *Voyage au bout de la nuit*. The nightmarish style overtakes a reality that always appears to be beyond the individual's control. This is the story of a poor Parisian student, a former soldier who immigrates to the United States and experiences the horror of working in the Ford factory. He disregards the mechanized carnage of World War I but observes the metamorphosis of human beings turned into mere objects. The daily indifference to the phenomenon of dehumanization verges on cruelty and the absurd and assumes colossal proportions. Civilization itself whirls like an automaton and subordinates social relationships to money.

Céline perceives endless cages of insects in the glass buildings of the Ford factory, which so many observers called a "temple of progress." He dwells on the noisy, harsh, deafening roar of machines, the grinding of gears, whirling, rotating, and whining. Outside the main door there are hundreds of poor foreigners in search of work. Scarcely anyone speaks English in that crowd, and between the smell of urine and bad breath all look at each other as untrusting animals. Subhuman men desperate for work jostle each other in the lines.

Landing a job is not a problem. Any person can work at Ford, any miserable person. First they have to remove their clothes and be examined. Here, having an education is not worth anything according to the doctor's comments to the French student; he also warns him to take care not to show his intelligence, to behave as an obedient chimpanzee, to turn himself into a machine:

> Everything trembled in the enormous building, and we ourselves, from our ears to the soles of our feet, were gathered into this trembling, which came from the windows, the floor, and all the clanking metal, tremors that shook the whole building from top to bottom. We ourselves became machines, our flesh trembled in the furious din, it gripped us around our heads and in our bowels and rose up to our eyes in quick, continuous jolts. The further we went, the more of our companions we lost. In leaving them, we gave them bright little smiles, as if all this were just lovely. It was no longer possible to speak to them or hear them. Each time three or four of them stopped at a machine.[29]

There is no time to stop and reflect. Facing this fatality, the human being shrinks and his life is reduced to nothing; he becomes the servant of the machines, a shrunken phantom of flesh and bone, fodder for the metal monsters:

> It's sickening to watch the workers bent over their machines, intent on giving them all possible pleasure, calibrating bolts and more bolts, instead of putting an end once for all to this stench of oil, this vapor that burns your throat and attacks your eardrums from inside. It's not shame that makes them bow their heads. You give in to noise as you give in to war. At the machines you let yourself go with the two three ideas that are wobbling about at the top of your head. And that's the end. From then on everything you look at, everything you touch, is hard. And everything you still manage to remember more or less becomes rigid as iron, and loses its savor in your thoughts. All of a sudden you've become disgustingly old.[30]

Céline's character Bardamu is never presented as a model worker, and from the outset he works poorly. We can imagine this lower-middle-class Frenchman, cynical and uncomfortable in the midst of American efficiency. A few days after being hired, he is transferred to another task, equally mechanized, where the person has to survive between stupor and delirium. The only thing that matters is the noisy clattering of thousands of instruments that command the men. When the workday ends at six in the evening, the worker carries away the racket of the machines inside his head, locked in for the entire night. He carries away, also, the smell of oil. It is as though he has a new nose and a new brain; the odor of oil instead of air; the racket instead of silence. A new man is born, resigned after some weeks of working at the factory, to forgetting the world and the warmth of other bodies. Machines, only machines. Until Molly the prostitute, with her money, patience, and kind nature, rescues the man-machine and frees him from the daily grind of facing the gleaming pipes at the factory, as intricate and menacing as metal lianas.

Brave New World, by Aldous Huxley, is the description of a fictitious, completely mechanized society. Human beings are produced in test tubes in a hatchery, conditioned from the outset not to deviate a single iota from the established patterns in the World State's motto: Community, Identity, Stability. This is the supreme vision of instrumental technology, hypnotic, fascinating, imaginatively informed by the French psychological theories of the masses and the behavior studies of an Englishman, John Watson, and a Russian, Ivan Pavlov. Who directs this enormous machinery of neo-Pavlovian conditioning? An American, Henry Ford.

When sailing from Malaysia to the United States, Huxley discovered *My Life and Work* in the ship's library. His initial reaction was one of fascination. Six years later, Huxley presented a radically different message in *Brave New World*. Jerome Meckier researched this transformation and suggests that, between 1926 and 1932, Huxley met "primitivists" D. H. Lawrence and Gerald Heard, read Pavlov and Watson with horror, and gradually identified the American inventor Henry Ford as a dangerous utopist, a false futurist, whose ideas could mean the end of humanity.[31] For Huxley the list of thinkers who threatened the future of humanity was quite varied: Pavlov, Watson, Wells, Helvetius, Bentham, Freud. No thinker more terrible than Henry Ford, because the assembly line turned efficiency and consumption into gods. With his organizational genius and fervent belief in technological progress, this action-oriented American was able to convert the abstract idea of a conditioned society into an enormous factory for assembly-line production.

We know Huxley considered his trip to be a transformative experience. The psychology of European civilization could be perceived best from abroad. There is, however, a book he read with care in Europe that helped him reflect on the relationship between machinism, psychology, and

politics and that confirmed to him Henry Ford's importance as director
of a society organized on an industrial base. In "Machinery, Psychology,
and Politics," which appeared in *The Spectator* in November 1923, Huxley
comments on *La morale de la machine*, a book by Alphonse Séché, who
recommended that modern industrial nations be organized collectively as
a group of companies, hierarchically ordered and led by a person such as
Henry Ford. But Huxley does not endorse the optimistic tone of the book,
for he feels that mechanization leads to uniform behavior both externally
and internally, limits aesthetic choice by producing standardized objects
that are usually ugly, and promotes stupidity with large-scale production
of spiritual narcotics and substitutes for thinking such as newspapers,
magazines, movies, and the radio.

Huxley's preoccupation with the consequences of managed reproduction is intimately related to Fordism. The Ford Motor Company is at the
core of this ordered and standardized panoptical society, with its laboratory, hospital, school, and managed consumer behavior. Mechanical creation and serial production, or the principles of mass production applied
to biology. The technological systems of the automobile and biotechnology intersect, approaching the limits of humanism and individualism in
the age of mechanical reproduction. Of course there are un-Ford-like
examples of inadequacy in characters such as John the Savage and Helm-
holtz Watson. Or in problems such as loneliness and unhappiness in the
midst of compulsive happiness; love instead of free, pragmatic sexuality;
and the search for transcendence.

Twenty years after *Brave New World* was published, Huxley explained
in the foreword to a newer edition the motives that had led him to imagine the future as a nightmare. He argued that the theme of the book was
not the advancement of science as such; rather it was the advancement of
science as it affects human individuals, starting with research in biology,
psychology, and physiology. The people who govern the Brave New World
are neither insane nor anarchical: their fundamental objective is social
stability. Scientific resources are available for that, with happiness being
viewed as a duty and as a reward.

Brave New World narrates dramatically the fear of converting the Earth
into a factory that produces standardized objects fed by genetically conceived and scientifically managed workers. The era: 632 AF, that is, After
Ford. The date the Model T was introduced marks the starting date of the
new era. Whoever is not aware of Ford is considered uncivilized. "Thanks
be to Ford" replaces "Thanks be to God," while the book *My Life and Work*,
edited by the Society for the Propagation of Fordian Knowledge, replaces

the Bible. Previously, there had been something known as Christianity. In the new age the upper ends are cut off all the crosses, transforming that symbol into the T of Ford's universal model.

Here nature (the wood of the cross) is transformed into machinism (the metal of the automobile) and the sacred mutates into something mechanical. A true mechanical genesis, a new world that eliminates the prefigurative meaning of the mast where Ulysses was tied as a Christ figure and does away with any sacred interpretation of history. The revolution that marks the beginning of modern history is mass production, the announcement that human beings could be manufactured in a laboratory. Psychoanalysis contributes to this as an instrument of control, the "Ford-Freud" complex, while the *Community, Identity, Stability* triad replaces the famous words of the French Revolution.

Hatching and Conditioning Center, Decanting Room, vials of pills and conditioned reflexes. The masses are conditioned to hate books and the outdoors, although not outdoor sports, for they promote consumption of means of transportation. The machine grinds tirelessly on. Why such extreme conditioning? What are the objectives of such overwhelming control? Less truth and beauty than power, the spell of comfort and constant satisfaction. God is incompatible with machines, scientific medicine, and universal happiness.

But restrictions are imposed on being able to participate in the perfect new world. Any upheaval between interior and exterior is forbidden. Happiness carries with it the renunciation of self-initiative, danger, and freedom: those who are fully adapted to the routine of the assembly line are rewarded. The unhealthy alternative of the utopian life—primitive life in an Indian village—is presented as an insane choice. Precisely, the defect in his novel the writer recognized years later is that it left no place for choice except between insanity (the utopia) and dementia (the primitive).

Literary works were inspired by mass production. Fiction was nourished by reality, and the assembly line morphed into the biotechnology of the future. Huxley's description of the egg-hatching process in *Brave New World* was directly inspired by the Ford Motor Company's assembly line. Flaps of sow's peritoneum, cut to the exact size, shot up in small elevators to the Bottling Room from the Organ Store in the basement. The Bottle Liner only had to reach out his hand, take the flap, insert it in a bottle, smooth it down and before the lined container moved beyond his reach on the moving belt another flap of peritoneum arrived, shot from the depths, ready to be slipped into the inside of another bottle. Thus, over and over, in the Bottling Room, the Liners Room, the Matriculators Room, the Social Predestination Room.

Theodor Adorno interprets the paralogism of identity in *Brave New World* and situated Huxley's novel in the context of American capitalism, where men lose their own individuation. With his unmistakable ill-humor, he denounces the curse of things "always being the same": *Brave New World* was a unique concentration camp where, freed of contradiction, it considered itself to be a Terrestrial Paradise. Oppression and domination live on in this deformed utopia, while individuals are as isolated from the spirit as they are from nature. In the mutilation of human liberty, Adorno detects the failure of reason and the proliferation of irrationality, the latter triumphant under the veneer of the perfect organization. Ideological criticism mobilizes against the whole, and thinking is accused of becoming a slave of total organization. This is the reign of terror, not of freedom or authentic pleasure. *Brave New World* presents a terrifying vision of capitalism and American cultural industry. Human beings have been reduced to being mere purchasers of the products mass-produced by the trusts and have been submitted to total predestination by social intervention. *Conditioning*, a term from biology and behaviorist psychology, is the method used to guarantee the unchanging social order and reproduce stupidity. It is the idiocy of the *everybody's happy nowadays* cult of the automobile, separate from any objective purpose, of the fetishist passion for owning perfect machines. Pleasure degenerates into miserable fun. In the name of culture, says Adorno, civilization is thrown into barbarism.[32]

If so many fears and hopes converged in the figure of Henry Ford, it is because, clearly, there is a threatening link between modern technology and total mobilization. Of course, this relationship cannot be understood merely as an abstract conflict between man and machine; rather it must be situated in the social environment of human relations and in the context of the secularization of the advanced industrial societies. While for Adorno the construct that denounced the totalitarian World State in *Brave New World* was already totalitarian itself, other authors extended the concept of panopticism to the modern utopian visions of the "perfect city" where power is exercised through the lens of a camera and by synoptism, a method of surveillance that includes mass means of communication.

Against the Object-King

Histories of the automobile tend to be radiant and excellent allies of kinetic modernity. They show pride and self-confidence. Miguel de Castro

Vicente presents several stages in his *Historia del automóvil*: Prehistory, Antiquity, the Middle Ages, and the Modern Age. The Prehistoric stage goes from the end of the eighteenth century to 1885 and covers the "first babblings" of automobilism. Antiquity is from 1886 to 1901, a phase that covers from the first builders to the appearance of the Mercedes, whose organic complex inaugurates a "new era." In the Middle Ages the organic complex model is perfected. It persists despite the high purchase price, a problem that Henry Ford solved with the manufacturing of the popular Model T, a "miracle" that marked a new Age in the History of the Automobile. The Modern Age is the era during which vast manufacturing complexes of the automotive industry are built.

Assembly-line mass production reached unimagined levels: vehicles mobilized the largest fortunes in the world and represented the greatest industrial opportunity of modern times. An object that has been capable of creating such enthusiasm and such dedication, affirms Castro Vicente, cannot be a bad object. In such a golden version of mobility and technological production, the automobile is "the crown jewel of Technology offered to Mankind by Man. Its history, as that of all useful, good, and beautiful objects, is destined to be even longer, perhaps as long as the life of our Civilization. For that reason we can say we have narrated only the first chapter of a glorious history."[33]

A contrasting version of this "glorious history" has been developing, especially since the 1960s. The crisis of modernization—environmental damage, traffic jams, fuel shortages, high accident rates, transnational monopolies—affects the image of the automobile. In the 1960s Ralph Nader, then a young lawyer in Connecticut, started his consumer-advocacy campaigns by riding in amusement park bumper cars in order to illustrate the dangers of cars.[34] Edward Hall, in *The Hidden Dimension*, compares the automobile city par excellence, Los Angeles, with cities for people, such as Paris, Florence, and Venice, and concludes that "the automobile was the greatest consumer of public and personal space ever created by man."[35] Who would say it: the "crown jewel of technology" on the bench of the accused, indicted for having isolated man from his milieu, created barriers to human contact, and stimulated competitive, aggressive, and destructive interaction.

Another critical evaluation, surprising because it comes from one of the prophets of the media in relation to social life, was from Marshall McLuhan. He situated the automobile in the Gutenberg Galaxy, associated with the mechanical technology of printing: uniformity, abstraction, linear continuity, and individualization. McLuhan recognized that the "mechanical bride" had transformed itself into an article of dress without which a person who was not one of the initiated felt uncertain, unclad, and incomplete. The driver was a cavalier armed with a misguided missile, propelled by the typical mechanical pressure of explosion and separation of functions, but it was a historical phase on the way to extinction.

The devaluation of the automobile's purpose as a means of communication made by McLuhan in *Understanding Media* has human integration in the postliterate era as a counterpoint. The future of the automobile, which the prophetic Canadian compared with the history of the horse, would be less in the area of transportation than in that of entertainment, as television questioned all the mechanical assumptions about uniformity and standardization characteristic of the assembly line: "To mistake the car for a status symbol, just because it is asked to be taken as anything but a car, is to mistake the whole meaning of this very late product of the mechanical age that is now yielding its form to electric technology. The car is a superb piece of uniform, standardized mechanism that is of a piece with the Gutenberg technology and literacy which created the first classless society in the world."[36]

Just as electrical force tended to put an end to the mechanical age of uniformity and standardization, the communication society would place the working automobile in a museum next to the horse, and as a simple source of pleasure it would return to its origin as an instrument of entertainment. While the realization of such a prediction still seems to be a dream, it is certain that vital transformations in the future of the automobile are coming, among them the possibility of a return to the electric automobile. The electric vehicle is seen as an alternative to traditional internal-combustion engines, in order to comply with strict emission controls. The wheel is not as obsolete as McLuhan thought: it continues to play an important cultural role.

Similarly, French intellectuals examined the function of the mobile object in contemporary society. Jean Baudrillard identifies the automobile as a sublime extension of the domestic environment, a phallic, narcissistic projection where the subjective system of needs is combined with the objective system of production.[37] On the other, hand Henri Lefebvre, in the Object-King that inscribed mobility as a social function and imposed its own law of disciplining and planning, raises it to a general symbol of self-destruction.[38] Quotidianness, for Lefebvre, is converted into the noise of motors, "rational" use, demands of production, and distribution of vehicles.

David Harvey points out there were currents of dissatisfaction in the Third World with the modernization process, which promised development and full integration into Fordism but which, in practice, delivered destruction of local cultures, oppression, and various forms of capitalist domination.[39] The benefits were meager gains in terms of living standard and public services for anyone but an affluent indigenous elite that chose to collaborate with international capital. In Latin America, Argentine Juan José Sebreli prolongs the criticism of Ezequiel Martínez Estrada and synthesizes the anti-utopian diagnosis in "El tótem del automóvil," an appendix added at a later date to his *Buenos Aires: Vida cotidiana y alienación* (Buenos Aires: Daily life and alienation). Sebreli argues that Ray Bradbury's forecast that pedestrians in the city of the future would be extravagant, even subversive, beings who would have to be locked up was not very far from reality. The difference, in the case of Latin America, continues to be the adaptation of Veblen's ostentatious consumerism to the national way of life: the idea of an artificial technology and of the automobile as a symbol of class identity and a totem of prestige.

In order to understand the meaning of these criticisms, it is necessary to set aside the crisis of industrial modernization and remember the prestige of motorization in the early decades of the twentieth century. The compelling need for standardization and the never-ending struggle of different companies to get ahead of their rivals had led to a search for perfection, harmony, and beauty of the vehicle, Le Corbusier said; he had compared the automobile with the Parthenon and projected a forerunner of the Volkswagen at the end of the 1920s, the *Voiture maximum*. Around the same time, visionary Buckminster Fuller was designing the Dymaxion.

In the mid-1930s, author and essayist E. B. White published a personal tribute to the Ford Model T—the last had been manufactured in 1927—based on his experience as owner of an automobile bought in 1922, which he had nicknamed "Hotspur"; he toured a large part of the United States in it. In "Farewell, My Lovely" (*New Yorker*, May 16, 1936), written under the pseudonym of Lee Strout White, he laments the end of the times of glory and indicates that for millions of people who grew up with the Ford Moustache, the Model T meant the American scene. White remembered that the Ford Model T referred to youth and excitement and evoked the joy of its owner when spring arrived, and emphasizes, "The driver of the old Model T was a man enthroned." The Model T was never complete: it was born nude as a baby and needed gadgets; it was a vibrant skeleton that had to be perfected with a number of optional accessories useful for its proper functioning, such as a rust-prevention liquid that forestalled radiator leaks. White's farewell is, symptomatically, the good-bye to an era in which the Ford Model T stimulated popular erudition and unlimited mythology about the mass-produced mobile object.

Sinclair Lewis also initially shared the euphoria for the automobile. His wife remembered her husband's reaction to his first car: "There were to be many thrilling occasions in the life of Sinclair Lewis—seeing an entire bookseller's window on Fifth Avenue devoted to *Main Street*, receiving the Nobel Prize from a king—but it's a safe guess that neither topped that moment when he stopped the Ford [his first car] neatly in front of the old stone carriage step and called out to his father and mother and me sitting on the porch after supper, 'How about a ride?' . . . Story-writing was one thing but owning and driving a car was another."[40]

In Lewis's first novels the automobile appears as a hero. However, that initial euphoria later became social satire and criticism of consumerism. It could be said that he narrated the experience of being dislocation. It was a rite of passage, the sensation of disorientation and uncertainty fomented by World War I and in particular by the ravages of the Great Depression of the '30s—a reformist criticism of moralizing character, marked by the loss of innocence and set down as literature that was at the same time realist and experimental, with elements of sociological reporting.

We know that all action is impure. The man who had been considered a genius in the 1920s did not survive the Great Depression and the end of the Model T unscathed. Everything was said about Henry Ford: that he was a cruel man, insensitive, ignorant, intolerant, anti-Semitic, that he hated beauty, freedom, and human dignity. Nor were his factories the eighth wonder of the world; they were prisons where the workers functioned, little more than hands and tired eyes, enslaved to the mechanical march of production. The well-known literary critic and essayist Edmund Wilson visited Detroit in 1931 and summarized these criticisms in his essay "Detroit Motors," included in the book that marked his shift to political writing, *The American Jitters* (1932). Wilson witnessed the massive melting down of old cars and interviewed workers in the Ford factories, such as an Englishman named Bert, who stated the worker left his brain and his freedom at the factory door.

Although Henry Ford had been compared with Abraham Lincoln, Jesus Christ, and Karl Marx, Wilson noted that his reputation as a benefactor of the American worker was visibly declining. Ford clearly was not adored by his workers: he was a hard man full of distrust and prejudice who had been depicted in an ambiguous way in many books used by Wilson to construct his profile—among them, Samuel Marquis, *Henry Ford: An Interpretation*; E. G. Pipp, *Henry Ford: Both Sides of Him*; W. M.

Cunningham, *"J 8": A Chronicle of the Neglected Truth about Henry Ford and the Ford Motor Company*; Louis Lochner, *Peace Ship: Henry Ford— America's Don Quixote.* Added to the testimonies of businessmen, newsmen, and Ford factory workers, the portrait of the "despot of River Rouge" is that of a mechanical genius and an industrialist who could not be relied on, an ignorant, old-fashioned American who could not avoid the collapse of the capitalist system.

Just like other writers of the so-called Lost Generation, John Dos Passos served in the ambulance corps of the American Army during World War I and worked as a newsman in Europe before returning to his country. When he published *Manhattan Transfer* in 1925, his style was that of an experimental writer who mixed facts and fiction in a panoramic view of life in America. For that reason it is not surprising that in *The Big Money*, he dedicates one-third of the epic prose poem *U.S.A* (*The 42nd Parallel*, 1930; *Nineteen Nineteen*, 1932; *The Big Money*, 1936), to the figure of Henry Ford and to his most famous automobile, the Tin Lizzie.

This hybrid novelist-historian that was Dos Passos, illegitimate son of a lawyer of Portuguese origin, describes, in his trilogy, the history of the United States from the early twentieth century to the 1929 Depression. And he does so by using short biographies that weave together representative historical individuality with the imaginative dimension, through newspaper-like writing based on a cinematographer's way of seeing things—dramatic writing, that of this anarchist, Communist, and idealist writer—indignant about the capitalist plot and the ruins of democracy.

His depiction of Henry Ford is coherent with the anti-epic character of the trilogy, which accuses materialism and social injustice. But do not think Dos Passos was a critic of technology, rather the opposite. His representations of Thomas Edison, the Wright brothers, and Frank Lloyd Wright are heroic, all associated with technological inventiveness. In contrast Henry Ford is marked from the time he was a young man by an imbalance. He was disturbed by machinery: locomotives, timepieces, tractors, electric carriages, and mechanical gadgets. The admirer of Edison and the genial inventor emerges: the dedicated businessman, and the richest man in the world, with aspirations of social engineering. Also the anti-Semitic pursuer of Jews, with a brutal capacity for getting the most out of his workers: "The great automotive boom was on. At Ford's production was improving all the time; less waste, more spotters, straw bosses, stoolpigeons (fifteen minutes for lunch, three minutes to go to the toilet, the Taylorized speedup everywhere, reachunder, adjustwasher, screwdown bolt, reachunderadjustscrewdownreachunderadjust, until every ounce of life was sucked off into production and at night the workmen went home gray shaking husks)."[41]

While mass production of the Ford car meant for many an expression of the progress of civilization, Henry Ford himself defended with vigor cultural values that the assembly line gradually made obsolete. That boy who had left farm life to dedicate himself to machines in the city was now a winner who deplored modern music and preached the spiritual values of rural America, to the point that he ordered built, in the town of Greenfield, Michigan, a replica of a small nineteenth-century town, with gravel roads, gas lamps, horse-drawn vehicles, and an old store.

Ford's reconstruction of the regional past reproduced history as a caricature. He did not discriminate, and, unlike refined collectors who are distinguished for the originality with which they select their objects, he bought everything. Not surprisingly, the project ran into hyper-realism at the same time his ideology clung to the American democratic tradition of the "usable past" and the popular museum. Neither was Ford an erudite type. His genius's disdain for beauty and the model is evident. The pride of a moralist moves him, and he has something of the European millionaire collectors described by Honoré de Balzac in *Cousin Pons* and cited by Walter Benjamin with delight in his essay on Eduard Fuchs. They are owners who dress like paupers, who appear unattached to anything and oblivious to women or expense; nevertheless, collectors are the "most passionate men in the world."

In John Dos Passos's representation, Henry Ford is a man overwhelmed by his work. He revolutionized the world with the application of Fordism, then delved into nostalgia for a purer, unpolluted past. He is the impassioned antiquarian who protects himself from amnesia through restoration and who ordered his father's farm rebuilt so he could return it exactly to the state in which he remembered it as a boy. That old, disenchanted man made a museum town for old objects, attempting to return to the era when everything depended on horses. Plows, water-turned mill wheels, wagons, furniture from old wooden houses. After the triumphant trajectory, the nostalgia of infancy and the search for a "Rosebud" in the pre-industrial world. And the reference to *Citizen Kane* is meaningful here. Because just as Orson Welles critically re-created the powerful William Randolph Hearst, Dos Passos wrote about Henry Ford from the relativization of culture. He is the critic of social injustice and alienation: Ford guarding himself like a lunatic, with a private army, against the new America "of starved children and hollow bellies and cracked shoes stamping on soup lines, which has swallowed up the old thrifty farmlands of Wayne

County, Michigan, as if they had never been."[42] The unhappy conscience does not allow the individual to reconcile himself with himself.

The same year *The Big Money* was published, Charles Chaplin's *Modern Times* came out. The cinematographic critique of the production system, in particular the assembly line, did not start with Chaplin. It was present in René Clair's film *A nous la liberté*. This well-known French director poked fun at Ford-inspired procedures in his 1931 social satire. But the theme of mechanization—first of the wooden horses mass-produced in the prison and then the assembly line of phonographs in the factory—is a clear indicator of the triumph of closed work spaces, of the control that manages to dominate the destiny of human beings. Chaplin took advantage of gags and corrosive humor to take questioning industrial society to the extreme. And this brilliant satire against modern times and the Taylor system was inspired by a visit Chaplin made to Henry Ford's Highland Park factory in 1923. Much more remains from that visit besides the photograph in which Henry Ford, his son Edsel, and Chaplin pose smiling in the row of turbines. From that experience images are derived that today are classics: the line of sheep entering the sheepfold and the workers in the factory, the machine trip, the threatening face of the chief in the bathroom, and the hilarious demonstration of the mechanized meal.

Modern Times juxtaposes various critical positions that were around in that time with regard to the assembly line, such as the one that appeared in the *Tri-City Labor Review* in 1932:

I ran into a fellow the other day who is awaiting for one of the new Fords. "Nice car," he told me.

But I always think about a visit I once paid to one of Ford's assembling plants every time any one mentions a Ford car to me. Every employee seemed to be restricted to a well-defined jerk, twist, spasm, or quiver resulting in a Flivver. I never thought it possible that human beings could be reduced to such perfect automats. I looked constantly for the wire or belt concealed about their bodies which kept them in motion with such marvelous clock-like precision. I failed to discover how motive power is transmitted to these people and as it don't seem reasonable that human beings would willingly consent to being simplified into jerks, I assume that their wives wind them up while asleep. I shall never be able to look another Tin Lizzie in the face without shuddering at the memory of Henry's manikins.[43]

For writers, movie directors, artists, and psychologists, mass production on an assembly line had a high human cost. In *The Flivver King: A*

Story of Ford-America, a fictionalized biography of Ford, Upton Sinclair insists on the contradictions of the character and on the damage of capitalist mechanization. Ford is at the same time a king and a victim of capital. While exploiting the proletariat, he engenders his own destruction. He ages badly, obsessed by the pastoral image, forcing himself to recapture what he had contributed to destroying. He is a dictator who distrusts everything and everyone.

Even today, in an era of crisis in the American motor vehicle industry, the persona of Henry Ford continues to present challenges. It is difficult to add new information about a human being that has been examined in such detail. The distinction is common between Ford realist entrepreneur and Ford moralist, between Ford engineer and Ford ideologue. Allan Nevins and Frank E. Hill pointed out in the 1950s some of the basic contradictions of the figure. Until then Ford's personality had lent itself to a Jekyll and Hyde type interpretation, which, according to these authors, simplified things too much, "for he was not two men but a dozen." Ford, a rural man and the son of farmers, had been projected into leadership of an industrial urban era, and that explained the internal conflict. Second, Ford, the practical industrialist, had to be understood as a dreamer, as a man of imaginative, artistic temperament. An artist whose desire was to reconstruct parts of the world in his image. Many victories and failures would be fathomable, according to Nevins and Hill, if Ford were perceived from the angle of imaginative and artistic temperament.

As happens in the classics, each generation adds new perspectives. The aforementioned contradictions continue in a story by Italo Calvino entitled "Henry Ford." It is an imaginary dialogue written for television in 1982 that was never produced but that synthesizes the historical turns of the screw. At the end of the dialogue an image of Ford is superimposed on scenes of slow, heavy traffic in a large city, of trucks in a jam on a highway, smoke from smokestacks, work at a steel-mill press, and work on an assembly line. But this person who changed the image of the planet thanks to industrial organization and motorization prefers to have little birds as a background on his gravestone. The announcer is not convinced that Ford, the person of the century, who exerted the greatest influence in the history of humankind and modeled our way of life, wanted to be represented among little birds.

The dialogue is full of such contrasts. On the one hand, they are Ford's opinions on freedom, the beauty of nature, waste, uniformity, history, tradition, art, the economy of his time, trade unions, and the financial system; on the other hand, the announcer points out the contradictions:

"You mean he invented and manufactured and sold automobiles so that people could drive away from the factories of Detroit and listen to the birds singing in the woods? . . . To sum up: you wish to save your workers unnecessary movements in the building of automobiles which allow us all to live in continual movement."[44]

The contradictions of this person who had been noticed by writers such as John Dos Passos, Upton Sinclair, and Italo Calvino continue in E. L. Doctorow's novel *Ragtime* (1975). Two decades after Doctorow published *Ragtime*, such conflicts appeared radicalized from the perspective of the multiple identities of the subject. Both Roger Casey and Jean-François Bayart point out in Henry Ford the conflict between the position of elitist paternalism and egalitarian populist feeling, as well as the tension between the belief in progress and conservative nostalgia.[45] The promoter of technological development who had declared that history was worthless verbiage spent a large part of his life decrying moral degradation, collecting old artifacts for his museums, and carefully rebuilding historic sites.

3. THE TRANSNATIONAL OBJECT

*AUTOMOBILE. All the millions of cars on this planet are stationary and
their apparent motion constitutes mankind's greatest collective dream.*

J. G. BALLARD, "PROJECT FOR A GLOSSARY OF THE TWENTIETH CENTURY"

The World as Adventure

At the beginning of the twentieth century, the automobile was the symbol par excellence of what was modern. Its arrival in different parts of
the world confirmed the irresistible trajectory of mobility. The snorting
machine, the new mechanical lizard, the car of fire arrived, enveloped in a
cloud of dust. And the harbinger of motorization came, riding the metallic horse. While the medieval herald bore messages and kept the nobility
in line, the driver introduced the unseen and the strange, in anticipation
of the future. As in myths, he came from far away, announcing the great
transformation. A few decades after the publication of Jules Verne's imaginative *Around the World in Eighty Days* in 1873, the automobile had proudly
circled the globe. In *La nuova arma: La macchina* (The new weapon: The
automobile), Mario Morasso anticipates F. T. Marinetti by comparing the
Winged Victory of Samothrace with the motor of an automobile. He seems
to admire the engine for its ferocious impatience, similar to that of the
Winged Victory of Samothrace, which reigns from the top of a flight of
stairs in the Louvre and holds the wind in her fluttering garment, showing the force of movement. For Morasso the comparison is not irreverent:
when the iron monster trembles and shudders from the inciting vibration
of the engine, it offers a revelation of virtual force and demonstrates the
"crazed" speed it is capable of.[1]

A few years later Marinetti noisily celebrated the coming of the automobile, which was slowly covering the globe. His images are masculine,
aristocratic, and associated with speed and freedom, but they imply
the celebration of mobility. The metallic horse gallops triumphantly in
"All'Automobile da corsa" (To the race car). It is the vehement god born
of a race of steel, intoxicated with space and hungry for the infinite, that
dances through the white streets of the world. It can be seen galloping to

the depths of the forests, its metal bridle loose, while at the sound of its voice the setting sun accelerates its blood-red palpitations on the horizon. It is a beautiful demon, and now and then the poet raises his body amidst the speed to feel the icy, velvety arms of the wind. This monstrous dancer races onward on oversized legs, while mountains and animals flee from its frenetic path.

The automobile runs on the "white streets" of world literature. Movement dominates everything in the poetry of futurism, as in "Automobile quasi te" (Automobile almost you), by Luciano Folgore, the author of *Il canto dei motori* (The song of the motors), or in "Battute d'automobile" (Heartbeats of an automobile), by Auro d'Alba (pseudonym of Umberto Bottone). The autolatry—love of self—of the futurists was poetically supported by a handful of owners who started to travel about the world on four wheels. Some were adventurous millionaires such as American Charles L. Glidden, who left London in 1901 in a 24-HP Napier, accompanied by his wife and some friends. The wheels of the Napier were special: the tires could be removed so the car could ride on rails. Six years later, Glidden returned to England in the same Napier. He had visited 35 countries and 11,000 cities, towns, villages, and hamlets. Of the 69,000 kilometers (43,000 miles) traveled, 12,000 (7,600 miles) were on rails.[2]

A new figure appeared: the haughty, powerful automobile collector. Early in 1900 the tsar of Russia, Nicholas II, had an impressive fleet that included a Rolls-Royce, several Delaunay-Bellevilles, and a Packard. Only the Revolution of 1917 could stop his voracious accumulation of automobiles. Another collector was the shah of Persia, Mouzaffar-ed-Din, who acquired music boxes, electric lamps, furniture, stuffed birds, medallions, and shotguns on his trips to Paris. Moreover, he purchased automobiles of various makes to give to his ministers and friends in Teheran, where he took one of the best chauffeurs in France and instructed him to drive very slowly: he rode about in his comfortable, luxurious, imperial car as slowly as in any carriage.

Collectors such as these amassed ultramodern items in a traditional environment. However, the image of the collector at the beginning of the twentieth century morphed into the variations that are familiar today: collectors of antique cars of certain makes or from specific years, and in general obsessed with restoring the vehicle by using only original parts.

The car salesman was another figure that contributed to the dissemination of the automobile. He had to present his product and demonstrate its advantages; for this purpose he organized trips, outings, and exhibitions. On occasion, anticipating the construction of highways and getting there far ahead of other salesmen, he arrived at distant towns riding a donkey in order to offer his merchandise.

Adventures were not always successful. On the contrary, most trips failed shortly after they began. The most notable case was that of salesmen E. E. Lehwess and Max Cudell, with their intended trip around the world in their "Passe-Partout." Unlike Phileas Fogg—the perfectionist British gentleman of Jules Verne's novel, who started his trip by train with his French manservant Passepartout—Lehwess and Cudell used a Panhard & Levassor special with a 25-HP motor. It weighed three tons and was an enormous car: two beds could be set up in the body. It was supposed to go everywhere, including Russia, the Gobi Desert, China, Japan, the United States, and Canada. But the enormous yellow automobile did not get beyond Nizhny Novgorod, where its owners abandoned it in the snow with two broken cylinders.

Then, as now, there were sportsmen. The traditional sports at that time were wrestling, marksmanship, swimming, horsemanship, and fencing. Games with balls and motorized competitions were a novelty, and automobile races were not so much a new sport as they were an activity for audacious millionaires. Drivers signed on for the privilege of winning a prize: instead of organizing solo excursions, they participated in competitions or expeditions that were increasingly risky such as the Peking-Paris and New York–Paris runs. At the outset competitions were from one city to another. In 1907 a monument was raised to Émile Levassor in the French capital: he had won the Paris-Bordeaux race in 1895, driving forty-eight hours almost nonstop in a test of speed, but especially a demonstration of the endurance of cars and drivers in very demanding circumstances.

The races were exhausting, often in automobiles without the protection of hoods or windshields and lacking adequate brakes and proper wheels and during which drivers had to traverse snow-covered fields, forge their way cross-country, and build bridges so they could cross streams. The lack of gasoline left many a driver—a blend of mechanic and adventurer—stranded on the roadside.

The Great Race (1965) was inspired by the automobile races at the beginning of the twentieth century, races that covered long distances. The differences are evident between Blake Edwards's comedy, in which Maggie DuBois (Natalie Wood) is a competitor, representing the introduction of women's demands in a field considered exclusively male, and the so-called race of the century (Peking-Paris, 1907). Besides requiring exclusively male participation in that race, the Chinese government refused to issue entry visas for the drivers, alleging political and economic reasons, saying they were coming as a group of engineers under the direction of an Italian prince whose main objective was to establish a rapid communication system that would be detrimental to the railroads. Some authorities even claimed that the drivers wanted to prepare a route so China could be invaded by an army of automobiles. European governments had to intervene energetically for the Chinese government to free up the passports.[3]

Land routes that connected countries combined technical, political, economic, and cultural elements. In the case of the Peking-Paris rally, as well as the American New York–Paris replica, different kinds of transportation systems converged. Drivers whose automobiles were pushed by coolies over short distances with the help of draft animals that accompanied the expedition drove part of the way on the tracks of the Trans-Siberian railroad. This line, which was concluded in 1904, linked Moscow in western Russia to Vladivostok on the Sea of Japan, passing through the harsh landscape of Siberia. It had been declared one of the wonders of the twentieth century at the Universal Exposition in Paris in 1900. As a matter of fact, this monumental iron road made possible the growth of cities and industrial centers along its route. One can now drive all over the planet by automobile—the planet that only with difficulty was circumnavigated by sailing ships during the Renaissance and yet was largely unified by trains in the nineteenth century.

Clärenore (Clara) Stinnes from Germany covered much of the globe in her automobile at the end of the 1920s. Kinetic modernity was expressed by the allure of the unknown, tourism, and the will to demonstrate the vehicle's efficiency. Hers had to be a German-made car because the German adventuress—who had hated school as a girl, shunned all activities considered feminine, and darkened her face with charcoal in order to play with the boys as an Apache Indian—wanted to use her trip to demonstrate the postwar recovery of German technology. She traveled around the world and wrote about her escapades. Stinnes recorded her feats in the pages of *Im Auto durch zwei Welten*. Unlike medieval and Renaissance travelers, who often mixed history and fiction when writing about remote regions of the world, this herald of motorization narrated the adventures of the automobile in distant lands.

Clärenore prepared herself as only an athlete could to carry out her mission, living the trip across the continents before setting out. She worked tirelessly in her father's automobile factory, competed in automobile races, bought maps, drew up itineraries, identified where she could get food, and organized letters and documents. She hired two mechanics, Victor Heidtlinger and Hans Grunow, and a Swedish cinematographer,

Carl Axel Söderström, to film all the incidents. From the 1926 Frankfurt Automobile Exhibition, she selected an Adler Standard 6 with Continental tires that would be accompanied by an Adler L9 with reserves of fuel, tools, picks, shovels, axes, three Mauser pistols, spare parts, a tent, and the luggage. The rear part of the Adler L9 was set aside for luggage and provisions; the upper part could be converted into sleeping quarters for two or three people. Besides the four adventurers, the team included Lord, a silky-haired black setter.

On May 25, 1927, the group made its proud departure before a group of journalists. They hurried as best they could to Moscow, hoping to avoid the Siberian winter. There was, however, another reason to hurry through Prague, Vienna, and Budapest: those areas were still "too normal and civilized to awaken true interest in us." This was not a scientific expedition to gather information, and the relief of the travelers was apparent when they discovered "signs of identity" along the way: in Chile they spent a night with countrymen in a naval vessel, delighted to be among "German sailors, young blonds with blue eyes and white uniforms." In general they sought out what was novel, although it often turned out to be distasteful or disagreeable.

The harshness of the trip took its toll. Grunow became so seriously ill that he had to be operated on in Moscow and sent home; Heidtlinger abandoned the group some weeks later. Clärenore and Carl continued the "German-Swedish exploit" without mechanics; nevertheless, they were able to enlist the help of local guides, members of automobile clubs, and government representatives. Those who came to their aid considered themselves as characters in the projected book, as in the case of Mr. Alinge in Ulan Bator, who confessed that he invited them to spend the night at his house because he wanted his name to appear in the account. A few humorous moments arose such as when in El Real, Darién province, Clärenore's masculine attire confused the Panamanians, who were unable to determine her gender. The doubts disappeared when an Indian woman approached her, asked if she was a man or a woman, and raised her hand to touch her breast. "A woman, despite the trousers!" declared the woman, in Spanish, to the circle of onlookers.

Clärenore cannot be considered a careful observer or a great writer. Otherwise the narration of her trip through Istanbul, Ankara (then known as Angora), Damascus, Baghdad, Teheran, Tbilisi, Moscow, Novosibirsk, Ulan Bator, Peking, Tokyo, Los Angeles, Panama, Lima, La Paz, Santiago, Buenos Aires, Vancouver, Chicago, and New York would be full of colorful descriptions and significant details. Just to be in another place fascinated this German traveler, who thought out the contrasts from inside the automobile and was delighted with exteriors. In order to satisfy the curiosity of village children, who had never seen an automobile before, the Europeans did not leave without visiting the local school and answering questions through interpreters. The ritual of showing the children the Adlers inside and out was a constant: a car is worth more than a thousand words.

The driver-geographer accumulated valuable information about old ruins, towns, cities, and countries during the 49,240 kilometers (30,600 miles) she covered in two years, one month, and twenty days of travel. But her interpretations of beliefs and behaviors are invariably superficial. The Persian's love of nature, Clärenore affirms, is visible in the tree-lined streets; the Turk is cruel and mistreats animals; the American respects and reveres from the bottom of his heart everyone who has had a role in the development of humankind; the Chinese think the structure of the universe is symmetrical.

To compensate for this, a number of her observations preserve the freshness of experience and help visualize aspects of daily life unknown at that time. In Ulan Bator camels and automobiles share the narrow streets with no particular sense of order. The city squares are full of pilgrims and prostrate penitents begging Buddha aloud to pardon their sins, kissing the ground, and exhibiting all forms of humility and repentance. Especially interesting are descriptions of daily life in Peking, where vendors noisily hawk their wares and use noisemakers and flutes to draw people's attention. The shoe repairman distinguishes himself from the knife sharpener and the flower seller with his characteristic patter and by the sound of the noisemaker, whistle, or flute, while the cries of the coolies are almost indistinguishable from the squeaking of the wheels of their rickshaws. All women, even those on the lower rungs of the social ladder, travel in a little wagon pulled by a donkey, or ride sidesaddle on some animal, because they cannot walk very far on their tiny bound and deformed feet. The ancient custom of binding little girls' feet, impeding their normal development, was starting to fall into disuse in the cities according to the German traveler, but in the countryside the peasants clung tenaciously to it.

By early 1929 the travelers were on the Argentine pampa, where they observed gauchos lassoing wild colts. The curious thing about this description of horse breaking is that she introduces an unusual element into her travelogue: she compares the violent methods of the gaucho with more modern and less brutal methods where colts are accustomed to being around people from the time they are born. Then breaking is gradual, without violence and cruelty. Traditional gauchos, Clärenore Stinnes admits, scarcely exist. With this observation about the transformation of violent customs into a gentler mode—the same could be applied to cows and bulls—the German traveler highlights the arrival of the civilizing process to the Argentine pampa.

However, the main character of the book is the automobile, the agent of the mobilizing process; hence, she usually dramatizes the passage of the vehicles through inhospitable places. The fantastic, which contaminated countless other travel accounts, is soft-pedaled, and the idea of culture as a "sum of social acts" disappears. Instead, images of the Adlers struggling against a river current, against impossible-to-cross rocky places, mountain ranges, and sand dunes proliferate. The Adlers are described when sunk in the snow, stuck in the mud, covered by a thick layer of clay, emerging from deep ruts, surrounded by rugged rock formations, attached to a yoke of oxen, towed by thirty men. In all these cases the most dramatic moments are associated with the impossibility of continuing the journey. Sometimes caution pays off, such as when they buy rawhide to place around the wheels to keep them from sinking too much in soft soil. In the desert there is no trail, much less a highway, to follow. And if sandy deserts are hard to cross, rocky landscapes are much more difficult. In order to continue they have to open the way with pickaxes or dynamite or else make a lengthy detour. Rocks dig into the tires like sharp knives and force constant repairs.

On one occasion they decided not to go on. Without food or drink, the situation was absolutely desperate. They even lacked the strength to stand when they had to abandon the car in a solitary mountainous area and start walking: "We started to cry like children. The rocks had destroyed our shoes. It felt as though we were walking on hot coals, each step causing pain and burning. Sometimes we crawled on all fours without the strength to stand up. Our mouths were full of foam, and because of the strange effect of thirst and fever, everywhere we looked we saw water that, unfortunately, did not exist, as we were hallucinating."[4] This suffering contrasted with their triumphant arrival in Berlin on July 19, 1929, when Clärenore Stinnes and Carl Axel Söderström drove into the city, each one at the wheel of an Adler, completely surrounded by an enthusiastic crowd throwing flowers, stretching out their hands, and acclaiming them as heroes.

The Great Adventure was not incompatible with economic and civilizing interests. The French colonies in Africa in particular stimulated the ambition of a visionary entrepreneur, André Citroën. He is often considered the Henry Ford of France. Although both believed in the principles of the Taylorist system, they had radically different personalities. John

Reynolds sums up the differences: Citroën was progressive, liberal, sophisticated, pleasure-loving, and Jewish; Ford was conservative, provincial, puritanical, pessimistic in his view of human beings, and anti-Semitic.[5] The optimism and idealism of Citroën motivated him to always be at the forefront of innovation. He did not intervene directly in the design of his products or in the construction of prototypes. An inimitable marketer, he enjoyed gambling in casinos and often dined at Maxim's. With his friend Charles Chaplin he crossed the snow-covered mountains of Saint Moritz in one of his automobiles, he received Charles Lindbergh after his famous transatlantic flight, and he forged strong commercial ties with the United States. On land and in the air his name was an icon of the era.

Citroën declared that the first words a child ought to learn to pronounce were "Mamma, Poppa, and Citroën." He started a lucrative business of miniature Citroën cars made by a company that specialized in making toys. No one could have imagined this would be the start of childhood education in the social meaning of the automobile. What seems natural to us today—that children recognize the makes of cars, and perhaps even their technical specifications and prices, and that they discuss details one would expect only specialists to know—confirms the legitimacy of a valuable collection system that first appeared in the early decades of the twentieth century. Childhood education in the social meaning of the automobile worked its way into childhood drawings. Even in places far from production centers, such as the southern Australian desert, from the 1940s the children of Ernabella drew cars as well as horses and the western windmills used to pump water. Diana Young observes that in the first drawings, the cars are shown with totemic animals—lizards and kangaroos—and rural elements such as rocks, trees, and ponds. Later on, in the collections of student drawings made in the 1940s, 1950s, and 1960s in Ernabella, cars and trucks appear frequently while camels—which up to then were the favorite means of transportation of many aborigines in the desert—appear much less. "Those children are the car owners of today. There was and is obviously something magical, enchanting about the car."[6]

Citröen's project surely had its share of nationalism, because children who played cars usually did so with imaginary Model Ts. After the horrors of World War I, lead soldiers lost some of their prestige in Europe. Neither Napoleon, the prototype of the military toy, nor armies with tiny blue flags attracted boys as they had in the past. Nor did the uniforms of generals, trumpets, drums, and tin swords. After the horrors of war, Miguel Ángel Asturias describes the French boys who "play at Henry Ford, building automobiles," next to their mother, who is mending clothes, their father, who is reading the newspaper, and an older sister, who is playing Debussy on the piano.[7]

André Citroën's generosity was legendary. He gave automobiles as tips to hotel employees and croupiers at the casino in Deauville. He gave a Cabriolet B14 to Josephine Baker, which the Black Pearl drove around Paris (besides her Voisin), while thousands of Citroën taxis circulated in Paris with the name of the founder on the doors. Despite being a millionaire, Citroën lived with his family in a large rented apartment. Nothing of castles or yachts. Few belongings. He loved music and the jazz era. The one who loved to drive was his elegant wife, invariably dressed by Coco Chanel. But Monsieur Citroën was always in the news, at times in the company of the Prince of Wales, Queen Mary of England, Josephine Baker, or Charles Lindbergh. All of this was part of his publicity strategy in which the generous person could not be distinguished from the automobile factory.

The pages the Russian novelist, poet, and journalist Ilya Ehrenburg dedicated to André Citroën in *Citroën 10 HP* are noteworthy. Published in Russian in 1929 and translated into German the same year, it is an unclassifiable book. It is not a novel, but a chronicle of its time. The heroes are not imaginary, nor was the story invented by the author, although in some passages false names replace the real ones. There are real people in the book such as Émile Zola, Henry Ford, Henry Deterding, and Giacomo Matteoti.

The book was written in Paris from February to June 1929. In order to explain the actions of his characters, Ehrenburg does not rely on official accounts; rather he offers his own explanations. The book is a mixture of history and fiction, an imaginative text drawing on historical material. In the table of contents he shows the characters are subordinated to a mechanism of motorization that irrevocably involves them. Each chapter highlights elements related to the automobile: The Birth of the Automobile (Chapter 1), The Conveyor Belt (Chapter 2), Tires (Chapter 3), A Poetic Digression (Chapter 4), Gasoline (Chapter 5), The Stock Exchange (Chapter 6), Roads (Chapter 7). The characters never lose their individuality, but they are devoured by a means of production that consumes them all equally. The fantasies interweave with the capitalist economy, marriage with work, the family with the assembly line, managers with workers, nature with the machine, and life with death.

Ehrenburg wrote about Citroën in the chapter on the conveyor belt. The image is familiar: a long line of workers manufacturing an automobile. While one group tightens a nut, another twists a bolt, a third group places mudguards, a fourth paints the sidewalls of the tires, a fifth bores holes in the axles. Each worker has exactly forty seconds for his task: the machine is in a hurry, and no one talks. Thousands of times the same action by a worker is repeated: the hand palm up, half a turn, and palm down. He gets fatigued while the conveyor belt moves ceaselessly on. Only with machines is it possible for kinetic utopia to continue to function.

The curious thing is that this image of the assembly line usually was linked with Henry Ford and Fordism. Citroën appears, consequently, as the follower of Fordist methods in France, as terrible for workers and managers as they were in the United States. The world globalizes around the intensification of speed. Faster! What did you say? Faster!! It is all the same for workers Pierre Chardain and Jean Lebaque as it is for the secretaries, the engineers, and André Citroën. It is life in acceleration, and the conveyor belt is always moving. Acceleration predominates even *outside* the factory, as what happened to taxi drivers: "Karl Lang often heard the word: 'Faster!' He didn't know who was hurrying him, the people or the taxi. Why were those restless shadows hurrying? And who hurried them—other shadows or merely the throbbing of the engine. Karl didn't think about it. He was just an ordinary taxi-driver, and there are so many of them, so many taxi-drivers, they all step on the gas, thrust out blood-red hand-signals and keep silent. The horns speak for them."[8]

Velocity defines modernity and is of its essence. Increase the speed of production. Increase the demand. Increase the factories. Improve the machines. Eliminate frontiers. Sell all of the production, to the French, to the Japanese, to the Russians, to the workers, to those who up to now dreamed of a bicycle. Advertising is a must in order to compete with Ford and Peugeot, with Renault and Fiat. So what if no one talks in the factories? So what if the workers hear only the sound of the machines? The racket deafens the workers, whether French or Chinese, and their eyes become glassy and absent. They forget everything, even the color of the sky and the name of their hometown. They go on tightening screws. They are reduced to being nothing more than hands.

In Ehrenburg's narration, the beauty portrayed in the advertising contrasts with the shameful reality of the factory:

> Citroën's ad men publicized the sea and the mountains, the banks of the Loire, Alpine passes, pine trees, ozone. Citroën's workshops were filled with the foul breath of machines. Noxious gases, the stench of hot oil, sharp acid fumes, alcohol, gasoline, paints, enamels. Metals were etched with acids—the workers had eczema. Metals were cleaned with sand—the

workers would be ambushed by consumption. Metals were painted with automatic spray guns—the workers were being poisoned by the vapors. In the foundries, the eyes of workers teared from the oil and sulfur. Little by little, they could no longer bear the sunlight. But there was no sun in the workshops. They continued carrying away the frames. Why have eyes, ears, or life? They had hands, they stood at the belt.[9]

Not even André Citroën could be saved in this imaginative history of dehumanization, for he was merely a small cog in the machine. His name might shine at night on the Eiffel Tower and be present in millions of minds. Bulgarian students, Polish ice skaters, diplomats, boxers, sopranos, journalists, and carnival queens could visit his factories. But he was not rich like Ford, famous like Lindbergh, or powerful like the Lazard bankers. Citroën might be a god for factory manager Pierre Chardain, but for the Lazard Frères Bank he was simply the manager of a few businesses.

If Ehrenburg had written *Citroën 10 HP* ten years later, the image of Citroën would have been more melancholic. At the end of 1934 the Citroën company was unable to maintain solvency and was put in receivership. On January 3, 1935, the factories were closed; André Citroën died the same year of stomach cancer. But the technological system that sustained the automobile was more alive than ever. Characters came and went, while kinetic utopia kept its promise and spread its mechanical angels about in the turbulent world of mobilization.

For Ehrenburg, the automobile was a decidedly global figure. The world was its fuel and its garage. From the jungles of Brazil, Java, and Ceylon, from Malaysia and Indochina came the raw material that kept the wheels spinning. Standard Oil, Royal Dutch, and Anglo-Persian fought for the crude oil market. Capitalist traders converted the world into a business and motorized vehicles crossed borders, generating fantasies of consumption:

Cars don't have a homeland. Like oil stocks or like classic love, they can easily cross borders. Italian Fiats clamber up the cliffs of Norway. Ever-worried specialists in Renault taxis jolt around the bumpy streets of Moscow. Ford is ubiquitous, he's in Australia, he's also in Japan. American Chevrolet trucks carry Sumatran tobacco and Palestinian oranges. A Spanish banker owns a German Mercedes. 10-H.P. Citroëns in display windows in Piccadilly or Berlin cause dreamy passers-by to halt. The automobile has come to show even the slowest minds that the earth is truly round, that the heart is just a poetic relic, that a human being contains two standard gauges: one indicates miles, the other minutes.[10]

Automobiles cross borders and the earth shrinks. Every year thousands of people die in car accidents, but the automobile is consolidated as the new divinity. The metal idol cares not for truth, but rather the progressive supression of distances and proliferation of its own kind. Cost reductions from mass production were imposed and the solution, according to Citroën, was to combine the Ford method with European conditions. However, dedication, the factory, and repetitive labor were not enough. Michelin tires were needed, and gas stations, highways, world's fairs, contacts with politicians, a team of specialists to attract customers, investments in the stock market. Above all else, plenty of advertising.

During the 1920s Citroën sent several expeditions to the heart of Africa, seeking to broaden contacts with the French colonies. From late December 1922 to March 1923 the first cross-Sahara Citroën expedition took place. It left from Touggourt, ten men in five half-track vehicles with movable tracks over the rear wheels, led by Georges-Marie Haardt. The group included their mascot, Flossie Sealyham, a white terrier that would be the model for Milou, the faithful companion of Tintin the adventurer. They also had many rifles, ammunition, potable water, fuel, and portable tents; in three of the five half-track cars there were clearly visible machine guns to dissuade potential attacks. Every day from five in the morning to ten at night they advanced across the sea of sand, where so many caravans had been lost without leaving a trace. All along the way skeletons of camels could be seen. But the expedition—in reality a tiny column of Citroën-Kegresse half-track cars in the vast Sahara desert—was destined not to fail; it transmitted news reports by radio and telegraph to Paris.

At the beginning of January 1923 the expedition proudly entered the gates of Timbuktu. It had once been forbidden territory for Europeans, under penalty of death, but it had been a French colony since 1893. In the main square the governor awaited them. They delivered to him the first postcard sent from France across the Sahara. Citroën responded from Paris on the level of what he considered a historic feat, referring to the "work of titans for the cause of humanity and the triumph of French industry." After two thousand years of service to humankind, John Reynolds affirmed, "the camel was dead, replaced by the Citroën motor vehicle."[11]

The most famous of the Citroën expeditions was the second Haardt/Audouin-Dubreuil mission. We know the details of this trans-African expedition from the report of the leader, Georges-Marie Haardt, and second-in-command, Louis Audouin-Dubreuil, *The Black Journey: Across Central Africa with the Citroën Expedition*. This was a carefully organized expedition, partly because Citroën himself and his wife planned to participate, along with the king of Belgium, the commander of the French army, and the governor-general of Algeria. That would not be possible, because a few days before the projected start the assassination of a caid in southern Morocco altered the political panorama and forced the French government to veto the journey. Although Citroën later found out the supposed disturbances were merely a political foil to ruin his plans (and he suspected his rival Louis Renault had something to do with it), he was forced to postpone the inauguration and promotion of the line. This meant the delay of a daring industrial and commercial venture.

Citroën had hoped to establish permanent communications between Algeria and western Africa through his automobiles. He had created a special department for this, the Citroën Trans-African Company, destined to organize biweekly contacts between Algeria and Timbuktu. The results were there to be seen: the construction of *bordjs*, hotels outfitted with all the modern appurtenances, in Colomb-Béchar, Benni-Abbes, Adrar, Timbuktu, Gao; the arrival of wheeled vehicles; the establishment of places suitable for camping in the intermediate sites. If we can believe Haardt and Audouin-Debreuil's account, worldwide curiosity mounted rapidly, and tourists from many countries put their names on the passenger lists. For 40,000 francs, the traveler could experience the adventure of the Sahara, sleeping in luxurious hotels next to an oasis all along the route. The hotels would be "lavishly furnished and decorated in the Arabian style. As the highlight of their tour, guests would spend one night of the twenty-four-day round trip under canvas, when an exotic and elaborate dinner would be served in an immense tent. After the meal, as the guests reclined on carpets, a cabaret would be performed by native musicians, dancers, jugglers and snake charmers. Fifty years ahead of his time, André Citroën had invented the Club Méditerranée Safari Holiday."[12] The project was abandoned for good when Citroën was forced to cancel the inaugural trip.

The first automobile expedition across the Sahara demonstrated the feasibility of establishing links between the colonies and anticipated the possibility of using motor vehicles as a means of exploring the continent of Africa. The second Haardt/Audouin–Dubreuil mission, popularly known as the "Croisière Noire" (Black Journey), was of interest to both commerce and science. It required over a year of methodical preparations. In the end the expedition would travel from one end of Africa to the other, from Colomb-Béchar to Cape Town and later to Madagascar over 20,000 kilometers (12,500 miles) of desert, brush, savannas, swamps, tropical forests, rivers, and lakes. It had to face hostile tribes with bows and poisoned arrows, and it traversed routes never before conquered by motor vehicles. Four support missions were sent out to preassigned sites between Algeria and the Indian Ocean so they could take care of receiving the objects collected by the expedition along with its films and documents.

The purposes of the journey clearly went beyond a rapid trip and a sporting effort. People were specially chosen for specific tasks. Ethnographic studies were entrusted to Alexandre Iacovleff, an experienced traveler and painter, who prepared more than 500 paintings, drawings, and sketches during the expedition. The person in charge of the zoological collections, who was also the expedition's doctor, gathered no fewer than 300 mammals, 800 birds, and 1,500 insects. An engineer and several mechanics, most of whom had been participants in the first crossing of the Sahara by automobile, were in charge of the technical oversight of the half-tracks.

There were eight vehicles, each propelled by a 10-HP Citroën motor and equipped with Kégresse-Hinstin B2 treaded tracks, towing a small trailer with various materials (maps, documents, firearms for defense and for hunting, spare parts, medicines, food, etc.). On the chassis, made entirely of duraluminum and painted white, a distinctive emblem adorned each car and gave it a particular personality. Nature, animal, and mythological motifs heralded the mechanical output of automotive technology: Gold Beetle, Elephant with Tower, Moving Sun, Winged Snail, Silver Crescent, Dove, Centaur, and Pegasus.

The importance given to cinematography as one of the basic means of documentation shows the growing value of images in ethnographic records. There were 30,000 meters (98,400 feet) of film and 8,000 photographs. Filming the expedition was so important that a well-known filmmaker, Léon Poirier, was hired. He put together a film diary of the expedition, *La croisière noire,* a movie that would be popular in its time. The premiere took place in London on January 16, 1928, with the Prince of Wales as guest of honor.

The expedition was also supposed to study ways to link the Algiers-Timbuktu line to Chad and extend it as far as Khartoum. It was not a spiritual mission, related to spreading the divine word; rather it was a commercial mission because of the growing importance of tourism. One of its purposes was to establish bases for future travelers to use along a circuit through Algeria, western Africa, Chad, Khartoum, Egypt, and Marseille. This was the beginning of exotic tourism, whose later development is well known.

The eight half-tracks that left on October 28, 1924, from the fort of the French Foreign Legion in Colomb-Béchar, in northwestern Algeria, followed a route that had been mapped out for them and that pursued a number of specific objectives. It is interesting here to mention only a few examples of the routes of globalization. To start with, it must be said that the rail line ended precisely in Colomb-Béchar. Haardt and Audouin-Dubreuil noted that "here the railroad stops. With it the intense life of western civilization ceases. Beyond Colomb-Béchar the desert begins." The desert here means a terrible image, an inhospitable sea of sand, completely primitive, where not even the "noble savage" lives. Civilization is measured, in part, by the arrival of technology. Open spaces are visualized in terms of being able to cover them mechanically by land and air. In the desert physical marks would remain to feed the technical imagination. The following passage is illustrative: "May we not say that it is a little in the interests of our winged brothers, the airplanes, that our caterpillars are on their way to creep over the soil of Africa for nearly 15,000 miles, reconnoitering sure routes and places suited for landing, in order that soon the air ways will be opened to regular communications, which will mark the beginning of a new era in the evolution of the Dark Continent?"[13]

Imagine their surprise when they discovered that "new era" had started before the arrival of the Citroën half-tracks. In the desert region dominated by Barmou, the sultan of Tessaoua, who had 100 wives, the French travelers were upset by the presence of an unexpected competitor from the United States: a Ford. Barmou had received a *brand-new* Ford as a gift from an American. By that time it was not all that new as it was a crank-operated model. In any case it was a clear example of the growing competition for influence in the changing colonial world and of the importance of motorization. For several days a native driver had tried to get it started without eking out the faintest ping in the cylinders—a problem the Europeans fixed easily by giving several turns to the crank.

It is now commonly understood that the perception of time and space changes according to the speed at which things are moving. Accounts by European train passengers during the nineteenth century confirm this by recording the changes in the way they observed the countryside. For this reason the arrival of the automobile to the Sahara meant, for the natives, a process of adaptation of their visual and temporal appreciation. Haardt and Audouin-Dubreuil noted that during their first trip across the Sahara they were able to prove that the fast pace of the automobiles disconcerted the natives, who were accustomed to calculating a day's journey according to the pace of a camel or a man on foot. "The speed at which the different districts are passed changes their aspect. In a native's reckoning, time and space, or distance, are one and the same thing; he no longer recognizes them and ends by losing all idea of direction."[14]

In Uganda, the convoy split into four two-car groups. Audouin-Dubreuil and his companions went on to Mombasa via Nairobi, crossing Mount Kilimanjaro. The second group went to Dar-es-Salaam by Lake Victoria, while a third group crossed southern Rhodesia toward Cape Town. The fourth group, led by Haardt, struggled to get to Madagascar. They crossed Nyasaland and the two Rhodesias (Malawi, Zambia, and Zimbabwe) by a route the English colonial authorities considered impossible. Between Kampala and Blantyre the group made practically no headway. Torrential rains and a fire almost ended their expedition.

The feeling that the world is shrinking derives from the acceleration of communications. After traveling thousands of miles through French West Africa, the Belgian Congo, and English South Africa, the travelers met again to triumphantly enter Madagascar. During the reception banquet, Governor Olivier referred to the automobile's union of cultures: the group had just traced a path across the immense Dark Continent. The arrival of the automobile, on the other hand, anticipated the arrival of regular air transport service. Through the desert and by air, kinetic modernity does not rest at its task of shrinking the earth.

Parallel to the triumphalist discourse on progress, a new element stands out: the end of an era because of technological advance. A sharp awareness of temporality emerges, manifested as disappearance and birth. The travelers remember with nostalgia the end of the adventure, nostalgia associated with the fatality of irreversible transformations:

> These were wonderful hours we shall never forget, but shall never live over again, not only because time never goes back, but also because the Dark Continent, now penetrated from every side, has been captured by storm and progress.
> The mystery of Africa is soon to end.
> Our white cars have been the advance guard; the faithful worshippers of Boula-Matari were not wrong in believing them to be heralds of a new Era. The old world is suffocating: in its conquest of space, it is annihilating distance—and also the charm of the unknown.[15]

It is not a matter of questioning the legitimacy of colonial expansionism, but of valuing the singularity of the historical moment. Despite a romantic attitude regarding the projection of a primitive authenticity, the

French notion of *civilization* defeated the particularist notion of *culture*. As heralds of motorization, these French travelers worked from an evolutionary perspective and recorded surviving cultural remnants destined to disappear. The idea of the unity of humankind is the grammar of civilization, and the cultural particularities were minimized with the arrival of motor vehicles. They symbolized the universal character of progress. While the members of the expedition may have justified the scientific meaning of their enterprise, transportation technology implied a sense of the normative. The backwardness of the colonies was less spiritual than technical and material, although such divisions can never be clear-cut, and it is difficult to escape the convergence of the descriptive and the normative. We are facing the idea of technological progress as the inexorable destiny of humanity.

The awareness of temporality as the dissolution of particularity is what relates and, at the same time, distinguishes the travelers' discourse about progress from the anthropological project of recording the moribund remains of preindustrial civilization in various regions of the world. It is also possible to detect in the Citroën expedition into the heart of Africa some aspects of a modern attitude in relation to the cultural order that James Clifford calls "ethnographic surrealism."[16]

Europeans had different interests in the preindustrial world, often existing side by side in an ambivalent way. On the one hand, we can find in the Citroën expedition the amassing of curious collections, enthusiasm for newness, and even a degree of cultural relativism. On the other hand, this also led to a rekindled interest in colonial control of the African difference, the composition of hierarchies, the classification system, homogenization by technology, and the prestige of technical objects. While in Paris the artificiality of the familiar was shown through African masks and sculptures, in the desert the half-tracks traced the "black route" and thus announced the arrival of modernity. Before mechanical objects transformed local cultures forever, it was necessary to collect the expressions of their former primitivism.

The pioneer character of the adventure ensured its originality, and any trip that came later would be merely an extension of the original endeavor. The presence of the automobile in the desert divided the history of Africa into a before and after for European travelers. Like the American astronaut's boot print on the moon, the tracing of rubber tires on the blazing hot desert sand marks the beginning of modern colonial history. No later episode could alter this, considered to be the inaugural moment. The automobile in the desert simply expressed the many changes in the world in a spectacular way. Although they appeared suddenly, and swiftly disappeared, the Citroën half-tracks were omens of what the future would be like.

At the beginning of the 1930s Citroën planned an adventure even more daring than the Black Journey: the Central Asia expedition, known as the "Crosière Jaune" (the Yellow Journey). Georges-Marie Haardt was the leader again. This journey lasted a year and produced 5,000 photographs, 230,000 feet of film, drawings, ethnological documents, mineral specimens, art and archaeological objects, and an unusual collection of flora and fauna.

Although Haardt would die from pneumonia in his hotel bed in Shanghai, other expeditions continued to use Citroën motors to travel across the world: the Rocky Mountains in Canada, and Antarctica, where it was promised the first motor vehicle to reach the South Pole would be a Citroën. These expeditions confirmed that the routes of globalization continued to be traced by the marks of rubber tires and increasingly powerful engines.

The drivers who achieved some of the first land crossings in South America were predominantly foreign, and mostly French. In 1908 Count Lesdain disembarked in Rio de Janeiro. An expert driver who had already experienced automobile adventures in Algeria, Morocco, and China, he arrived with his famous Brasier, which had a 16-HP gasoline engine. When asked the reason for his trip, he merely answered that he was a tourist drawn by the wonders of Rio de Janeiro. However, the count soon announced he would climb the Corcovado in his car. No one believed him, as there was no road (the statue of Christ the Redeemer, which was built in 1931, did not exist yet). According to Vergniaud Gonçalves, the count proved his skill and calmly scaled the hill, rolling on the narrow-gauge tracks of the Corcovado rack-rail tramway.[17] At one point, however, the Brasier slipped off the rails and almost fell into an abyss, the only serious incident of this unusual ascent of the Corcovado by automobile.

Count Lesdain's fame was assured. But the ascent of the Corcovado is insignificant when compared with his next automobile adventure: the journey from Rio de Janeiro to São Paulo. This is an ordinary trip today of around five hours by highway. It took Lesdain and his companions some twenty-six days to cover the distance. And not only did they take almost a month to get to São Paulo, they lost their way, they crossed flooded fields, they almost ran off a precipice, they improvised a small wooden bridge that collapsed just after the Brasier had crossed it, they had problems with their gasoline supply, and they traveled twenty-eight kilometers (eighteen miles) of the way on train tracks. In reality what saved the disoriented Frenchman was the fazenda owner and political chief of the region, Luiz Barbosa da Silva, who decided to join him in the municipality of Barra de Piraí and show him the way to São Paulo.

When Lesdain finally arrived at his destination, he was received as a hero by the crowds. This is a typical example of kinetic modernity: its representatives were acclaimed at the time of departure and arrival. The *Jornal do Brasil* reported on March 6, 1908, that the Frenchman's trip had been "a new milestone in Brazilian automobilism." And the *Correo Paulistano*, on April 12, referred to this feat of strong will and idealism: "The journey undertaken by the fearless chauffeur was an enterprise replete with danger and difficulties that was only achieved because of the bravery and perseverance of the count himself, and because of the love this dedicated sportsman had for motoring. It is really necessary to be endowed with strong will and obstinacy beyond the commonplace to have achieved this genuine tour de force, which will remain engraved in the history of Brazilian motoring."[18]

Another picturesque figure was a French engineer named Roger Courteville. On September 12, 1926, Courteville started out, with his wife and a mechanic, from Rio de Janeiro to La Paz and Lima by land. As there were no roads, the objective of the expedition was to map out the route of a future highway linking the Atlantic and the Pacific. This project covered 14,000 kilometers (8,750 miles) and envisioned an initial land route linking three countries and three capital cities. The expedition did not have the official support of the French government, and the official government representatives always had the same response: a transcontinental journey by automobile was not feasible at that time, impossible. In order to implement it, the French engineer appealed to his friends, merchants, industrialists, and private institutions, such as the Brazilian Automobile Club, for help. He spent a year organizing all the details. The misadventures of this expedition would be recorded in his *La première traversée de l'Amérique du Sud en automobile, de Rio de Janeiro à La Paz et Lima* (The first journey across South America in a motorcar, from Rio de Janeiro to La Paz and Lima), published in Paris in 1930.

Courteville wanted the car to be of French manufacture. He selected a six-wheel Renault and filled it with objects. A movie camera and 10,000 meters (32,800 feet) of film, a map 32 meters long and one meter wide (103 × 3.3 feet) on which he had marked his probable itinerary, several letters addressed to the authorities of the capitals he was to visit in the course of the journey, an artificial-horizon sextant for his astronomical calculations of longitude and latitude, compasses, altimeters, stopwatches, food for three weeks, 300 liters (83.4 gallons) of gasoline, 30 liters (34 quarts) of oil, Tecalemit vehicle-servicing equipment, firearms, ammunition, and camping equipment. The result was a varied mix of human beings and objects that gave the sensation of an acrobat's cart mounted on balloon tires.

The small group left Rio in the morning from the building of the Brazilian Automobile Club. Petrópolis, a town built 1,300 meters (4,300 feet) above sea level on the mountain slope above the Parnaíba River, was the destination of the first stage (a trip that takes an hour today). They were supposed to arrive in São Paulo two days later. The expedition almost ended in the bottom of an abyss 30 meters (100 feet) deep because they set out on roads that were totally unsuitable for motorized transport. From Barra Mansa they traveled on a good highway at an average speed of 55 kilometers (34 miles) per hour, enjoying the contrasts between the tropical landscape, the exuberant vegetation of the State of Rio de Janeiro, and the Europeanization of the farmland in São Paulo, where every speck of land was carefully cultivated.

The commentaries about the cities are informative but not very interesting. Courteville states São Paulo is a thoroughly cosmopolitan city and the Paulistanos are extraordinarily busy people, generally not very talkative, but dominated by a single concern: the price of coffee. He tells us little about La Paz and Lima. Arequipa, Peru, is a curious case. On each corner there is a church or the store of a German tradesman. At times, according to the French traveler, the volcano has the effect of electrifying the air in the city, and the people suffer from the influence of the phenomenon, which translates into perpetual ill humor. It is not unusual for two close friends to go two weeks or more without speaking to each other. The descriptions of the small villages, such as San José de Chiquitos, founded as a Jesuit mission in 1748, are particularly interesting. At any rate the account is a source of valuable information in an era devoid of the abundant images and information that characterize the modern tourism industry.

A crowd was always on hand when the travelers left, showing a lot of curiosity about the foreigner and his machine on wheels. The monotonous life in these remote areas was briefly altered by the arrival of the automobile. In Puerto Suárez, Bolivia, the entire town turned out to see them off. In Santa Cruz de la Sierra, when they heard the noise of the motor, everyone poured into the streets, and the crowd escorted the car to the main plaza. But in San José de Chiquitos, where no car had ever been seen before, the travelers were confused with Brazilian revolutionaries coming to take over the city, and they were met with distrust. The press made it possible for the travelers to be recognized in the later stages of the expedition. Even the gendarmes had heard that there was a six-wheeled automobile on the roads of Peru.

The narration is certainly not to be commended for its sense of humor. Some comic episodes are interspersed in the various chapters, however, and give a certain flavor to the text. This is the case of the story of the American owner of an oil business who offered several liters of oil free of charge and then, taking advantage of his gift, transformed the car into a multicolored rolling billboard, every word of which was intended to inform the native population about the economic benefits of his products. What can be said about Dr. Morbeck, the mayor of Santa Rita and absolute ruler of 20,000 gold and diamond prospectors? Courteville had imagined him to be a fearsome man, based on the stories he had been told about him, so much so that before visiting him he checked to see if his revolver was loaded. What a disappointment awaited the Frenchman when he got to meet this potentate from Mato Grosso! A short man, very agreeable and attentive, whose appearance and demeanor were those of a university president. He lived in a rustic house completely devoid of material comforts.

Other anecdotes reveal a number of details about the circulation of human beings, objects, expectations, and beliefs in the heart of Brazil. The foreigner intended to film a village of Bororo Indians. When he arrived at the village, all of the Indians suddenly disappeared and from the main cabin was heard a voice shouting in bad Portuguese, "If no give ten thousand *reis,* white man no see Bororos." We can only imagine the Frenchman, who considered the Indians as objects to be recorded for Europeans, being told to pay to film the "exoticness" of the Bororos. They were demanding payment so the tribe could be filmed, just as today visits by Jeep to the shantytown *favelas* of Rio de Janeiro have become entertainment organized by travel agencies. In the case of Courteville, the "white man" refused to pay. Betting on the curiosity of the natives, he placed his camera in such a way that the Indians were motivated to stick their heads out of their hiding places in order to see it. Little by little the Bororos came closer so they could inspect it. Courteville invited one of them to look through the lens, describing at the same time in a loud voice the marvelous visual spectacle. Within ten minutes the entire tribe was disputing the honor of being able to contemplate those incomparable visions. Acting like a charlatan from a country fair, in the little bit of daylight that remained, the "white man" managed to run through 120 meters (400 feet) of film.

A different encounter, nonetheless rich in implications, was the supposed dialogue between Courteville and Colonel Fawcett, in the middle of
the Mato Grosso plateau. Col. P. H. Fawcett, an Englishman, had arrived
in Rio de Janeiro in 1920 to prepare a rigorous, daring expedition in search
of the City of the Caesars. World War I had convinced many of the decadence of Europe. In Fawcett's case, he added to this the conviction that
there was a magnificent city hidden in the jungle, remains of an ancient
civilization spotted by slave hunter *bandeirante* Raposo in the eighteenth
century. Maps were useless: Fawcett got lost in the jungles of northern
Brazil and was attacked by ticks, mosquitoes, flies, swarms of bees, and
constant rain.

One of the surprising features of Fawcett's expedition was that the
tiny group traveled by foot at about the same time the French engineer
Courteville sought to unite distant regions by means of the automobile.
The curious thing is that both travelers came across each other about 150
kilometers (94 miles) from Cuiabá, "in that immense solitude, lost so far
from the inhabited world." Whether Courteville's account is true or not,
this encounter gives us a metonymic representation of the triumph of
mechanical travel. Fawcett was gray haired and had an unkempt beard
and droopy eyes and had stopped caring about his appearance. He was
dressed in undershorts, a khaki-colored shirt, and a broad-brimmed
hat. The mosquitoes were devouring him, but he did not seem to care; in
fact the calves of his legs were landing fields for all kinds of mosquitoes.
Courteville sent his mechanic to Cuiabá in search of water for the motor.
This suggests the condition of those who crossed Brazilian territory in a
vehicle in deplorable condition was far from idyllic.

In any case, at the same time the airplane was conquering airspace, the
automobile was crossing land masses, and together they announced the
great transformation. The transcontinental route was the great dream of
those emissaries of progress. If, on the one hand, modernization is perceived as inevitable, on the other hand, it is only possible to bring it about
through technology. It is not a matter of men lost in the jungle in search
of mythical objectives, but of individuals who mapped the territories and
brought nations closer together.

The automobile contributed to the discovery of nature and the recognition of the artificiality of European culture. There were always traces
of the romantic traveler in these first motorized characters who traveled
across unknown regions. Man became small, nature gigantic. Curiously,
the automobile served to bring the individual close to nature, not to distance him from it. The mechanical tended to disappear as an insignificant

dot in this natural scenario, never before altered by human intervention. It was the charm of the primitive and untouched, expressed in the vision of the variety of birds, the size of the trees, the enormous ferns and the magnificent flowers that grew down to the banks of the river. The result was a profound sense of solitude and silence. Mother Nature exuded a sort of infinite calm in contrast to the feverish image of industrialism and the complications of urban life. Nature versus culture, silence versus noise, ineffable calm versus movement, Eden-like landscape versus reinforced concrete, simplicity versus complexity. Nevertheless, the presence of the automobile in the jungle indicated a change of perception in relation to nature.

Nature is compared to culture and functions as a symbol of hostility against the onslaught of progress. It is kinetic utopia itself that is at risk. For that reason the figure of the automobile, which must triumph over all the obstacles on the road, becomes more important. The progress of the motor vehicle always has the risk of failure, whether for the lack of highways, for tree trunks hidden in the grass, for ruts in the road, for car-nivorous animals, for forests, mountains, or rivers outside their banks. On the edge of the Tunas River, the travelers had to find a way to protect the motor so that it could continue to function under water. In order to move forward they had to morph into improvising inventors. Such solutions can never have a proper laboratory for experimentation, or adequate materials to fix the problem. Moreover they had to solve the problem in the simplest possible way. The solution for crossing the Tunas River came about, as a consequence, in a simple manner (although the language seems highly complex to the person not versed in mechanics). An air chamber was cut in such a way that it formed a tube; one end was wrapped around the carburetor and the other was tied to the hood like a periscope, keeping the sensitive part of the motor from being drowned out. They wrapped the sparkplugs and connecting wires with a little bit of gutta-percha, while they ensured the ignition coil was perfectly insulated with an exterior cas-ing of clay. Thus it was possible to drive through water almost two meters (six and a half feet) deep.

When they arrived at the banks of the Río Grande, it seemed the expe-dition had come to an end. They faced a river of liquid mud two kilome-ters (a mile and a quarter) wide with a current stronger than that of the Rhone. It was necessary to organize a team of thirty swimmers to pass the vehicle to the other side. But the two rafts built for the purpose sank under the weight of the automobile. The only solution was to disassemble the engine, chassis, and body. It was not easy to transport the automobile in parts, but they finally managed it, and the vehicle was reassembled on the other side of the river.

In addition to the formidable obstacles of nature, there were equally terrible mechanical difficulties. Many times the travelers were afraid to turn on the headlights as they worried about running down the battery, and they drove with the help of a handheld flashlight. There were stretches where they had one or two blowouts every 100 meters (330 feet), forcing them to stop and remove the wheel so they could repair the damage. Undoubtedly, the worst moment of the trip was when the car stopped suddenly with the sound of a hammer banging on the engine block. The crankshaft had cracked between the third and fourth connecting rods. In other words, the engine was broken.

What to do? A return to Três Lagoas meant more than ten days on foot. When they thought they were done for, five Ford trucks appeared on the horizon, full of armed soldiers. They were their unexpected saviors. The trucks were in a deplorable state but did, miraculously, still run. Any problem was resolved by the soldiers with a few kicks. A few violent blows to the ignition coils and the truck would start up again. This is the well-known image of the durable, reliable Ford, quite the opposite of the sophisticated European automobile. Lt. Luiz Moreira de Paula told Courteville that in order to get along with European machines, one had to have the skills of a watchmaker in order to fix them. On the other hand, the Ford trucks had no brakes or reverse gear; a branch tied with wire took the place of the front springs, and the lieutenant's shirt served as a clutch.

From Corumbá, Courteville asked the Renault factory for a replacement engine. The car was still under warranty. That was no help at all. Since there was no motor in Corumbá, Courteville had to travel to Campo Grande, where he found a Ford engine that was not in service. He decided to attach the new motor to the gear box: the Renault-Ford marriage worked. It was now a hybrid automobile, a rare mixture with a French six-wheeled chassis and an American engine.

It was with this inconceivable Renault-Ford blend that Roger Courteville, his wife, Marta-Emma Seedorf, and mechanic Julio Kotzent traveled through Brazil, Bolivia, and Peru all the way to Lima. They crossed the Andes with the car disassembled into small pieces carried on thirty-eight mules. Who would have imagined this would be an expedition to scale the Andes with the automobile disassembled and carried on muleback? They had to tackle sharp inclines, switchbacks, at times a narrow gorge between sheer walls, at other times an abyss between two rocky slopes. Only rocks and stones, nothing of vegetation; a day's journey went from seven in the morning to six in the afternoon. When they finally got to Chorrillos, a slum on the outskirts of Lima, after a trip of eleven months, they were met by the Brazilian ambassador and a car from the Brazilian embassy, with a caravan of official cars as a cortege that accompanied them into Lima. The automobile was a shambles: its fabric top destroyed, the curtains looked like frayed pennants, the color was indefinable, the exhaust pipe was missing, and gas fumes emerged directly from the cylinder block. One connecting rod was melted, the valves were greased by crude oil, and the motor was noisier than a 400-HP airplane. The final resting place of the Renault-Ford was the Lima museum, where it was exhibited to show the potential of the automobile and as a symbol of the future transcontinental road. It was the ambiguous triumph of kinetic modernity, materialized in the hybrid automobile, broken, yet replete with flowers and decorated with the insignias of all Peruvian sporting entities, the emblem of the Automobile Club of Brazil proudly mounted on the radiator cap.

The Automobile in Latin America

The cultural history of the automobile in Latin America has still not been adequately researched. Álvaro Casal Tatlock provides some essential information.[19] He discusses the pioneers who risked their lives and their cars in inhospitable regions. In 1905 Argentine José Piquero ventured through the Andes in his Oldsmobile, and in 1914 John Martin managed a more extensive trip in a Buick. By then car magazines were being published and races were being held.

Automobiles began to reach South America in significant numbers at the beginning of the twentieth century. Prior to that only a few motor vehicles ran on streets that were in a deplorable state, attracting attention wherever they went. This happened in Argentina, where a Benz Victoria, imported in 1895, caused varied reactions, including jokes in which the owner was called a *cacerola* (cooking pot). Imports increased in the early decades of the century. But there clearly was rivalry between cars and carriages, especially the luxury models. In the first issue of the *Álbum Sud-americano* (South American album)—an illustrated monthly magazine published in Buenos Aires that first saw the light of day in October 1902 and "circulated profusely in all the Commercial, Industrial, Financial, Livestock, Agricultural, and Social centers of Europe and America"— Casa Remon, located at 102–134 Avenida República, advertised its luxury carriages, which had been awarded an honorable mention and the highest rating at the National Exposition of 1898. The A. Remon Carriage Factory offered its distinguished clientele new-model Coupés and Milords built with materials received directly from the major European factories. These modern carriages, with rubber wheels, were distinguished for their elegant styling, unlike "those heavy, horrible vehicles in poor taste, true funeral coaches, instead of carriages to ride in."

In no country in Latin America was the interimperialist rivalry between the United States and England as intense as it was in Argentina. From 1918 to 1939 the United States sought to topple England from its supremacy in the region. Raúl García Heras studied this rivalry and affirms that the principal American automotive concerns played a significant role in the immigration of American industry to South America.[20] Both Ford and General Motors set up assembly plants in Argentina and established efficient marketing networks, bringing about qualitative changes in consumer habits. They fostered local demand for motor vehicles through advertisements in the principal newspapers and magazines, radio advertising, and automobile salons or expositions. All this happened while the country still lacked a network of roads to satisfy the needs of those who were starting to use automobiles to get around.

At the outset they were limited to urban surroundings, in particular the city of Buenos Aires; later they started to expand to outlying areas. Nevertheless, by the end of 1920 the large number of cars on the roads—the result of Argentina's burgeoning economy—had risen so much that only Germany, the South African Union, and Australia surpassed it.[21]

During the postwar period of the 1920s, the American automotive industry came to dominate the Latin American market, not only because of low prices and the durability of their automobiles, but also because the U.S. government cooperated with the American private sector's expansion abroad. García Heras states that this policy was fostered by Herbert Hoover, who conceived it as a joint venture between the government and private business. He adds that the American automobile companies studied various sales strategies in Argentina in order to meet the technical requirements of potential new customers and then established an efficient sales network. This joint government–private sector program was so successful that by the end of that decade American companies controlled practically the entire Argentine automotive business. The Ford Motor Company even offered free mechanical service to drivers who were preparing to travel to the main tourism sites, took advantage of the radio as an advertising medium, and published a magazine of general interest, *Mundo Ford*.[22] Ford's advertising accentuated the freedom and pleasure of driving: "There are many beautiful places near the city that you and your family are not aware of. Buy a Ford and get acquainted with all the neighborhoods of the city and its picturesque environs. Drive yourself. Take the street or road that seems the most interesting. If an object or a sight attracts your attention, stop. Without violence, without hurry, with complete comfort, with utter calm. You are the owner of a Ford. You are in command."[23]

Argentina is a relevant example in Latin America of the state's role in building roads as a way of modernizing the nation. During the 1930s a broad highway development program was carried out to facilitate transportation by motor vehicle. Anahí Ballent and Adrián Gorelik certify the American preeminence in the automotive market and point out that the prestige of this kind of transportation combined diverse elements, including technical modernity, entrepreneurial novelty, the possibility of developing local businesses as suppliers and cargo carriers, and a political argument that had the transportation industry challenging the railroad, seen as emblematic of British imperialism.[24] Highway construction was growing rapidly: in 1932 Argentina had some 2,000 kilometers (1,250 miles) of highways; ten years later the nationwide network had more than 30,000 kilometers (18,750 miles) of paved roads, contributing to the development of weekend outings and country clubs. One of the advertising slogans used by the government company Yacimientos Petrolíferos Fiscales (YPF) was, in fact, "YPF builds roads, YPF builds the nation." It was used with photographs illustrating the contradictory trail of kinetic modernity in distant places, with a picture of an automobile running on a recently opened road, or the opening of a brand-new service station in a small village.[25]

Although the Argentine case is a bit different, as, according to Ballent and Gorelik, it combined state intervention and the economic model of substitution of imports with the idea of the nation's territory as a key to solving its problems, the example is not exceptional. Road building was an international trend. What set Argentina apart is the relatively early date— shortly before the New Deal work groups and Hitler's plans.[26] In that sense it is a clear manifestation of a broad phenomenon of territorial modernization based on motorization and road building.

Buenos Aires had two automobile clubs at the beginning of the century, the Argentine Automobile Club and the Argentine Touring Club. One of the functions of the clubs was organizing races, first on public roads, later on rural highways, and finally on racetracks. The very first races, from one city to another, led to exploring the countryside. In the 1920s Rafaela was an unknown town in Santa Fe province, but it was where three Argentines got together to organize a race that imitated the Indianapolis 500. From the start the 500 Miles of Rafaela was a prestigious race for Argentine drivers.

While on the one hand, the routes of globalization implied discovery of one's own country and increased risk of death on racetracks, on the other hand, it meant that drivers went abroad as well. For many Argentine drivers Europe and the United States were much more than car-manufacturing centers. Before Juan Manuel Fangio and Froilán González, Martín "Macoco" Alzaga Unzué became famous competing on the racetracks of Monza, Marseille, San Sebastián, and Indianapolis.

The literary elite in Argentina is not characterized by technological images. Gonzalo Aguilar explains the dearth of technology in the work of the Argentine avant-garde in terms of a stratification of the cultural field: there was probably no "technological dimension" in the intellectual elite's prestigious corpus of knowledge.[27] Unlike Oliverio Girondo's rushed poetics, in Jorge Luis Borges's itinerary the automobile appears only on the sidelines: "I am a more or less bereaved man who travels by tram and chooses deserted streets for a walk, but it seems good to me that there are cars and automobiles and a street called Florida with shiny display windows."[28] With few exceptions, Aguilar concludes, Borges's metaphors have objects found in nature as their main references.

The major chronicler in Buenos Aires in the 1920s and 1930s was Roberto Arlt, the author of "Aguafuertes porteñas" (Etchings of Buenos Aires): not only automobiles, but also trolleys, buses, airplanes, telephones, popular entertainment, the figure of the boxer, the man in the kiosk, the man who sells happiness for a peso, the violinist who arrives late at the orchestra rehearsal, the chess player, the people of Buenos Aires, and the custom of picking one's teeth. Arlt dedicated many of his essays to the automobile, among them "El vendedor de automóviles" (The car salesman) (September 14, 1928), "El acompañante del que maneja auto particular" (The private car driver's companion) (December 1, 1928), "El automovilista incipiente" (The novice driver) (January 30, 1929), "El arte de robar automóviles" (The art of stealing cars) (May 22, 1929), "Disquisiciones automovilísticas" (Automotive digressions) (September 10, 1929), "Capacidad del automóvil familiar" (The capacity of the family car) (July 29, 1930), "Tipos y subtipos del mundo automovilista" (Characters in the automotive world) (December 9, 1930), "Automovilistas desconfiados" (Mistrustful drivers) (February 24, 1931), "El cementerio de los automóviles" (The automobile cemetery) (June 20, 1933), and "Sin ruido de automóviles" (Without the noise of automobiles) (February 2, 1940).

What can be done with the messy pile of rusty pieces, used tires, and worn-out parts? As inert objects, they become a bothersome problem. Such unserviceable items must be removed from the consumption cycle:

hide them in dark places, bury them, destroy them, make them disappear inside roofed enclosures. They cannot be present if they are absent. Society reorganizes itself and puts things in order again, getting rid of "things that are out of place" when cleaning up. But often objects and their parts remain as shadows. They are the phantasmagoria of capital and consumerism turned into waste.[29] Such rubbish does not disappear magically; it is moved to less important places.

Roberto Arlt named the desolate landscape of useless parts that he found in a corner of Buenos Aires "a paradise for inventors." Along Rivadavia Street he discovered that in a certain area there were many junkyards with unusable motors, piles of automobile parts "incapable of serving as a spare part in any car": a fast-buck artist's arsenal, as they were machines good for nothing. Arlt asked himself who were the ones who went to an "automobile cemetery," or "swindler's necropolis," to buy a set of nonworking rods or a radiator akin to a watering can: "Who are they, then, who trade, buy, and make those hypothetical steering wheels, those impossible car bodies, those fantastic wheels, rods that kick violently instead of ticking, roller bearings that are so oval shaped they are almost oblong, and scrawny off-kilter crankshafts, all finally given up for good for ever and ever?"[30]

That mishmash of parts is a Mecca for those who have invented something but do not have money to make a prototype, for the water sports fan who wants to convert his humble canoe into a car moved by propellers and an unlikely transmission mechanism, for rural people who want to generate electricity for their own houses, for the amateur mechanic who seeks to dampen the sound of a noisy motor. In contrast to those who have enough money to be able to indulge their fantasies as much as they want is "the poor, haggard inventor, who, when he is down on his luck, entertains himself by taking the street leading to this graveyard and resignedly gazing at the discarded remains, while thinking that if he had the money he, too, would be able to finish his invention and he could do so precisely with that iron block that is an eight-cylinder motor in a series of two by two."[31]

The first automobiles to come to Brazil on large ships show the importance of the Europe–Latin America relationship. Henrique Santos Dumont, a brother of the inventor, had bought a Peugeot in Paris. When it arrived in Brazil it was quickly reembarked for return to France because of a manufacturing defect. A Daimler motor opened Brazil's age of the automobile. It was the car seen by pedestrians in downtown São Paulo in 1893.

Henrique Santos Dumont did not have to pay taxes, as there were no regulations yet for motor vehicles, yet he dared to protest to the authorities about the potholes in the streets. His car did not even have a license plate. The original plate dates from 1903, when it was issued to the first owner; plates were usually not transferred when an automobile was sold, and this explains why low numbers were so prized. Industrialist Francisco Matarazzo was the fortunate owner of plate number 1, which Dr. Walter Seng sought to buy. The symbolic power of the number caused some buyers to wait for months in order to obtain a desired number, such as 2222 or 8888. National license plates, numbered sequentially, with a single model for all cities, were adopted in Brazil in 1936.

The automobile spread throughout Brazil. There were automobiles in Rio de Janeiro, Petrópolis, Porto Alegre, and Salvador. The first automobile reached Recife in 1903, a two-seater Renault 80 with the gearshift on the outside. In the first decade of the century, body shops were established and taxis appeared. So did the first drivers authorized by the official examining commission, automobiles for cargo, and automobiles used for advertising. The São Paulo Automobile Club and the Automobile Club of Brazil were founded, inspired by the French Automobile Club. The bylaws of the São Paulo club set forth the club's objectives: "to ensure government authorities keep the existing roads in good repair and build new highways; take charge of road maintenance through a technical commission or a trusted professional; obtain greater facilities for automobiles and spare parts to be imported, providing there are no equivalents made in Brazil; protect automobile and spare parts industries; organize competitions, races, and all kinds of contests that stimulate the development of automobilism."[32]

From the outset the automobile clubs stimulated occasional contests and automobile and motorcycle races, often comparing them to those in Europe, as appears in the announcement in the *Estado de São Paulo* on July 26, 1908, on the occasion of the first automobile race in South America: "Today the name of São Paulo will be taken to the farthest reaches of the universe, thus placing the name of the most important state of Brazil next to the principal European cities, where nearly all automobile races have been held." In a general way, whether slowly or rapidly, changes in the urban landscape were taking place in all the capitals and important cities of Latin America. In different countries, the motto was similar: "To govern is to open roads."

A fascinating example of how objects can circulate was the arrival of four German Protos in Brazil. In 1908, on the occasion of the National Exposition in Rio de Janeiro, by then the capital city, they were expecting eleven thousand exhibitors and one million visitors. The Baron of Rio Branco, at that time the minister of foreign relations, was in charge of receiving international dignitaries, and he decided to complement the fleet of automobiles with four Landaulet Protos models: one for the president of the republic, with a siren just like the German emperor's; another for the Ministry of War; two for the Ministry of Foreign Affairs. The Brazilian consul in Berlin assisted with the negotiations with the German manufacturer. That was to be expected, as each Protos cost twenty-four thousand marks, equivalent to half a million dollars today. While this amount may be somewhat exaggerated, what is certain is that the Rothschild firm lent the money so the Banco do Brasil could close the transaction.

The Protos had recently become famous. The small German factory had reached international fame by winning the New York to Paris race of 1908. The trip around the world! Six competitors—Protos, Thomas Flyer, Züst, De Dion Bouton, Sizaire-Naudin, Motobloc—covered 21,000 kilometers (14,125 miles), including the ice at the North Pole. The route had to be altered because of the snow. The Protos was the first to reach Paris, 165 days after leaving New York. However, the title of champion went to the Thomas Flyer, which crossed the finish line four days later, after crossing parts of Alaska and Japan the Protos had avoided. It was then that Siemens–Schuckert Werke bought the controlling interest in Protos and started to manufacture gasoline-fueled cars under the winning carmaker's name. One was a popular model and one was a more sophisticated model, but neither had an electric starter. They still had to be cranked.

It was obviously the sophisticated model—the one preferred by the German imperial family—that was brought to Brazil. It was a model 17/35 PS, with a gasoline motor, four cylinders in a line, with two side valves per cylinder that cost a fortune, weighed 1,550 kilos (3,400 pounds), and it was capable of a maximum speed of 80 kilometers (50 miles) per hour. It also had a Claudel carburetor, Bosch magneto ignition, wheels with wooden spokes, and tires with Michelin inner tubes.

Following the exposition, one of these sophisticated Protos went on to be used exclusively by the Baron of Rio Branco. This car was well known to the citizens of Rio at the beginning of the century. It rolled down the Avenida Central daily, while on Saturdays it was parked aristocratically at the Leopoldina Station, where the baron took the train to Petrópolis. The baron used the Protos until his death in 1912. A few years later, when it was sold to the commander of the Federal Capital Police Brigade, it was no longer so luxurious. Commander Olympio Agobar de Oliveira used it for official ceremonies and his daily trip from his home to work. He had a chauffeur, a mechanic, a car washer, and two guards. But after Agobar left the command in 1918, it was used to deliver food to the barracks. In 1924 it was considered unserviceable and was decommissioned. It was a complete ruin, less than two decades after its costly manufacture. The National History Museum asked to place it in its collection. Only at the end of the 1980s did restoration work commence, and that went on for ten years. Today it is exhibited in a small room of the museum, as noble and shiny as ever. By the way, the last Protos to leave the German factory did so in July 1927, adorned with flowers and a sign that said "Finis."

Journalists showed particular interest in the topic of urban transformation. When *Vida vertiginosa* (Dizzying life) was published in 1911, João do Rio emphasized the importance of analyzing the current period of history in his preface. He was concerned about what was happening around him. His writing is marked by an awareness of the particular singularity of the historical moment and the changes in practices, habits, and ideas. Using a Baudelairian approach, he recorded the material and spiritual changes that were taking place in the tropical city.

"The Age of the Automobile" depicts, at the same time it projects, how the sensibilities of the era were changing. The age of the automobile had taken off suddenly with dialogues that would have been inconceivable up to that moment, fast business deals, chauffeurs, and machines. Among other things, João do Rio examines the theme of the subordination of nature to technical forces. He refers particularly to the "disappearance" of nature:

> Thanks to the automobile the landscape died; the landscape, trees, waterfalls, the beauty found in nature. We go by in a flash, with our goggles thick with dust. We do not see the trees. The trees are the ones that look on us with envy. Thus the automobile did away with our modest happiness of delighting in a patch of forest and showing nature to foreigners. We do not have nature anymore, or Corcovado mountain, or Sugar Loaf hill, or large trees, because we no longer see them. Nature has withdrawn in shame. As compensation we have palaces, high palaces born from the exhaust from the gasoline of the first automobiles and a fever for large things that is devouring us.[33]

The automobile required the building of roads and service stations. Although it was admired by pedestrians, it murdered the landscape with its speed. It also killed men and women, nannies and children. This aspect of the perverse effects of mobility seems to be an underlying theme of vital importance. While progress is inevitable, it must not be transformed into need. This leads to the obligation of recording the things civilization is destroying.

World War I altered trade relations with the Old World. High prices and difficulties in obtaining materials from Europe during the war consolidated the import market in Latin America for American cars, which were simpler, more reliable, and more affordable. Henry Ford did not let the opportunity go by, and in 1919 he established an assembly plant in São Paulo, producing the popular Model T. A few years later General Motors opened an assembly plant in São Caetano do Sul, with a production capacity of 25 vehicles per day. During the 1920s auto imports increased considerably, reaching 53,928 cars imported in 1929, but then the number plummeted because of the stock market crash in New York and the revolution in Brazil.

During that same decade, the first automobile road caravan took place between São Paulo and Rio de Janeiro, sponsored by the Associação de Estradas de Rodagem and led by the pioneer of Brazilian automobilism, Américo R. Netto. Many details had to be coordinated: the speed at which the group would travel; contacts (for which a system of signals was implemented based on colored flags and blinking lights); provisioning of gas and oil, water and food, shovels, hoes, pickaxes, mallets, short and long planks, ropes, steel cables, and spare tires. It was a time of meeting challenges and planning the building of road networks.

If government was opening roads, the country's progress and future greatness depended on having modern transportation throughout the nation's territory. Does this idea sound familiar? Do we know where it originated? The sign of movement and the trend toward motorization are justified by the notion that the automobile increases contacts between neighboring countries. A Hupmobile made the trip from São Paulo to Buenos Aires. There were four in the car: Francisco Davidson, a mechanic, a movie camera operator, and a companion, who were photographed when they left São Paulo and when they arrived in Buenos Aires, always wearing neckties and hats. This excursion crossed the Brazilian states of São Paulo, Paraná, Santa Catarina, and Rio Grande do Sul, entering Argentine territory through Uruguaiana. They continued through Monte Caseros, Curuzú-Cuatiá, Chajarí, Concordia, Paraná, Santa Fe, and Rosario to Buenos Aires. An Argentine newspaper recorded the event, confirming its educational function: "Mr. Davidson and his companions have covered approximately 5,000 kilometers [3,106 miles] on this educational trip with undeniable benefits, for the showing of their film—which we trust will be shown in our theaters—will enable a high percentage of our Buenos Aires population to become aware of many unknown regions, and we are not necessarily referring to the parts filmed in our territory."[34]

In Brazil it is well known that avant-garde poetry made use of technological images and recorded the circulation of objects in the era of motorization: "The mist follows us as a guest / But lifts somewhat near Loreto /
Coffee plantations / Cities / Cut by Paulista Avenue / Corona gathers and
spreads about in harvests / The new poetry travels in Gofredo / Which
waits for us in a Ford," writes Oswald de Andrade in "Versos de Dona
Carrie" (Dona Carrie's Verses).[35] Mário de Andrade wrote poetically of
the automobile itself: "In a luxury car, / Sixty times per month, / Clean-
shaven and with a good cigar, / King of kings . . . / Oh, all you, men, men,
/ Men, you will be slaves, / If in a short time there are no Fords / King of
kings!"

Oswald de Andrade is usually associated with "the meek, green Cadillac of illusion." His poetry, however, includes various references to American mass production and to "Forde" automobiles as would be expected in
modern industrial poetry of "primitive" sensibilities. Mário de Andrade
also includes the Ford image and the impact of "Americanism" on Brazilian culture, themes that draw less from the transgressor language of the
European avant-garde than from the assembly lines and the mass-production characteristic of Fordism.

In his poem "Louvação da tarde" (In praise of the afternoon), Mário
de Andrade fully develops poetic imagery that draws on the figure of the
automobile:

Immeasurable afternoon, vast afternoon,
Daughter of an aging Sun, sickly daughter
Of one who ignores the rules of eugenics,
Empty afternoon, pale rose in color,
An afternoon long in coming and particularly late
Immobile . . . almost immobile: it is pleasant
With a blond-headed parrot of a light breeze
Resting on my hand, to lose myself
In the islands of your perfume, rolling
Along on the deserted highways.
Only you, vast afternoon, can release me
From my work. I go freely,
Forgetful of life, slowly,
With a foot idly pressing the accelerator.
And the small machine drives me, lost
To myself, among the resplendent coffee groves,
While my glance mechanically translates

The American language
Of tire treads in the dust.
The gentle breathing of the Ford
Joins the sharp cries of the birds,
Calming my blood and my breath.
They are repeated harsh murmurings,
That order my pulsating being
To a healthy beat. Only in the exile
Of your silence do I feel
The rhythms of the engine
Methodically regulating
My body. And perhaps even my thoughts.[36]

American language becomes entangled with European poetics and national tradition. Different sides of the modern sensorial, affective experience are juxtaposed in the figure of the Ford: American technology, English reflexive poetry, Brazilian coffee plantations, history and literature of the nation, the impossible love for Maria.

Antonio Candido made a thorough study of "Louvação da tarde." In his article he reports the poem was written in October 1925, corrected years later, and published in 1930 as the next-to-last composition of the series "Maria's Time" in the book *Remate de males* (Fire sale of evils). This book, according to Candido, occupies a central position in the oeuvre of Mário de Andrade, for it represents the shift from more external poetry from the early times of the Modernist struggle to the most internally oriented poetry of the final stages.[37] As a matter of fact, in a letter to Manuel Bandeira, Mário de Andrade told him his intention was to construct a poem that could not be read on a trolley and that need not be recited (December 12, 1925). A few days later Manuel Bandeira answered him, confirming that the poem introduced precisely the impression of inner ardor and purity that delights. The technique and the rhythm were new: neither meter nor free verse (December 16, 1925). Written in blank decasyllables, "Louvação da tarde" does not, according to Candido, point to English reflexive-type poems, with references to nature, but instead to meditations in blank verse from the pre-Romantic and Romantic literature of Brazil. But in this poem Mário de Andrade introduces a different feature: the automobile. A 1920s Ford rolling down the highway as the afternoon wanes. If we remember the automobile of Marinetti the futurist, we can clearly observe the contrast. Instead of rupture, this is clearly in the modern tradition. Nothing of the din of the avant-garde, of reckless speed or of urban dynamism. On the contrary, a drive through coffee plantations at dusk, where the cinematographic element of movement and vision leads to the interior of the being. A portrait that is more internal than external, more psychological than physical, more imagined than real: less a look than contemplation.

Candido notes in this poem not only the passing of a more outwardly directed poetry to one that is more inwardly directed, as Mário de Andrade's work and Brazilian Modernism were becoming, but also the itinerant poet who invented the modern meditative poem starting with a trip in an automobile. He highlights the invention of a moving meditation inserted in the mechanical era that inverts the futurist cliché and discards the philosophy of speed, preferring instead the contemplative context of the Romantic tradition. A poem likened to an animal at one with the rhythms of nature in which traveling in this humanized machine at sunset leads the traveler back to his fazenda through the contemplation of nature and self. Neither on foot nor on horseback, rather, in an automobile, but in a movement exempt from the futurist spirit of speed and force: a poem where quiet, sweetness, gentleness, and slowness prevail. In conclusion, "Louvação da tarde" shows how "an idle dream can lead to a momentary fleeing from reality and how the construction-dream is born from it, which is the process by which literary works are produced."[38]

It is interesting to point out the technical motifs in the poem, because they are subordinated to affectivity and imagination, unlike Italian futurist poetry, which imposed such emblems as expressions of the conquest of time and space. In "Louvação da tarde," the theme of the trip is returned to, a very old topic, but one that appears renewed as a fundamental feature of knowing one's homeland. But there are also fans of motorization who go back to the subject of travel, no doubt quite ancient, but one that appears renewed as a fundamental trait of knowledge of the homeland. There were also motorization fanatics who sang only to the object of mobility and composed verses about its power. Such is the case of Américo Netto, a well-known Brazilian driver and sometime poet who took advantage of his column "Carro e turismo" (Car and tourism) in the magazine *Ariel*— which often ran advertisements for costly Talbot, Lorraine Dietrich, Bugatti, Lincoln, Oldsmobile, and Cadillac automobiles—in order to disseminate the dizzying pace of modern life.

The trajectory of the fanatic of moving metal is intimately intertwined with speed and the conquest of space, as in the 1920 poem by Américo Netto, "Automóvel":

Mass flying forth
On invisible horses
That calculations hid
In the hollow souls of the cylinders. . . .

Song of steel passing by,
Scratching out routes and snoring
As it runs into the quiet space

Song of force, angry and hot
Where metals clash
And gears engage
Pulling the molecules out
Of the blonde voluptuousness of light oil.

Brazil also has a "father" among Formula 1 world champions: Francisco
Landi. This early Brazilian racing myth was born in São Paulo in 1907, when
the city had only sixty-eight automobiles. While he was growing up he spent
a lot of time in car repair shops and often participated in races with cars
borrowed from friends, with no seat belt, and with the scant protection of a
cloth helmet. He first gained worldwide attention in 1933 at the first international trials on the Gávea Circuit race. For years he made headlines winning
races with a car inferior to the Italian cars that were the world standard
racing cars of that era. Chico Landi was a successful driver in all categories,
sometimes defeating Argentina's Juan Manuel Fangio and Italy's Alberto
Ascari. However, he died poor after working in a mechanic's workshop in
his later years. His ashes were scattered on the Interlagos racetrack.

A high society woman from São Paulo, Dulce Barreiros, participated
in several races at the end of the 1920s. In one of them she overturned in
the Bugatti that Count Matarazzo Suplicy had given her to drive. It was
thought she would never race again, but she not only returned, she won
the Pacaembú race in 1929. Another woman, Hellé Nice, dazzled the Brazilians at the Gávea Circuit in Rio de Janeiro in the 1930s. But the woman
who made the automobile popular was Carmen Miranda, when she and
Sílvio Caldas recorded the duet "Fon-Fon" (Beep beep), by João de Barro
and Alberto Ribeiro in 1937:

BEEP BEEP
The sound on this horn's no good at all
I prefer when it goes like this: beep beep

But don't go through the traffic light my dear
You might just ruin the shiftin' gear.

Your green eyes say to me: Come through!
So I accelerate and now can't stop
You've got more curves than a trampoline
And a precipice of a mouth to fall into.
I won't do that!

When I drive by, over in Leblon
To people on the street: I'll say beep beep!
But I'm not driving in a race like that
A crazy mess to snare just me!

Don't be scared, I'm alright at the wheel,
I don't speed much, and I'll stay in my lane,
Will you make me yours to keep, my sweet?
You won't hear me going beep beep beep!

The tension between machine and nature took on various forms, particularly in those regions of the world where modernization was an irregular phenomenon. In Brazil the automobile appeared on the coffee plantations, in the jungles, in the towns, in the cities, driven by offspring of immigrants, the wealthy, and taxi drivers. Many times the automobile merely crossed precapitalist enclaves: it crossed sparsely inhabited places of deeply rooted local traditions. For Agenor Barbosa, in "Canto real da estrada de rodagem" (Royal song of the road), the tranquil old towns awaken to the sound of the motor passing through. The local people react; they stop to gape, while young girls silently gaze out the windows and one of them throws a kiss to the passengers, who will surely never come this way again.

Life in the technosphere leads us to easily forget the traditional opposition between technology and nature. Literature is full of examples where the machine triumphs over nature or where nature avenges itself furiously over some technical encroachment. Since the invention of the automobile, different traditions evolved to relate it to what is considered "natural." These are explanations that depend on degrees of modernization that place us within different value systems. Thus, Mário de Andrade, in *Amar, verbo intransitivo* (To love, intransitive verb), contrasts the joy of the German Fräulein with the happiness of the Brazilians, when they drive through the Tijuca forest in an automobile: "Fräulein was happy because she was going to revitalize herself in contact with the unspoiled land, to enjoy a little virgin air, to live in nature. The Brazilians were happy because they went for a ride in an automobile and mainly because they had found a way to spend an entire day, thank God!"[39] A very modern European pleasure, going for a walk in the unspoiled thick growth, with its promise of innocence and revelation; a high-class Latin American pleasure, going for a ride in a car, without much effort, through the dense forest, showing off the triumph of civilization.

In one case the body becomes a wholly integrated part of the land; in the other the body glides as an Olympian on wheels. One variant of this contrast is found in the address by Blaise Cendrars on the general trends of contemporaneous aesthetics, given on June 12, 1924, in São Paulo, in which the autonomy of technical forms in the context of nature is recorded. The aesthetic evolution of the automobile, for reasons of utility, led to using more appropriate materials—tempered steel, thin glass, copper bars, and aerodynamic shapes—lower body styles, converging lines, elongated profiles, smooth surfaces. Nothing resembles the old horse-drawn carriage.

Despite his having only one arm (Cendrars had lost his right arm in World War I), the automobile fascinated him. An old Ford had been placed at his disposal on the fazendas of São Martinho and Santa Veridiana, owned by Paulo Prado, and it became his faithful companion on excursions throughout Brazil. In that open-air Ford he went about as a modern-day explorer through plantations, jungles, and neighboring cities. With his motorized excursions he exemplified the typical transition of movement to adventure, both of which are present from the very first written accounts of the automobile. On a number of occasions in Cendrars's poetry, the "old Ford" awaits him at the door so they can go on an adventure. In Europe he eventually purchased an Alfa Romeo: he felt free behind the wheel, where he could see "the face of solitude."

Argentina and Brazil had no reason to envy a European country such as Portugal. It was still a monarchy when the count of Avilez imported the first automobile, a Panhard & Levassor fitted with a V-2 cylinder Daimler motor, in 1895. The peculiarity of the Portuguese example of automobility is found in the monarchy: His Royal Highness Don Carlos and His Royal Highness Infante Don Alfonso encouraged automobilism. The automobile was, initially, a symbol of distinction, typical of the aristocracy, the great bourgeoisie, and some liberal professions, such as lawyers and doctors. It progressively went from being an object for taking a leisurely ride or going on an excursion to being a work tool, signaling a more democratic adoption of the car as merchandise.

This evolution was slow but constant: in 1900 there were 13 automobiles sold in Portugal, 20 in 1901, 51 in 1902, 118 in 1903. "This rapid dissemination of the new 'horseless carriages' profoundly altered many aspects of the country's sociology, culture, and economy," Barros Rodrigues observes. "The urban landscape started to be invaded by the new trends of the century: stands where dealers exhibited their automobiles, garages and service stations where repairs and maintenance work was done on vehicles, and stores that sold accessories, which established businesses that sold elements destined for the automobile such as tires, gas, lubricants, flashlights, trunks for luggage, tools, etc."[40] The difference between Portugal and other countries was in the details. Also in Portugal there was advertising in newspapers and magazines, highway codes, official competitions, speed checks, the Automobile Club, the Automobile Salon, and racetracks. In the first official competition, in 1902, there were three competitors, two of whom were foreign; the first Salon was held in Porto in the Crystal Palace. The general model of the arrival and development of the automobile was repeated along similar lines in most of the world.

While in Brazil Mário de Andrade traveled poetically in a Ford; in Portugal a Chevrolet inspired the imagination of the poet Fernando Pessoa (Álvaro de Campos):

At the wheel of a Chevrolet on the road to Sintra,
Under the moon, and, dreamily, on the deserted road
I drive alone, I drive almost slowly, and it seems a bit
To me, or I make an effort so it will seem to me, that I am
Going along another road, in another dream, in another world.
That I go on without having left Lisbon or Sintra where I am to go,
That I continue, and what else is there but not stopping and only going on?
. . .

Responsive to my subconscious movements of the steering wheel,
The automobile they lent me glides along under me and carries me.
I smile at the symbol, thinking about it, and turning to the right.
I continue in the world in so many things that were lent me!
I cling to so many things that were lent me!
How much was lent me? My goodness! I am myself!

To the left, the ranch—yes, the ranch—on the edge of the road.
To the right, open land, with the moon in the distance.
The automobile, which a short time ago seemed to give me freedom,

Is now a thing where I am shut in,
That I can only drive if I am shut in it,
That I only can control if I am inside it, if it includes me. . . .

On the road to Sintra under the moon, in the sadness, seeing the fields
and the night,
Driving the borrowed Chevrolet disconsolately,
I lose myself on the future road, I disappear in the distance as I get there,
And, in a terrible desire, suddenly, violently, inconceivably,
I accelerate . . .
But my heart remains in the pile of stones where I turned when I saw it
without seeing it,
At the door of the ranch,
My heart empty,
My heart dissatisfied
My heart more human than I, more exact than life. . . .

This is not the futurist Pessoa. Nor is the description of Sintra the important part; at twenty-eight kilometers (around 17 miles) from Lisbon it sometimes seems to be wrapped in a thin veil of mist, and at other times it is bathed in a glorious splendor of light. In reality, little is said of the external landscape and instead much of the narrator's inner life. The road of life, that old theme, reemerges now recycled with the figure of the automobile and motorized movement.

Imagination that does not want to be confused with fantasy has its limits. It takes off when it has been released and extracts material from daily life, but organizes it in peculiar ways and transforms it into creative mental activity. This capacity for imagination is not the exercise of memory either, for it multiplies one memory with another self that meditates on the trip as such. If imagination is the capacity found at the heart of poetry, as Francis Bacon thought, in the modern era it finds its place in the automobile: it is imagination on the move.

Unlike in Paraguay, where automobiles were introduced gradually and shared the roads for a long time with horses, donkeys, and oxen, the experience of Uruguay was much closer to the situations in Argentina and Brazil. Jewelers Moreau and Labat imported the first four-wheeled motor vehicle in 1900. By 1905 there were already 59 cars in Montevideo; in 1906, 109; in 1912, 704. In the first decade, the government had already imposed taxes, drafted traffic regulations, implemented taximeter service, and some physicians made house calls by automobile. Dr. Pouey's trip to Piriápolis in 1906, the first automobile trip to the interior in Uruguay, was amply documented in the newspaper *El Día*, and the first automobile accident resulting in a fatality happened that same year. Women did not drive yet, but in 1911 the municipal authorities in Montevideo granted the first license to a woman to drive on public roads. María Amelia Behrens passed the required examination, paid fifty cents for the driver's permit, and drove about triumphantly on the streets of the capital city. A few years later buses started to circulate and the first automobile race was held. At an exceptionally late date, compared to neighboring countries, was the founding of the Automobile Club of Uruguay, which took place around the end of World War I.

In the 1920s architects started to design houses with garages in the space formerly occupied by carriages or horses. When possible, rooms were added for the chauffeur, still needed to start the engine and other car-related tasks. The first national Automobile Salon took place in the pavilions of the Prado in Montevideo in 1923, sponsored by the Centro Automovilista del Uruguay. There were sixty-one stands and a luxurious catalogue was published. Little Uruguay adapted to the demands of motorization: enthusiasm for car races grew, as did the number of traffic accidents; the use of gas pumps was imposed (the pouring of naphtha from one container to another in other conditions being prohibited); a school for chauffeurs was founded; and the magazine *El Auto Uruguayo* began publication. Newlyweds left the church in vehicles from Rossi's rental firm, while the deceased were transported in black limousines. Not surprisingly, the most popular car was the Ford Model T, with a bronze radiator, imported since 1910 by the Casa Shaw shop, followed by the Chevrolet.

When the New York Stock Market crashed in October 1929, Uruguay was not noticeably different from other countries in Latin America. In 1930 there were 37,000 automobiles in the capital, including 8 Bugattis. The inhabitants of Montevideo continued to attend certain events, such as the car races in Carrasco, without understanding that this was the end of one era and the beginning of another.[41]

Some avant-garde writers availed themselves of technological imagery. Henry Ford had established assembly plants throughout the world, and consequently the Model T became popular. *El hombre que se comió un autobús (poemas con olor a nafta)* (The man who ate a bus [poems that smell of naphtha]), by Alfredo Mario Ferreiro, published in 1927, was written in the context of such transformations of mobility. The dedication to "dear Chuchú" indicates the general tone of the poems: "You and I are made in the image of wonderful motors: we never break down. We have never been seen in our underwear. Our triumph of love—with pedal to the floorboard—runs on the highway of happiness, despite the potholes that enemy hands and souls have dug. With our headlights on—joy of light in the darkness—our motor of pure love propels the chassis of illusion. And on we go, with the speed of a Packard, the sound of a Gramophone, and the reliability of a Ford."

Ferreiro's avant-garde rewriting of a famous poem by Rubén Darío is proof of the impact of Fordism on literary production and of the elasticity of poetic language. In the first verse of "Lo fatal" (What is fatal), Darío writes, "Happy is the tree that is scarcely sensitive / and happier is the hard rock because it no longer feels / for there is no greater pain than the pain of being alive / nor greater nightmare than conscious life." The human being faces, in the following verses, the "sure fright of being dead tomorrow," without knowing "where we are going, nor from whence we have come." There is not, of course, any reference to the automobile in this poem of disappointment. Alfredo Mario Ferreiro did so in "El dolor de ser Ford" (The pain of being a Ford):

> What a pain it must be
> to always be a Ford!
>
> To be a Ford . . .
> And not to be a winged Packard,
> A solemn Lincoln,
> A long-nosed Renault,
> Or a wide Cadillac.
>
> To be a Ford,
> To always be a Tin Lizzie.
>
> And that everyone says,
> "There goes a Ford."
> As one would say,
> "There goes a nobody."
>
> Knowing that deep down inside
> The sparkplugs and the carburetor,
> That automobile is the same as other cars,
> And, maybe even better . . . !

While parody is not a new phenomenon, it takes on special importance in the context of the avant-garde, to the extent that it is often considered a critical instrument characteristic of "Modernist" epistemology. Hutcheon defines parody as a modern form of self-reflection, since it is a repetition that denotes a difference.[42] More than being a parasitic and derivative modality, an enemy of creative genius and of vital originality, parody artistically reorganizes the past and re-creates tradition from the standpoint of the present. It is an acknowledgment and a coming to terms, an ironic inversion that does not take value away from the original text; rather it reformulates it with a renewed sensitivity. It is thus distinguished from mere imitation, plagiarism, or pastiche.

Ferreiro attempts to do with Rubén Darío what Apollinaire did with Verlaine and Joyce with Homer. Let us remember that the "divine" Darío is one of the most prominent figures in the history of Latin American literature. For a time he represented the new poetry movement, and he is regarded as the premier poet in the Spanish language, comparable only to Garcilaso and Góngora. Parody works best when the original text is part of a tradition and is recognized as a cultural reference of its time. "Lo fatal" in *Cantos de vida y esperanza* (Songs of life and hope) is such an example for the Latin American avant-garde. When Ferreiro parodies Darío's poem in "El dolor de ser Ford," he celebrates the arrival of a new poetic sensibility, relying on mechanical images and on "recently built models."

As happens with most "machinist" artists, Ferreiro is only partially one of them. Machines fit into a broad range of interests that have to do with the representation of modern reality. Thus Jorge Luis Borges's comment on *El hombre que se comió un autobús* is quite accurate: "Alfredo Mario Ferreiro is the only futurist I have known. He is not, like the Italian orator Marinetti, a declaimer of machines nor is he dominated by their momentum or their speed; he is a man pleased that there are machines, yet he is also pleased that there is wind, and colts, and lives. In other words, reality pleases him."[43]

Borges's lesson here is inevitable: any repetition signifies a difference. In Ferreiro's "El dolor de ser Ford" the external replaces inner concerns, which are not accorded much value. Darío's esoteric interests, his studies of the occult, his fear of death, and his fears of the presence of beings from the hereafter are converted into daring juvenile references to the external aspects of urban life: instead of metaphysical terror, the socioeconomic classification system; instead of the educator and spiritual guide of the people, the irreverent avant-garde poet. Ferreiro depicts the world around him and rewrites a Darío who hated automobiles. Darío's world was full of princesses, carriages, gondolas, and swans; Ferreiro's world was mostly filled with the emblems of technological modernization. Men become the brands that protect and envelop them: Ford, Cadillac, Lincoln, Renault, Packard. Clearly, the Uruguayan avant-garde would have enjoyed listening to the tango "Packard," by E. de la Cruz and C. de la Púa, performed by Edmundo Rivero ("It was a gold mine / it was a great car / it was a pleasure Packard / it was a gem / a car that always worked at night / always with its taxi flag down").

Toward the end of 1927, a writer for the magazine *La Pluma* noted that the new poets had started the year "hearing the screechings of the ordinary Ford that had fallen in love with the distinguished *voiturette*, and ended the year shouting from the Salvo skyscraper [at that time the tallest building in Latin America]. Automobile horns greeted its arrival, illuminated signs bade it farewell."[44] Despite the free verse, irreverent humor, and the anything but solemn metaphors of Alfredo Mario Ferreiro, vanguard poetry in Uruguay had little effect on the dominant aesthetic models.

Del pingo al volante (From the saddle to the steering wheel) is a Uruguayan silent film from 1928, directed by Roberto Kourí, photography by Humberto Peruzzi, and screenplay by Antonio Soto "Boy." As the title suggests, it contrasts rural and urban life. There are scenes of ranches in the countryside, although most of the film focuses on urban life and shows areas of the capital, especially Montevideo's elegant neighborhoods. It is a romantic comedy: a young socialite (Susana), whose parents are planning a marriage of convenience for her, hesitates between the wealthy rancher (Juan Alberto) and a libertine dandy (Eduardo). The happy conclusion—marriage to the rancher—corresponds to Uruguay's golden age of aristocratic customs in the 1920s. There is an unusual twist to the filming of this movie, which extended over a period of two months and was made with amateurs. Guillermo Zapiola reports that the director, Roberto Kourí, was a Lebanese immigrant who disembarked in the port of Montevideo in 1928, saying he knew how to make movies, was hired to make the film, did the job, collected half of the international going rate of that time, boarded a departing ship, and disappeared.[45] It seems that Kourí was his last name but Roberto was not his real first name. At least there is no record of his having made a movie, before or after, in Uruguay or elsewhere, except for *Del pingo al volante*.

The film deals with the classical theme of a "trip to the city." But it innovates by representing the adaptation of the millionaire who arrived as an unpolished rancher but, with spotless ethical behavior, manages to triumph in the city. His love for Susana defeats the strategies of the dissolute Eduardo, who does everything possible to bother him: he cuts him down in the presence of ladies with inappropriate questions—"Do cows still have horns in the country?"—he cheats him at cards, and he steals his car.

The one who had lived the rough country life and had developed his muscles from simple athletic events and working the land faces an unknown world in the city. He finds himself lost among mansions, butlers, chauffeurs, electric streetcars, cocktail parties, black-tie affairs, ladies in fur coats and boas and fashionable flapper's hats and necklaces. He does not know how to go through a revolving door: he keeps on going around and around while the women laugh. His gifts are socially inappropriate, he steps on his partner's feet at dancing classes, and he does not get up the courage to declare his love to Susana. When the town dandy Eduardo steals his automobile and escapes with Susana, Juan Alberto follows them in another car, catches up with them, and bests them in a dangerous race on the sands of Carrasco beach. He risks his life on a mechanical steed to show his love, but he is criticized by Susana, who feels they all could have died because of his recklessness. Worse still, deceitful Eduardo steals his car keys, and the rancher, unable to use the automobile, is forced to walk back to town. Although the scene of the "good Creole's" return on foot is sad, Juan Alberto has again proved his love for Susana, who finally realizes she loves him. Love is approached this time through mechanized mobility.

Uruguay, like other countries, has its local idols, for example, the race driver Héctor Suppici Sedes. He won many trophies and medals and appeared in countless photographs and songs. In his honor Pintín Castellanos composed the *milonga* "Meta fierro" (Press the iron) after Suppici Sedes won the Grand Prix of the South in Argentina in 1937. In 1938 the people of Uruguay paid tribute to him on the pages of the magazine *La Tribuna Popular*; this sports idol died in 1948, ironically, in an automobile accident.

During a number of years in Colombia, self-propelled vehicles coexisted with animal-drawn vehicles. According to some versions an automobile was offloaded in Barranquilla in 1897 and then was sent up the Magdalena River to the city of Honda. Whether this is true or not, it has been confirmed that a vehicle entered Medellín on muleback on October 19, 1899, the very day the Thousand Days' War broke out. Ramón Giovanni reported it was a De Dion Bouton manufactured in France, shipped disassembled with a chauffeur, who, despite his training, was unable to make it run.[46] When it finally was made to work, those who asked how many passengers the car was for were told it was for four, "two on board and two pushing from the rear."

The first automobiles, imported at the beginning of the century by Mr. Duperly (an entrepreneur also credited with the introduction of other inventions such as bicycles and movie cameras), reached the interior of the country by rail or by river, usually disassembled. They were mostly intended for recreational purposes rather than for trustworthy transportation. Only a privileged few—generals, governors, and the wealthy classes—had access to them. One of those cars, a Model A Cadillac, arrived from the river port of Cambao with its driver-mechanic, who assembled it so it could be driven on to Bogotá. In the first trials on the streets of Cambao, the Cadillac rolled off a bridge and was ruined. Another Cadillac was imported, which arrived at the train station in Facatativá. It was put together almost in secret because of Mr. Duperly's desire to present it in Bogotá as a surprise, ready to roll and running.[47]

Those first automobiles in the hands of the wealthy were at times associated with loose morals and scandal, as happened in the city of Cali. At the end of 1914 the mayor of Cali, through Decree No. 11, regulated the functioning of cars, because, "unfortunately it is an evident fact that quite a few young men and persons of notoriety use the automobile at night to associate with women of ill repute, sometimes accompanied by minors, and they drive about town, especially in the rougher neighborhoods, singing lewd songs, drinking heavily, making a racket, and disturbing citizens, who cannot sleep, while these people are involved in all manner of racy behavior."[48] According to the mayor, every automobile would have to bear a number in a visible place on the vehicle so it could be identified and the guilty punished.

Highways in Colombia were virtually nonexistent. Cargo was shipped by river on both the Magdalena and the Cauca, which, with a few complementary train lines, linked the heart of the country with the ports of Barranquilla, Cartagena, and Santa Marta on the Atlantic and with Buenaventura on the Pacific. But the arrival of the automobile led to transformations in urban and rural life. Numerous import firms hastened to become representatives of all sorts of American and European cars, while public transport companies were organized offering bus and taxi service, and repair shops appeared. In 1917 the Tropical Oil Company had been established in Colombia for the purpose of exploiting petroleum-derived fuels: it would no longer be necessary to consume five-gallon cans of imported gasoline. Soon electric pumps replaced pumps with cranks at gas stations.

We should not assume, however, a panorama of intense traffic. By 1927 Colombia had only 5,740 kilometers (almost 3,600 miles) of roads that could be used by automobiles, which led to the creation of the National Road Council. From the 1930s on, the construction of a highway network would become a determining factor in national development, although it was not until 1938 that there was talk of paving roads. The first tire factory, Icollantas, was opened in 1945.

Improved roads permitted hotels and tourism to flourish. Distances were shortened, making way for a summer vacation culture in hotels and recreation centers. This meant modernization of the notions of time and space. In contrast to these modern forms of bureaucratization of the spirit, an intellectual minority arose, which included poet Cristina de Arteaga, who wrote "Lo intrazado" (The uncharted), which appeared in *Tierra Nativa*, of Bucaramanga, on January 1, 1927:

Highways like reptiles
are long
and bitter,
filled with vile traffic
by the damned crowds, the servile crowds . . .

I am horrified by a planned road!
I prefer
an unpretentious
forgotten trail,
where cattle tread,
a stretch of empty trail,
so mine
I will never desire
another way.

Equally revealing of the resistance to modernization (especially poetic resistance) is the "Poema del caminante" (The walker's poem), by G. Castañeda Aragón, published in *Tierra Nativa* on August 13, 1927, where rallies are criticized and the sandal is exalted:

I praise careful walking.
Pilgrimages.
Moving about in all directions
But without lending a foot to the motor.

Because machines feed on space
And do not let us savor
The incomparable joy
Of not arriving soon.

Motors have killed the world,
Speed is killing us.
It is probably all right for the spirit to fly,
Or to roll on the roads.
But let your eyes travel
In their indolent diligence
With bells and shepherds.
How delicious are the innkeeper's wine
And the barmaid's caress!

I question rallies to London, Peking, and Paris.
They are but sparks and oil.
Only dizzying speed,
Paralyzing all sensations.
I sing the praises of the sandal.

These are poetic expressions that confirm that, in Colombia, avant-garde poetry was virtually nonexistent. *Suenan timbres* (Bells ring), by Luis Vidales, is an exception. It is a book of disconcerting images tied to mechanical life, where the electric light bulb's light evolves into a mirage of fingernails and where, by means of microscopes, microbes observe the learned sages, and the umbrella shaft inflates silk balloons so that the sky can insult them. In "La ciudad infantil" (The children's city) young Vidales, twenty-two at that time, mocks the seriousness of industrial society with the typical humor of the avant-garde: "Men passed by driving their cars, their trains, their trolleys, their automobiles. / What were they doing? / They were playing / They were out with their giant toys. / They continued to be boys. / And the great toy store of wheels flew around. / Oh, the children's city!"

In Venezuela, at the beginning of the century, there were only animal-drawn vehicles. The baker delivered bread riding on a donkey, and merchandise was transported in wagons parked at the door of a department store in downtown Caracas.[49] In 1904 the wife of the president of the republic brought back the first automobile from a trip to Europe, repeating the model of a direct purchase in France and its transfer into the local context.

With the subsequent importation of European and American automobiles came intense adaptation of roads so that they could accommodate the new means of transport. During the next decades, and despite the conversion of carriage houses into garages, the automobile had to coexist with horse-drawn vehicles. Symptomatically, in the 1920s the Touring Automobile Club was founded, sport cars appeared, and women began driving.

Fords and Chevrolets were the most popular cars because of their low price and efficient network of sales agents throughout the country. The Ford Model T in particular could be found in the most unlikely places, because where there were no roads the Model T arrived in boxes and was put together at the train station. Guillermo José Schael comments that, in Venezuela, Henry Ford was a pioneer in the adaptation of colonial roads to roads suitable for automobiles and that Fords were the champions of overcoming all manner of obstacles in that country.[50] One example was a tiny town in the mountains. The owner lived in the coffee plantation region of Bergantín, bought a Ford, and had it taken apart. He transported it by muleback to Bergantín, where it was reassembled and made to function again. "On the four streets of this tiny village hidden away in the mountains, Mr. Bajares gave himself the luxury of a motorized transport."[51]

Ford advertisements referred to how far the Model T had spread throughout the world. Besides being advertised as a small, economical, lightweight, powerful, and durable car, it was also added that Fords were used in many places in the republic and that their owners were satisfied with the good results they obtained from them. Newspapers and other periodicals praised the transformations in the natural and social landscape of the country, such as the magazine *El Automóvil* in mid-1928, when the Great Trans-Andean Highway was inaugurated.

A quick comparison provides an idea of the importance of mobility brought about by the automobile. In January 1928 the first issue of *Auto-Magazin* was published in Germany. In the editorial foreword of the magazine its launch was justified as a function of the enormous diffusion of automobilism. No industry had grown as much as the automobile industry: in the late 1920s Germany had approximately 750,000 cars on its streets. A magazine was necessary, according to this editorial introduction, to give information about new developments in the automobile field, both German and worldwide. Keeping up-to-date on automotive news, which now included abundant photographs, had become relevant.

As in so many other places in the world, the Ford Model T dominated the automobile market on Venezuela's Margarita Island. But the most desirable car there was the Overland, to the extent that the expression "he is an

Overland" came to mean someone who was well dressed. In 1922 there were no more than 30 automobiles on the island. Ten years later there were 122 motor vehicles, mostly Fords. The first to arrive was a De Dion Bouton, at the beginning of the century, with three cylinders, a three-gear transmission, and 10-HP. In the early years license plates were not necessary. The make of the automobile and the name of the owner were enough to identify it ("it is so-and-so's Overland, Ford, or Chevrolet"). However, by 1919 all automobiles had painted numbers to identify them.[52] History repeats itself when the topic is motorization, although on a smaller scale on Margarita Island: taxis, salesmen, advertising, women being kidnapped, automobile accidents, and the prestige of having a chauffeur.

The case of Cuba is fascinating. To be sure, in twentieth-century Cuban history, the automobile is replete with ideological significance and was never a neutral object. Before the Revolution, the American car was not only a symbol of what it meant to be civilized but also of having access to what was modern. With the triumph of the Revolution, however, the perception of the automobile changed: it became seen as an artifact of a corrupt, decadent society.[53] The first automobiles started to arrive in Cuba near the end of the nineteenth century, with the waning of Spanish domination. They represented the postcolonial future. Hundreds of different makes were on the streets of Havana by the early 1920s. The "democratic Ford," popularly called the *fotingo*, rapidly spread through the island and could be seen in cities such as Matanzas, Cienfuegos, and Santiago. Wallace Stevens was impressed when he visited Havana in 1923 and noticed the streets were full of Fords. And author Rodríguez Acosta, in *Sonata interrumpida* (Interrupted sonata), characterized the arrival of the *fotingo* as a true revolution in itself.

Close proximity to the United States facilitated trade during the years when the price of sugar was rising, and this continued until the Depression of 1929. The island then had 28,303 automobiles, a figure surpassed only in Argentina (205,000), Brazil (60,800), and Mexico (38,110). There was real fanatical enthusiasm for the automobile, for its appearance, and how it ran. In the words of Louis Pérez, it was surely the automobile "that most fully transported Cuban sensibilities across the threshold of modernity. The automobile early seized hold of the popular imagination and quickly became a national obsession. It symbolized progress and modernity, available for purchase and possession. The automobile occupied a strategic and complex place in the rendering of national identity and individual self-representation. Indeed, probably no other product so fully possessed the capacity to corroborate civilization as the Cuban condition."[54]

Popular and literary culture lost no time in incorporating motifs of motorization. A new sort of freedom was in the air, and particularly for the upper-middle-class women who bobbed their hair as flappers. Adultery and divorce appeared as a consequence of being able to move around easily and the possibilities offered by the large city. Literary titles say it all: "Infidelidad" (Infidelity), "Lo irremediable" (Beyond repair), *La mulata Soledad* (Soledad the mulatto girl). Emilio Roig de Leuchsenring expresses it clearly in "Once soluciones a un triángulo amoroso" (Eleven solutions to a love triangle), arguing that a husband can only presume his wife's faithfulness based on faith. A wife went out alone, visited many places, used the telephone, went to the movies. With an automobile she could quickly cover great distances. Not even security guards could ensure her faithfulness.[55]

Various writers used urban changes stemming from the automobile as subject matter. Rubén Martínez Villena (1899–1934), in his story "En automóvil" (In an automobile), describes the frightening new sensation of speed: "I did not know what it was to ride fast in an automobile. The car had barely gotten up speed, but it seemed to me it had grown wings. The terror, the uncontrollable terror of dying in an accident paralyzed me completely."[56] Many magazines, such as *El Fígaro, El Mundo, La Lucha, Gráfico, Havana Post,* and *Bohemia,* addressed various kinds of worries. Gustavo Robreño, in his article "El automóvil nos reivindica" (The automobile vindicates us), which appeared in *Gráfico* magazine in 1915, argues that until recently people left for work very early, but they moved very slowly. The automobile had noticeably changed this. It seemed to Robreño that in Cuba the proportion was lopsided: too many cars for the number of inhabitants. An avalanche of automobiles of various makes invaded the city, causing traffic jams on the streets and complicating getting around, all of which confirmed the changes in the city's appearance for Robreño. Havana, which had been the capital of lethargy, had become abuzz with movement, thanks to the automobile that had arrived to resuscitate the Cubans.[57] The automobile was no longer a luxury for many people but had become a necessity instead. "Civilization" seemed to require it, and Cuba, despite its burgeoning problems and accidents, had to imitate traffic patterns such as those of New York, Paris, London, Berlin, and Vienna. An English tourist observed in 1921 that nowhere, not even in London, had he seen such a large number of automobiles as in Cuba, from luxurious Buicks and Cadillacs to the infinite variety of Fords, each with its own siren or horn.[58]

When the automobile arrived in Puerto Rico there were no highways, garages, or gas stations. The only roads were made of stones, gravel, rough rocks, and, dirt, sand, or clay and became impossible to use when it rained. For some years there were steam-combustion automobiles and even electric motorcars, both European and American. The first car was a steam-powered Locomobile in 1904, whose boiler blew up when it attempted its first race. Fixing it was an ordeal, because even though car mechanics did not exist, there were mechanical "geniuses." From then on, many went to the United States to study to become mechanics, while others learned the trade by taking cars apart and putting them back together.

Automobilism developed rapidly in Puerto Rico, as did the highway network, repair shops, and domestic tourism. None of that is surprising. Despite those who announced the end of what they considered to be a passing fad and emphasized the problems (frequent accidents, blowouts, lack of mechanical aid, difficulty in obtaining fuel), the planet was being taken over by automobility. Puerto Rico, of course, did not miss out on the fever of movement. From the capital city of San Juan, roads extended to Ponce, Mayagüez, Aguadilla, Arecibo, Humacao, Caguas, Guayama, and Fajardo. Emilio Huyke recounts what cars were like in Puerto Rico at that time.[59] One climbed into a car with difficulty despite the running board, which helped somewhat. The top was of rubber or canvas and could be removed easily. The windshield was a single piece of glass, and its position could be changed at will. It had six carbide lamps that had to be lit one by one.

The first automobiles came equipped with a complete tool box. Among the tools was a jack for changing tires, a screwdriver, pliers, a hand pump, a measuring stick for the gasoline tank, a box of patches for tire repairs, extra inner tubes, a monkey wrench, copper wire and thread, replacement belts, talcum powder, a large file and a small one, sandpaper, rubber adhesive, a roll of *tiraempalme* tape, electric cables, carbide for the lamps, and an assortment of small parts to repair the motor. They also carried extra gas and oil, a canister of water, a flashlight, rags, wadding, fan belts, sparkplugs, ropes, and soap.[60] Gasoline—of only one kind—was imported in cans and sold by gallons or liters in drugstores, hardware, and liquor stores. There were no automatic pumps for the gas or for air for the tires. Nonetheless, it was advisable on any trip to carry spare gas and tires because it was difficult to find adequate services on the road. During the 1920s gas stations were becoming more modern and more helpful, favoring driving and tourism.

Mexico was a unique case because of its shared border with the United States. The first automobile entered Mexico by land from El Paso, Texas, at the end of the nineteenth century. From that moment on, the economic, commercial, and financial expansion of the United States led to a model of neocolonial development. The first automobiles that circulated in Mexico fulfilled the same "luxury whim" function as in the rest of Latin America: distinguishing small groups of wealthy people. Later on, Ford and General Motors set up assembly plants and expanded their network of sales to the entire country, which progressively transformed Mexico City into a hell on wheels.

In the 1920s the young Mexican poet, playwright, and journalist Salvador Novo, a car enthusiast, studied the progressive mechanization of society using the transformation in the distribution of bread as a case study. Novo argued that in the colonial towns bread was still being sold in the plazas in large baskets and that families had their favorite baker, the one who would flirt with the maids and was a delight for the children. But he noted, also, that the "favorite baker" was being replaced by the bread truck: "But now American firms were springing up that distributed bread by automobile: toast and raisin bread—so little imagination up north!— for all purposes. Those large assortments of sweet bread for the evening meal were disappearing and American style birthday cakes were being cut at birthday parties. . . . Mexico was becoming un-Mexicanized."[61] The Stridentists, inspired by Marinetti, celebrated the emotion of movement with stark imagination. Manuel Maples Arce wrote in the first Stridentist manifesto: "In half a glass of gasoline we have literally swallowed Juárez Avenue, at 80 horsepower. I mentally turn aside at one end of an unforeseen ellipse, forgetting the statue of Charles IV. Accessories for automobiles, Haynes spare parts, tires, batteries and dynamos, horns, sparkplugs, lubricants, gasoline."

Very early on the Mexican film industry adapted the American taste for adventure and episodic narration to local conditions. Serials, in particular, used the automobile as a creator of movement. There were still not many cars in Mexico when *El automóvil gris* (The gray automobile) opened in December 1919, but its directors, Enrique Rosas and Joaquín Coss, breathed in relief. At the beginning of the year an opportunist distributor had shown the film *The Scarlet Runner* using *El automóvil gris* for its title in Spanish. Months later another director, Ernesto Vollrath, concluded a new version of assault and crimes that he planned to title *La banda del automóvil gris* (The gray automobile gang). Rosas tried to prevent it, although the most he was able to manage was not having the color of the automobile mentioned in the title. In September Vollrath's *La banda del automóvil* or *La dama enlutada* (The automobile gang or The lady in mourning) started to run; it was the first Mexican serial film.

All this confusion was justified. The film that was being announced, *El automóvil gris*, promised to be a spectacular hit. In the words of Enrique Rosas it was a "Mexican film of palpitating actuality." It was based on real happenings. In 1915 a gang dressed in military uniforms went about in a gray car terrorizing Mexico City. The films showed, precisely, how an organized group of criminals used a car and military uniforms of Carranza's forces and robbed the homes of the wealthy. Moisés Viñas helps explain how the films differ, since they both depict the gang that assaulted the capital of the republic in 1915, albeit told from different points of view.[62] He states that while Vollrath's film moves from reality to fantasy, passing through melodrama with the action centering on an anguished mother, Rosas and Coss imaginatively uncover deeper aspects of reality and present the multiple social facets of the city.

It is, as a matter of fact, the discovery of the reality of urban life, of the contrasts between mansions and the poverty belt, between the wealthy, the criminals, and the police. There are nine assailants in one car who commit a number of crimes in different parts of the city. They do not use masks, but rather uniforms. The false authorization to immediately inspect the residence—a spurious search warrant—enables the viewer to see how the bourgeoisie live. But the cramped hovels of the bandits also appear, along with the police station, cock fights, shootings, and telephone calls. The robberies were filmed at the places where they actually happened, the execution of the guilty is authentic, and the chief of police, playing himself in the movie, is the very one who managed to capture the bandits.[63] In reality and in the made-up story, the gang broke up and some members escaped to other states. They were pursued and captured in different areas of Mexico.

Critics agree that *El automóvil gris* is the most important Mexican film produced between 1917 and 1920. Reyes bases this view on three arguments: the film is the last chapter of early Mexican cinematography; it announces the trend away from the "new cinema" movement, and it expresses both Italian and American influences. González Casanova asserts that Rosas's film is the culmination of the so-called Mexican School, a narrative that "maintains a sense of unity in a storyline based on real events, fictionalizing them but still maintaining the veracity of the account, in the final scene of the firing squad, by using actual footage of the attackers' executions."[64]

The filming of the police executing the occupants of the gray automobile—Mercadante, the man with the slashed face and the other accomplices—is horrible documentary footage of its day. Clearly, the bandits are discredited without the slightest attempt at explaining their motives. They appear simply as criminals. It was necessary to moralize in order to avoid censorship, because it was always rumored that people in power had been actively involved in the band's operations. It was also necessary to lighten somehow the brutal image of justice with an ethical lesson: death is the only outcome the criminal can expect; work is the only noble way to earn a living. Automobiles are for enjoyment or for work, not for banditry.

Advertising of the French car *De Dion Bouton*

Marcello Dodovich, Bugatti, 1932

Marcello Dudovich, Fiat Balilla, 1934

J. Carlos, 1935

Margaret Bourke-White, *At the Time of the Louisville Flood*, 1937

Tamara de Lempicka, *Self-Portrait (Tamara in a Green Bugatti)*, 1925

The automobile and sexuality, 1920s

Erotic photographs from
the 1920s

First crossing of South America by automobile, Rio de Janeiro to Lima, 1926

Publicity for the documentary *Raid Citroën* (Long Journey by Citroën)

Olivia Guedes Penteado and her daughters, Paris

Olivia Guedes Penteado and her daughters in the same car decorated for the Battle of the Flowers, Paris, 1908

Aerial view of Ford manufacturing plant in River Rouge, Michigan, 1930

Workers in the Ford factory,
ca. 1910

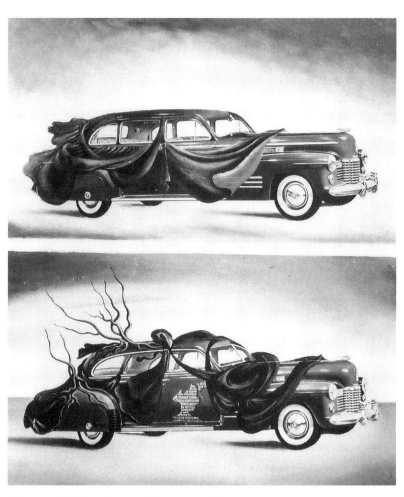

Salvador Dalí, *Phantasms of Two Automobiles*, 1925

Walker Evans, *Joe's Auto Graveyard*, Pennsylvania, 1936

Cover of the first Superman comic, 1938

The Batmobile

4. CONTRADICTIONS OF MOBILITY

A Precarious Tradition

In kinetic modernity, tradition still retains somewhat of a regulatory role. However, its authority is increasingly limited, because the sign of movement directly threatens it. Tradition tends to be understood as a series of activities carried out unconsciously, as a body of norms and beliefs incorporated by institutions and individuals. They were forms of continuity filtered and transmitted in diverse ways, which ordered conduct and determined social practices. With their utility, mobility, and visibility, automobiles intensified the problem of the relationship with new objects. If the stability of tradition became threatened, this suggested the emergence of "opposites" that placed the unquestionable nature of its character in doubt.

Although the term *mass production* became popularized at the end of the 1920s, this production method was associated even earlier with the United States. While the aesthetic of the machine was an international event, the mass production of automobiles was regarded as an American phenomenon. Eccentric writer-aristocrat Raymond Roussel is an interesting example of the symbolic value of the automobile. In the 1920s he acquired a "house on wheels" to travel through Europe. This model allied the aristocratic prestige of the private coach with the advantages of motorized transport. The magazine of the Touring Club of France published an article on Roussel's carromata, referring to "a highly ingenious shape and comfortable for a complete camping experience." Unlike the camping model of the "Spartans," who traveled around the world on foot or by bicycle, with their house on their backs, the "Sybarites" were the ones who transported their house with an automotive vehicle and sought the greatest comfort possible. They aspired to enjoy all the comforts and advantages of the home right in the midst of the forest or countryside.

Roussel's house on wheels captured an aristocratic ideal based on movement. Jules Verne had only imagined this hybrid car and dwelling in *La maison à vapeur* (The steam house). Now it was an automobile that measured 9 meters (29.5 feet) long by 2.3 meters wide (7.5 feet) wide—a genuine miniature house, according to the definition of the Touring Club of France. It had a living room, a bedroom, a study, a bathroom, and even a small bedroom for servants. It was the very image of modernity: it had electrical heating, a gas-fueled chimney, a radio set up to receive all European broadcasts, and a safe. Nevertheless, this "genuine chalet on wheels," in which the extravagant French writer traveled through Europe, was a mark of resistance given the signs of a world on the path to extinction.

The car promised a new form of freedom that questioned the distinction between aristocratic and democratic mobility. To illustrate the changing idea of movement, just compare Raymond Roussel's luxurious carromata, decorated with mirrors, wide windows, heavy curtains, and suede-upholstered armchairs—a veritable fin de siècle drawing room—with the image of transcontinental travel in the United States. While houses asphyxiate us and large books bore us, poet Vachel Lindsay writes, the car liberates us. For the poet, the United States was the vast space of continuous movement of cars from Concord, Boston, Topeka, and Austin, from Chicago, Alton, Oswego, and Toledo, from Buffalo, Kokomo, Lodi, and Kansas.

The first "autocampers" in the United States offered a way of avoiding the rigid schedules of trains and hotels. "Free will" and "anywhere" were the watchwords. People who yearned to set up camp anywhere shared in the desire to flee from convention. They were not rebels, although it was common to identify them with hoboes and gypsies. In any event, the sport of camping created the right conditions for the birth of the motel,[1] a standardized nationwide business that made the road recreation industry official and found a provocative literary guest in the character of Lolita.

Soon nature became a tourist attraction, a natural artifact to be captured by the eye and in photos. "Picture ahead! Kodak as you go" appeared on thousands of billboards set up in the 1920s by the Kodak Company along roads to advertise scenic landscapes.[2] It structured the gaze of the modern tourist, aimed at settings far away from everyday experience. Consequently, places formerly regarded as primitive became signs of authenticity. They were experienced as uncontaminated by civilization, as "profound."

This shift in the perception of nature was a significant step forward in the appraisal of the nation's landscape. The rustic West emerged as a glowing space that could be crossed with unparalleled freedom by car. "See America First" read the slogan of a movement that the automobile contributed to consolidating, particularly during World War I. Finally, people were free from the tyranny of the castles of the Loire, the canals of Venice, and the glaciers of Switzerland, as declared one columnist from the *New York Times*. In the open air, in parks and on mountains, freedom reigned—from European culture in the arid Southwest, and at the Grand Canyon, at Yosemite, and at Niagara Falls.

Parallel to the elegy to mobility, the ghost of alienation arose. A sensibility of loss disarticulated the image of belonging to a place or a tradition. In Europe this feeling of belonging to a sort of collective experience that could be communicated entered a crisis phase stemming from World War I. At that time the United States was unaware of the nightmare of war. It had no image of destruction, only accelerated transformation. However, movement had a powerful effect on the direction taken by the sense of loss. There were roads that crossed wastelands devoid of nature for those who returned from the disenchantment of exile. The account by Malcolm Cowley in *Exile's Return*, a story of the writers of the "lost generation" until 1930, ties the feeling of estrangement to the changes produced by means of transport. The return of such writers to the United States caused conflict. They were overwhelmed by a vague feeling of alienation: "being at home" vanished as part of a mythical undertaking. They returned physically, but spiritual return proved to be impossible. The relationship of the spirit with movement was always an ambiguous one, but given the civilization of efficiency, standardization, and mass production, contradictions assumed a predominant role.

The landscape was unrecognizable, and people wandered about like ghosts in a forsaken land. For Cowley, modern transportation facilitated this process. Airplanes, buses, trains, and highways went everywhere, even to the place of birth. Traveling toward the west, a writer suddenly found his own region, the town where he went to school, the forests where he gathered nuts and listened to the call of squirrels as they cut cones of fir trees. The writer could pass by the house where his grandmother lived and stop on one side of the road, asking himself what would happen if he bought it from strangers and planted himself a new garden in place of the old. He could live and die there just as one of his ancestors had. But no, the door held two locks preventing his return; the house would no longer accept him. He was after something that did not exist. The writer ceased to belong to the country now crossed by the new concrete superhighways, which did away with forests and put the remains of trunks and branches in their stead. It was useless to rue the loss of the past: he had to keep moving forward, driving ahead toward an uncertain destiny.[3] The strange country that stood between the individual and memory indicated that kinetic modernity invaded even the most intimate reaches of memory and identity. Whoever returned to his place of origin became lost on endless highways and in images of no return. Closed doors stood where there was once hospitality, unknown roads where forests and homesteads once rose. In the modern era of mobility, roving had no end, nor any final destination.

In rejecting the transformations brought about by mechanization, several forces of resistance converged. Depending on the specific contexts, this rejection led to the adaptation of extreme measures, although in general it was a partial phenomenon resulting from contradictions of mobility, as expressed in the resistance to transmitting messages of love by phone or typewriter. In *Afoot in England* W. H. Hudson explains his decision to walk through the English countryside instead of riding a bicycle, in order to preserve the connection with his fellow man and with "the wilderness of the human heart." Later the advantages of the bicycle become indisputable for him, despite the fact that he continues to protest the noise of automobiles, the clickety-clack of streetcars, and the speed of motorcycles.[4]

A close connection linked the desire to walk in the "wilderness of the human heart" and the evolution of means of transport. Until the end of the eighteenth century in Europe, walkers were viewed with mistrust. Only in the nineteenth century did the habit of walking in the countryside begin to gain legitimacy. Then this activity was no longer regarded as idle, because it was thanks to the spread of means of transport that the association between walkers and needy, down-and-out drifters lost its meaning. Instead, the countryside was perceived as invigorating, a means of fortifying body and soul, giving rise to the emergence of the "cool walker," equipped with hat, shorts, socks, boots, and other products specifically intended for walking as an outdoor activity.[5]

Arguments against the use of mechanical means of transport ranged from the inhumanity of the technological object to the loss of direct contact with nature and human beings. In an essay on speed, Paul Morand mentions the danger that, according to Emil Ludwig, threatened the European spirit: the new technological spirit. It took considerable time for European monarchs to admit the dignity of the automobile. One of them, Emperor Franz Joseph, never rode in a car, never used the telephone, and never wrote a letter on a typewriter.

There was, of course, in the United States an important trend of privilege in consumption committed to the aristocratic tradition, exemplified by the production of luxury vehicles: Duesenbergs, Cadillacs, Lincolns, and Pierce-Arrows. Inversely, what gained force in France were movements tending to popularize the automobile, which began to lose its aristocratic character. André Citroën's visit to Henry Ford's factory in Detroit led him to apply the assembly-line production model. He proposed to build a French version of the Model T, solid, lightweight, with low fuel consumption and low cost. His vision: a work tool for the middle class. The Citroën Type A, the cost of which reached 7,250 francs in its simplest model, was an instant hit. Unlike other European cars of the time, it came ready to take out for a spin. However, celebrities of the likes of Rudolph Valentino, Josephine Baker, and H. G. Wells bought the Voisin C1 model, produced by the pioneering aircraft designer and manufacturer Gabriel Voisin.

Why were there suddenly so many references to movement? In *Orlando*, Virginia Woolf, who never even drove a car, describes her hero-heroine crossing parks in a motorized vehicle. At the same time, Count Leinsdorf, a character in Robert Musil's *The Man without Qualities*, rides in a carriage with a coachman and reddish-brown horses, but reserves the use of a car to express his modernity. Surely the aristocratic connotation of the car/chauffeur combination persuaded Thomas Mann, in the mid-1920s, to acquire a handsome Fiat sedan for six passengers, from which he could comfortably wave to passersby. However, in his short story "Disorder and Early Sorrow," the sole car owner is a young financier.

There are indications of the disappearance of the aristocratic luster of the car, which joined the new generation's technological milieu with its pragmatic qualities.[6] Although motorization imbued fiction with new vigor, it was because modernization of images demanded it. The contradictions of mobility reached the stateliest of souls and subjected it to the dilemma of movement. With acceleration, the aristocratic sensibility was shaken, but it was impossible not to recognize that the sign of movement invaded its very existence.

Cities were not exempt from the trend toward motorization. Oxford, England, is an interesting example. From 1912 to 1935 a series of decisions made by one man, William Richard Morris, produced a brusque change in this city, dominated in days of yore by the hallowed British university. William Morris, a bicycle manufacturer who also offered repair services, decided to enter the automotive industry and opened a factory, the MG (Morris Garage), in Cowley, a few miles from Oxford. The changes in urban structure set in motion by the arrival of the train and the expansion of the university publishing house dramatically intensified when Morris began the production of automobiles, particularly in the mid-1920s, when he formed a partnership with the Budd Company of Philadelphia to create the Pressed Steel Company of Great Britain to produce steel car bodies. Morris's activities violently upset the social and political equilibrium

of Oxford and gave rise to unions, strikes, increased rent for accommo-
dations, and rural displacement.[7] In fact, Morris's contribution was so
decisive that in the early 1930s, writer J. G. Sinclair declared in *Portrait
of Oxford* that to be a success in that city, the main requirements were as
follows: possessing at least one pair of plus fours, a repertoire of pornographic stories, some skill—legendary or otherwise—at golf, a sneer on
your face, an inexhaustible capacity for suppurating self-conceit, and a
Morris car.

When we focus on the study of daily life in an American town in the
Midwest, the contradictions are all the more apparent. The relationship
between the automobile and enthusiasm and concern is unequivocal.
Robert and Helen Lynd, in their classic study *Middletown*, published in
1929, devote a chapter to the transformations in Muncie, Indiana, with
the advent of the automobile, movies, and radio. Of the three, the most
important was the car. One interviewee claimed it was not necessary to
study what was transforming the Midwest in the United States because it
could be summed up in four letters: A-U-T-O. Symptomatically, in 1909,
the car replaced the horse as the official means of transportation for presidents. That year two million horse-drawn vehicles were manufactured in
the United States, a number that fell to ten thousand in 1923; the inverse
was the case with the automobile, eighty thousand in 1909 and four million in 1923.

A group of new habits arose around "horseless wagons." If one takes
into account that the first car appeared in Middletown in 1900, the speed
of its assimilation into everyday life is astounding. By 1923 there were
more than six thousand passenger cars in the city, one for every six people,
and most of the vehicles were Fords. The introduction of Fords in the U.S.
heartland accelerated change in small towns, which still figure in Sinclair
Lewis's *Main Street* as extremely traditional places. At stake was the feeling of union and the breaking apart of families, who used to get together
on summer afternoons and weekends in their own yard; now they were
subjected to the centralizing and decentralizing force of the newcomer.
Some people mortgaged their homes to buy a car, while others cut back
on the money they spent on clothing, food, or gardening. The automobile
also seemed to make its presence felt in the space between the home and
religion, generating emotional conflicts, because leisure, at least in certain social groups, was transformed into a regular expectation instead of
an occasional event, stimulating the trend of taking vacations. The number of rearticulations in Midwestern cities with the introduction of cars,
movies, and radios—concluded the Lynds at the end of the 1920s—made

it impossible to study small American heartland towns as self-contained communities.

In that decade William Ashdown, a banker in a small town in the Midwest, noted that the household revolved around the car and that the art of walking had been lost. Going to the local store on foot was a faux pas even though it was only a few blocks away. Even his laundress came to work by taxi and returned home the same way. Ashdown paid the price.

The pedestrian established a more careful connection with the street and roads. A symbol of speed, the driver was a threat to the passerby. He was the enemy of the *flâneur*, out for an idle stroll down the street, because appraising space is related to delayed vision. In the street, the driver established a rivalry with the pedestrian. At the end of the 1920s, Gilberto Freyre recorded this rivalry with concern in northeastern Brazil.[8] Tradition, everything from rituals surrounding death to the simple exercise of walking, stood on the verge of check in a game of chess. If people want nothing to do with an unhurried walk, Freyre denounces, it is because the car has taken over the streets with the violence of a tank in enemy territory, eliminating the peace of mind necessary for leisurely ambles, unconcerned at being forced off one's path at any moment.

Public streets, formerly the domain of carriages and pedestrians, became showcases for electric, steam, and combustion engines. The conflict between horse-drawn and motorized vehicles was a common theme in the first decades of the twentieth century in Latin America. Chroniclers recorded this initial moment of the machine replacing the horse as a means of individual transport. In Montevideo in the 1900s the carriage lined with blue satin no longer dazzled pedestrians, and the curious ceased to flock to see the Argentine "sportsman" mail coaches leaving the Hotel Oriental. People no longer bothered to turn their heads to watch them pass with their four horses driven from above by the owner, dressed in elegant London style, with gray tails and a top hat. Cars were what stirred awe and admiration, perhaps because there were only two of them in Montevideo. And contrary to what might be expected from a highly expensive machine, they did not always run properly. One of the cars often refused to start. Therefore, the proprietors returned to using their old horse-drawn carriage and had the automobile await them elsewhere in the city.[9]

A keen observer of the likes of José Carlos Mariátegui wrote that World War I accelerated the process of displacing the horse with the machine. "In short, the last bellicose encounter marked the final decline of the cavalry," wrote Mariátegui in 1927.[10] While displacement was a historical event, it, paradoxically, contributed to highlighting the aesthetic value of the animal. As a means of transport, the horse appeared to be too individualistic. As an instrument of speed, it had fulfilled its task in dominating time and space. As a war apparatus, it was a thing of the past. In fact, during the war, there was a massacre of horses in Europe, which hastened the mechanization of transportation. On the other hand, it is estimated that in the United States there were at the same time thirty million horses and mules, which mechanization swiftly shifted to a secondary position.

Metal machines and the urban context are paradoxical factors that contributed to the reappraisal of what was regarded as "natural" and the protection of animals. This can be perceived as a result of difference. The beauty of the mare stands out from the asphalt pavement of the city, and the "noble horse" marches elegantly in an essay by José Vasconcelos.[11] Just like the phenomenon of immigration, the net balance of which went from a positive sign to a negative and vice versa—depending on historical circumstances—the horse disappeared from everyday city life to become a figure of the past, relegated to nostalgia.

As the horse ceased to be used as a work implement and was confined to closed spaces, it became the object of specialized treatment, thereby increasing the sensibility of urban inhabitants to its presence. It became an object of contemplation or an artistic symbol bearing diverse meanings. The gaze reappraised it, with a clear tendency to transform it into an aesthetic object. This aesthetic process worked in highly different ways from what operated in the field of industrial product imagery. Nature refused to die in the representation of the horse. References were made to freedom and energy (the herd of horses galloping on prairies) or the aristocratic character of the product (possession as a symbol of distinction). Therefore, two complementary phenomena were engaged, in which the horse was accompanied by its prestige to sublimate the evolution of the car.

The first phenomenon had to do with the persistence of the animal quality of mechanical beasts by "forming part" of a tradition and with the desire to establish analogies between the organic and innovative technologies. Why did the automobile displace the horse as the main attraction in circuses throughout the United States from the end of the nineteenth century? How did the animal quality persist in the mechanical? In an article entitled "H.P." [horsepower] sent from New York to the *Diário de Pernambuco* on May 13, 1926, Gilberto Freyre keenly discerns the transformation of the horse into a symbol of American progress: "And when what remains of the animal in the formidable horse of New York disappears in its entirety; when the horse is completely mechanized in the steel horse of this enormous Barnum & Bailey circus that is American civilization; when the machine completely conquers the last horse, usurping Roman sculpture, the strong beauty, the music of trotting, then the memory of the noble animal, a prehistoric species of the Triumphant Machine will persist in the initials H.P."

It is the lack of awareness of nature encoded in mobile objects of modernity. The automobile stood as if a reminder of the prolonged evolutionary process in mobilization, voluntarily clinging to its animal origin, but in fact detached from it, insistently begging for forgiveness for its historical demolition. That automobile spoke in a mysterious language, simultaneously contemporary yet remote, a product of material culture where hope and terror of history converged. Seeing it meant feeling the remorse of development beyond our control; it was the same as experiencing the contradictions of mobility from the perspective of nostalgia.

The second phenomenon had to do with consumption. U.S. advertising was adapted to sell the Buick automotive brand in Latin America. A polo player on horseback appeared on the upper part of the page and an enormous Buick below. That car, at least according to the ad, was "as powerful [and] agile as a polo pony." The new Buick, Fisher's masterpiece, was the great car of the year, thanks to the bold lines of its design, bright colors, grace, and luxury of its body. Together with its breathtaking beauty, the new elements of speed, power, acceleration, comfort, and safety could not be surpassed by any car.

We are well aware of the role of advertising, including examples from sports referring to leisure and the good life. Nevertheless, what draws attention here is the presence of animals. They are emblems of power and speed that energize the motor: jaguars, lions, pumas, horses. In the origin of brands, there is a veritable small zoo and of all the animals, none stands out more than the horse, the species that the automobile ousted from urban transport in the first place.

There were instances of the proud display of the automobile on a cart drawn by horses, as published in late 1905 by the *Cronología de Montevideo*. It reported the automobile was paraded triumphantly down the main avenue while the sidewalks were crammed full of people who cheered one of the amazing victories of human ingenuity at the end of the nineteenth century while its driver undertook the route clad in special garb, almost resembling an astronaut, with proud elegance that the photo captured for posterity. And most noteworthy is the fact that the car was carried on a horse-drawn cart. Montevideo had the invention, but did not yet know how to use it.[12]

The automobile was mounted on a cart drawn by animals, while the public applauded an operetta chauffeur. The image is eloquent. It was the era of movement, with all of its contradictions, and given the car's power, the cart pulled by horses soon became an obstacle. It was not long before voices clamored that this type of vehicle was getting in the way of progress and had to be eliminated. Such was the extent of power of naturalization of the modern era of mobility.

A significant document in this regard is the *grotesco* (grotesque) play *Mateo* (The horse-drawn cart), by Argentine playwright Armando Discépolo. The most representative work by Discépolo, born in Buenos Aires in 1887, was written in the context of the crisis in Río de la Plata realism and the issue of theatrical genres. Moreover, the fidelity of the settings and the characters was set amidst the conflicts in an urban society in violent transformation, principally among the humble classes and the bourgeoisie. Río de la Plata writers experimented with the expressive possibilities of psychological drama that they learned from Pirandello without discarding traditional forms of realism with a marked social commentary. Contradictions stemming from the impious nature of mobility arose on all sides. At home or on the street, in public or private arenas, people lived in a state of crisis, without communication, where rebellion was impossible.

When *Mateo* premiered on March 14, 1923, in the Teatro Nacional in Buenos Aires, no one recognized the innovative nature of the work. The two rooms of a small convent in the port city, the father powerless to deal with the disintegration of the home, the suffering mother, insensitive children, meddling and judgmental friends, the use of local color in the Río de la Plata idiolect and popular language—all seemed to be elements that continued the short farce tradition.[13] But the dramatic recasting of the subject of the immigrant, which at the same time was the product of mobility, suggests that the much feared hell was movement itself. Whoever hoped to find a new life in another place, exercising the profession of his ancestors, discovered the logic of movement in the alternative space.

The main character, Don Miguel, is an honorable man, a father concerned with his family commitments and the future of his children, whom he cannot support because he lacks the financial means. Don Miguel clings to the outdated public service coach and the old horse with which he makes a living, although he is a figure displaced by the new means of transport. His faithfulness to the old mode of conveyance earns him criticism from his children and his friends until he falls into delinquency, utterly failing in the process, and is forced to pay the price in prison for a crime that society is quick to condemn.

Don Miguel's crime is his lack of adaptability. In other words, the new technologies make conversion and retraining a necessity. How can a public service coach and an old nag compete with the mechanical novelty? The old horse even hits his head against a car and continues to work with difficulty. However, Don Miguel sees him as a "creature of God" and stoically tolerates his old age. The owner and his horse are bound by an emotional bond that is threatened by the machine. Throughout the play, the dialogue is full of sorrow, marking counterpoints between the end of tradition (the coach) and progress that devours the heart (the automobile): "The coach is done for, Carmené. The automobile's killed it. People are witnessing a terrible spectacle in the street; the coach's agony . . . but they don't move a hair. They look at you in the driver's seat of the coach with pity; you see the load and it makes you stop . . . one-armed [like an idiot] for the idea! . . . because they mumble to you a car [is] better than the horse. Have you heard of walking death? . . . It's the car."[14] It is the pathos of circulation formulated in *cocoliche*, hybrid Italian-tinged slang in Argentine Spanish. The dramatic element in all transitional situations is perceived from the perspective of the straggler who lacks real opportunities of salvation. The automobile kills, undoes, dismembers. The "Matagente," or "People-Killer": "The automobile! The wonderful discovery? Whoever made it can be proud. A statue should be put up in his honor . . . on a pile of dead bodies yet! Diabolical vehicle, repugnant machine that I am condemned to see come and go always full of passengers with a crazy look on their face, while the trumpet, the horn, I honk it and filthy pigs they boo at me and they leave me deaf."[15]

Given the response of his son Carlos, who declares that it is a matter of progress, Don Miguel refers to the "era of road killers," where protest is futile. What can he do? Buenos Aires is full of bridges and tunnels, electric streetcars and automobiles. There is no other recourse than to await inevitable disaster. Children and friends, however, do not share this notion of fatality; they argue that "you have to join in." In other words, you have to become a driver. Don Miguel avoids the idea as if it were the plague. He was always a worthy coachman, and becoming a driver implies losing his identity. If he were president for two minutes, he would toss all automobiles along with their drivers into the dike, cover it with a mountain of earth, and hang a sign declaring the end of danger. He prefers to die with the whip in his hand and the wagon ready, just like his father and his grandfather before him. He prefers to become a thief to becoming a driver. But the reality is that now few people ride his coach; they prefer the speed and prestige of the taxi.

To join in or to self-destruct, his son Carlos decides to become a taxi driver. He does not reproduce his father's work [according to family tradition], instead he enters the same logic of movement. Work to live like his father? One night he comes home with his brand-new chauffeur's uniform and twenty pesos to help with the household expenses. The hour is late: Don Miguel is not only tired, but he has also committed a crime. The police drag the old man away. Don Miguel "joins in." However, not in the business proposed by his son; instead, he is taken to prison. The hostility of the surroundings and uprooting in the new city lead to conflicts brought about by mobility.

Mateo represents the drama of movement. There is no room for slowness in the era of acceleration, when old age and velocity are pitted against each other as enemies. Traveling by carriage, unless for entertainment, is useless, and those who do not adapt to life's new conditions are added to the list of social outcasts.

However, passionate defenders of the world of mobility abound. For them the model of substitution is equivalent to progress, through the new industries that crop up. The transition of coachman to chauffeur is precisely the example used by Mr. Slang, the "Englishman from Tijuca," Monteiro Lobato's character in his book *América*. According to Mr. Slang, who paraphrases a passage in Henry Ford's book *My Life and Work*, all new machines or inventions create conditions of life that lead to the displacement of men as workers. With the appearance and spread of the automobile, thousands of coachmen and grooms lost their jobs. Was it a crisis? On the contrary, it was merely a social displacement with the potential for benefit: "The new machine did not come to diminish work, but rather to increase it, as the facts show. It only created new work. The job of chauffeur arose and that of people who repaired cars, those who washed them, sold gasoline, and that entire world of the automotive industry. And here is the point. The coachmen and other men who were cast out by the automobile were a much smaller number than the quantity of men summoned to carry out the new jobs created by the use of the automobile."[16]

Along the same lines of reasoning, Renato Almeida maximizes the kinetic utopia to fantasy in *Velocidade*. The model of substitution triumphs without resistance, failing only before the mystery of life and communication with God. Cars and buses displace electric streetcars, which in turn had relegated streetcars pulled by donkeys to oblivion. Each new mechanism cuts the time needed to travel distances and makes urban reconfiguration possible. There is no room for melancholy or weariness of life. The story is the uninterrupted progress of speed, which threatens the never-ending renewal of means of transportation.

This model of replacement generally appeared in connection with a simplified perception of time and space. It was an attractive model, easy to visualize: alterations in spatial and temporal perception corresponded to technological changes. However, the opportunity to experience such changes was far from homogeneous. On the contrary, the impact of technological modifications was distributed unevenly, depending on variables such as social class and professional group. Albeit obvious, not all people had the same opportunities to experience technological change, a fact that often went unnoticed.

Drilling through Air: Speed

Speed is the powerful ally of kinetic modernity and its best means of propaganda. Furthermore, it is a mysterious synesthesia and an experience of intoxication. In a car at high speed, our body is semi-immobile and euphoric, feeling the vertigo of the thrust of movement. We are the synergic arrow that cuts through space with a slight trembling movement, generating on its course a form of fleeting and elusive beauty, which has characterized modernity since the mid-nineteenth century.

Speed has much of the warrior's world, although here the confrontation is against limits. Typical of the imperative of movement is the ongoing challenge of barriers, by individuals who take the risk of driving increasingly powerful vehicles. At the end of the nineteenth century, Belgian driver Camille Jenatzy broke a new record: 105.9 kilometers (65.75 miles) per hour. He used a car called "Never Content," with an electric motor that he had built himself; it had the shape of a torpedo and was equipped with Michelin tires.

It took only a few individuals, but the craze for speed gradually spread to society and went on to contaminate ways of experiencing time. This mania for speed also sparked its opposite, the appreciation of slowness: "fast" things are badly made, poorly planned, and ill executed. One critical trend reproached the acceleration of modern life and regarded speed as contradictory to progress.

At that time, France was the foremost car producer worldwide and Paris was the global automotive capital. It had long, straight roads from the Napoleonic period that crossed the country, and it was more successful than industrialized England, the bastion of the equestrian world, in dealing with prejudices against the new machine. In France in 1900 there were some 3,000 automobiles; a little more than a decade later, the number had shot up to 100,000 vehicles. A panorama of similar growth took place in the United States, where the number of automobiles rose at a dizzying pace. In 1904 the United States surpassed France as the world producer. Under these circumstances, European immigrants, such as Scotsman David Buick and French-Swiss Louis Chevrolet, found favorable work conditions. Car magazines proliferated, and it is not strange that despite the academic disapproval of the representation of mechanical objects, particularly in Europe, there were writers and artists who focused part of their production on recording the impact of speed on the human psyche and on art forms.

The early experiences in an automobile of Belgian poet and dramatist Maurice Maeterlinck, known for his interest in spiritism and boxing, offer food for thought. "In an Automobile" narrates the impact of this recent mechanical creature on the writer's life.[17] In particular, the mysterious apparatus for changing speed drew his attention; hidden in its wrapper it held a furious temperament confined in a narrow cell. Man, with the support of the untiring machine, was pitched against time and space, two enemies of humanity. Once they were conquered, man would be like the gods.

This projection of the prosthetic individual as a divine being implies considerable imagination. Chronicles of the time indicate that the automobile was not particularly reliable. Georgette Leblanc, Maeterlinck's actress wife, confirmed that the couple bought one of the first automobiles made, and both of them embarked on short excursions. The ventures were triumphant. The sound of the engine drew the attention of neighbors, who waved handkerchiefs, while chickens went wild in front of the car. But soon after that everything went downhill. The lack of windshield wipers prevented the driver from communing with the road and enjoying speed; at the same time the trip generally ended in carsickness. At the end of one day the motor died irreparably, forcing them to spend the night on a farm. They returned home the next morning on a packhorse. On another occasion, Maeterlinck, in a letter to Georgette, told her that tomorrow he would be in Gruchet, "if the monster does not become too monstrous."

In any event, speed imposed itself as the foundation of modern civilization. Despite the fact that a number of automakers despised races—Karl Benz, Henry Ford, especially André Citroën—they were forced, for reasons of publicity, to participate in such events. At the beginning of the century, Octave Mirbeau perceived speed as a fundamental factor of daily life. For Mirbeau, fascination with the automobile was a mental illness that had a lovely name: speed. In speed, the human being existed, thought, felt, and loved swiftly, with movement like the charge of the light brigade. It was better not to think, or at least to do so in an unbridled way, for thought was an obstacle to action when the body was thrust into the adventure of displacement with total frenzy. Excitement envisioned space being crossed like a challenge full of danger and heroic characters, in which the American film industry was its most fanatical mouthpiece. Quite unlike the journey in mechanical terms, it was where they drove madly and space was merely an obstacle to be easily overcome. This was the paradox of speed: in one we are overly excited beings; in the other, mere packages.[18] It was often said that the nineteenth-century train turned passengers into packages, a transformation that the urban bus had perfected years later.

Changes in speed spurred contrasting reactions ranging from enchantment to horror. The modifications that had been taking place on different parts of the planet over the past few centuries were intensified by the massive export of British industrialized products, as was the case of sturdy shoes in discreet colors that replaced colonial footwear and altered the way people walked in Brazil. On the other hand, the adoption of the English type of lightweight carriage dazzled the Brazilians in the nineteenth century. By that time Rio de Janeiro was known as the city of excess when it came to speed, with the new carriages barreling down narrow streets at a gallop, startling pedestrians and frightening Europeans like Radiguet, for whom the "extraordinary speed" had suddenly made the city's streets dangerous.[19]

The owners of carriages, from high above and protected by the wooden structure of the vehicle, took to the streets as if they were private racetracks. Consequently, the cabriolet became a public threat: the coachman directed his horses at high speed at the multitude. Much earlier than the combustion engine, these horse-drawn vehicles were associated with luxury, liberty, and licentiousness.[20] Therefore, the automobile did not produce this taste for speed. It was, instead, its most powerful promoter. Automobile drivers continued the tradition established by coachmen and car owners, the tradition of carriage owners. Gilberto Freyre raised the question of why Brazilians were fast only when it came to driving. He sought explanations for the fact that public functionaries labored at a methodical snail's pace at work but at a terrifying speed when they left the office and jumped into their cars. Then they did not waste a second, and the ones who were sacrificed to speed were children, the elderly, women, country bumpkins, foreigners, tourists, those who should "know how to leap like acrobats, dance like ballerinas, balance like trapeze artists in the circus, disappear like magicians, so that no one diminish the sovereign, absolute, voluptuous speed that private cars and even lorries judge they have the right to use on the streets of Rio de Janeiro."²¹

The technological revolution that affected modes of transportation, work, and leisure time made the constant increment in speed possible and relegated the past to a primitive state. Many problems arose as a result of incessant mobilization, and they inspired nostalgic visions of a past that were swiftly dispelled. On the surface, comments Stephen Kern, one was in accord in that Taylorism and futurism, the new technology, the new music, and film were what made the world run. On a deeper level, expressions of resistance underscored the uncertainty brought about by these changes.²² The "insanity of speed" invaded the Paris of *marcheurs* (walkers) in an alarming way and outraged poet Rubén Darío, who in the poem "El hipogrifo" (The hippogriff) voices the idea that the future will arrive by car, "with speed, unbridled, killing, exploding."²³ For Darío, in the era of mechanical mobility, a skilled, daring driver enjoyed triumphs and acclaim that a Pasteur or Anatole France would never receive.

Italian futurism was the first avant-garde artistic movement that openly glorified the automobile. It fully exploited the possibilities of art to celebrate speed: literature, painting, sculpture, design, music, and theater. On October 15, 1908, F. T. Marinetti was thirty-one years old when he had an accident at the wheel of his four-cylinder Fiat Cabriolet on the Via Domodossola. Months later, in the "Manifesto of Futurism," the car signals the advent of urban modernity and serves as a literary tool to distinguish the vanguard sensibility from fin de siècle decadence. The race car paid homage to the mobility of the modern spirit in a gesture that Whitman, one of Marinetti's favorite authors, would have appreciated.

Speed reigned glorious in the "Manifesto of Futurism." It reinvigorated an aesthetic that preached war on the past: "We affirm that the world's magnificence has been enriched by a new beauty: the beauty of speed . . . Why should we look back, when what we want is to break down the mysterious doors of the Impossible? Time and Space died yesterday. We already live in the absolute, because we have created eternal, omnipresent speed."²⁴ The man-machine was displaced in another landscape, one that was geometric and technical. It was filled with railway tracks, high-tension power lines, and the turbulence of water. The human motor was converted into a common reference of the era, sparking the will to surpass the limitations of muscles and prophetically blurring the distinction between the living organism and the machine.

The modern subject is the individual in movement. Mobility is glorified. Speed excites the modern subject. This form of acceleration, which disdains obstacles and continually longs for novelty, is the new moral religion. On trains and in dining cars, on bridges and in tunnels, in weapons and motors, Marinetti discovered sites inhabited by the divine. Wheels and rails belonged to the realm of the divine to the extent that the intoxicating feeling of speed evoked the rapture of being joined with a singular divinity. While Giacomo Balla drew cars at high speed and lines of force on hundreds of his canvases, Luigi Russolo mixed the sound of motors in his concerto *The Meeting of Automobile and Airplane*. At the beginning of the century, Umberto Boccioni contrasted cars with horses and hunting dogs in his tempera sketch *Automobile and Fox Hunting*, an illustration for the Automobile Club of Italy, in which the fox jumps onto the car to escape from dogs in hot pursuit. The work of Gino Severini, Carlo Carrà, Mario Sironi, and Gino Galli, among others, followed. The disintegration of the object, begun with Impressionism, found a faithful line of continuation in futurism. Curiously enough, the continuity of a swift action in space dissolved the object. Futurism was so closely identified with the automobile and the representation of speed that English writer Wyndham Lewis described it as mere "auto racing."[25]

Among the examples that express the perception of the historical break beginning with the car's speed is the early text by Marie Holzer, "Das Automobil." The moving vehicle is portrayed as a powerful anarchist. Free of ancient norms, it accelerates, spreading fear throughout the world. No rail dictates its path: it is the lord of unlimited possibilities. Its driver mocks the rules, for there is only one law for him, that of his own will. It is the tyranny of the devil and the triumph of individual will over collectivity. The automobile destroys customs and defeats limits, it overcomes carriages, it occupies streets, it invades causeways, it threatens pedestrians and markets. What a lugubrious hour in our life, Holzer concludes, when the automobile tyrannically imposes its power to dissolve everything over tradition.[26]

For some, it was the victory of the devil, for others, the feeling of freedom. The automobile was particularly important in avant-garde poetry, where it symbolized the historical rupture that tended to legitimate the bold vocabulary of modern poetry, as in the volume *Automobilian Advance*, by Vadim Shershenevich. Peruvian poet Alberto Hidalgo celebrated the arrival of futurism and opened the section known as "Plus Ultra" of his book *Panoplia lírica*, defining himself as a new bard of concept and form. He was a seer of the future. The poet had to abandon the reasons dreamed up late at night, the sorrowful word, and the tears. He had to sing to Muscle and Force and Vigor, all capitalized.

Let us do away with schools, molds, and methods, intoned the Peruvian poet almost a decade after the "Manifesto of Futurism." Poetry was the cannon's red smile, the man's muscular arm, the engine's force. It was the shining steel of the locomotive, which in motion, made verses to speed, the potent airplane on whose two wings the shameless wind whistled, the elusive motorcycle (the modern horse) lost in the blue confine. Didn't electric streetcars perforate the air and create symphonies to acceleration? Poetry was hundred-story houses with hundreds of elevators and trans-atlantic ships bursting with grace and obese with progress. An intense feeling of liberty was linked to technical emblems and the modern city. The mold was undoubtedly futurist, although the sense of humor gave Hidalgo's poems a unique tone.

The automobile could not be absent from the new poetry. In *Panoplia lírica*, Hidalgo dedicates the poem "Oda al automóvil" (Ode to the auto-mobile) to the "mechanical pachyderm," from which I have selected a few passages:

> I feel aristocratic emotions
> Driving a 50-HP Mercedes
> The free and pure air bathes my restless brow
> and I intensely enjoy the wind that tosses
> my South American poet's hair.
> The mighty tires of my automobile, which
> tears up the silence with its hoarse horn,
> run dashingly on the gray asphalt
> while a man in a top hat who bustles
> on the arm of an old woman with a cynical nose
> remains
> ecstatic, absorbing on the pathway
> the smell of gasoline. . . .
>
> The (Car) means the triumph of Civilization:
> when passing a hallowed old monument
> or an inveterate museum,
> it roars like a lion
> that wishes to furiously devour the Past
> and bury Tradition. . . .
>
> Driving a magnificent automobile
> aristocratic emotions fill me

when before the immobile sky
the free and pure air bathes my restless brow
and the wind tosses
my South American poet's hair;
and going down the city streets
full of splendid exhilaration
I rejoice in
the notable vertigo of Speed.[27]

The automobile is the futuristic version of the vanguard, more in terms
of theme than form. The iconoclastic gesture, without being original,
supposes a previously unknown freedom. Hidalgo burst on the scene of
Latin American poetry with his bold images: metal eyelids, drill piercing
the air and rending the silence, the smell of gasoline. But still the auto is
"more artistic than Day," "more serene than Night," and "more beautiful
than a Woman." Nature and femininity act as counterpoints of a poetics
that seeks a constant means of emancipation from traditional styles. Little
does it matter that the poet does indeed drive a 50-HP Mercedes. The
poetry takes control of the vertigo of speed, emotion, the open air, and
enthusiasm, prolonged in the context of Latin America, unknown by its
museums, and where cars were scarce, the Marinettian sermon against the
past and tradition.

The automobile is the new poetic muse. Hidalgo incorporates Marinetti's shining discovery as the triumph of civilization. It is strange that
Hidalgo's book dates to 1917. The war in Europe was raging; thus it was
submerged in its first major crisis of civilization. At the same time that
Oswald Spengler expressed his *Kulturpessimismus* (culture pessimism)
in his first volume of *The Decline of the West*, diverse authors intensified
their criticism of civilization. Hidalgo probably did not share Marinetti's
ideas of war as purification ("We want to glorify war, sole cleansing of the
world"). As European youths died in the trenches, for the restless Peruvian poet, the car was "a clear source of poetry."

A world of rejuvenated values emerged from the first postwar period.
This was known as the "era of the machine," film, radio, telephone, the
automobile, and the airplane. For the first time, some young people produced the dominant ideas. The steering wheel directed culture and cinematographic sensibility. Although for our taste, the world was going too
fast, writes Paul Morand in his essay "De la vitesse" (About speed), it was
because we still had not managed to adapt, because speed did not mean
disorder, but rather a new order that we were forced to adopt. Often this

overpowering presence of change was defined as conquest of time and space.

Speed was associated with renovation of life; with mobility, anonymity, youth, and freedom. It rewarded circulation and looked down on old ties with land and family. Paul Morand recorded that a friend, thanks to the small car, had four vacations instead of one: a month at the seashore, a month in Paris, another in the countryside, a month in Italy. It was enthusiasm for adventure and effortless physical displacement, because the bourgeois traveler, free from train schedules and its imprisoning tracks, let himself be guided by the machine and the chauffeur.

On the train you do not really cross the country, there is no direct communication with the inhabitants, declared a car lover like Octave Mirbeau. This novelist and political pamphleteer, initially reactionary, antirepublican, and anti-Semitic, at that time a fervent collaborator on libertarian and anarchist magazines, crossed Europe at the start of the twentieth century and raved about the enormous freedom afforded by the "magic beast." The automobile not only led him from the plains to the mountains to the sea, on endless routes, contrasting landscapes, and picturesqueness in unceasing renewal, it also transported him through hidden customs and ideas in the making toward the living history of the present. Referring to the "miracle" of crossing, in a few hours, a diversity of customs and cultures, he had the sensation of having lived several months in a single day.

It was an updated version of the conflict between old and modern, even in writers who did not belong to avant-garde movements. Octave Mirbeau died in 1917, at almost seventy years of age. However, the automobile was a watershed. Mirbeau loved it more than his library, which for him was asleep, dead, and immobile. It was more useful for him. He thrilled when he saw the "fabulous unicorn," when he heard the vibration of that admirable organism that was his car's engine, with its steel lungs and heart, the vascular system of rubber and copper, the electric nerve system. It was not the quixotic discourse on weapons and letters, but rather the modern account of the preeminence of the vertigo of motoring over the insipidness of books.

Summer vacation hotels, where the well-to-do family tended to spend an entire month, waned in popularity. Motorization rebelled against sedentary life, converting repetition into boredom. The modern tourist was an anti-Aschenbach who planned to visit multiple attractions in a short lapse of time, the antithesis of the tuberculosis patient: here today, gone tomorrow. Motorization heralded the advent of the tourist who wanted a glimpse, always in passing, ever hungry for new sights. According to Paul

Virilio, modern tourists of desolation have taken the place of tourists of spleen, of neurasthenia, of tuberculosis, who were drawn to the foreign decoration of nineteenth-century train stations, as prisoners of hatred for the real world.[28] All of this was utterly different from the journey of the immigrant, the worker, the servant, who rarely achieved the status of "traveler."

Wherever tourists went, the number of places where they could spend money increased. However, these spots had to adapt to the new conditions of automotive mobility. The example of Ontario, Canada, is a case in point. Once it discovered in 1926, by means of a questionnaire, that the U.S. tourist thought that the speed limit was very low, it was altered. And because many of the tourists who went to Canada were trying to escape from the restrictions of Prohibition, the government of Ontario opened eight liquor stores on the border. At the same time that the motorization of Canada improved, the government invested money to expand the highway system inland, where tourists could spend money in the poorest districts.[29] In contrast, in Latin America, the highways could not be turned into "rivers of gold" by filling them with U.S. tourists. Although the Mexican border offered some similarities to the Canadian example, including domestic automotive tourism, such tourism was minimal between the countries of Latin America. There was a dearth of facilities and an abundance of difficulties.

The desire to go out for a spin in the car became popularized. Sundays were certainly a must (the shadowy figure of the "Sunday driver" was consolidated in the United States, as a social type in the 1920s). Even a bishop observed in 1919 that automobiles harmed ecclesiastical discipline and that members of the clergy must never, "unless necessary," go out for drives on Sunday or be "accompanied by members of the opposite sex."[30] "Joyriding" can be regarded as a variant of the car outing and was cited as an example of the loss of paternal authority over children, which contributed to breaking down family ties. In Midwestern towns, girls known as "flappers" were the ones who agreed to go on a "joyride" with "flippers," boys who seemed to live only for pleasure-seeking. For the moralizing conscience, both figures embodied the deterioration of youth at that time.

Writer-journalist João do Rio spoke of mothers who pretended to protect their daughters from experiencing the sensation of car rides. In Rio de Janeiro (the example is repeated in other urban centers in Latin America) local traditions of family protection were blended with the will to experience new sensations. Only a small number of boys were in a position to offer girls a ride in a car. When possible, the mother went with them; when the mother did not go along, these became cases for the moral voice that João do Rio interspersed in his chronicles of the degeneration of youth.

Now the memory of noisy excursions by car could be added to the memory of train rides. It was still an adventure to travel relatively short distances. Often it was necessary to get out of the car to push it. Stops were made on the way to eat sandwiches and to drink pop. Everything suggested the liking for gasoline, even the passengers, who ended up smelling like gas. And these excursions awakened more often than not in children and adolescents an enthusiasm for mechanical things. That pleasure in taking apart and reassembling an engine. Changing a tire. Tightening a hose. Adjusting a sparkplug. Not always, for there were also other young people attuned to the charm of new landscapes and to different kinds of people.

"Emotion" and "intoxication" are words repeated insistently when it comes to motion on four wheels. Marcel Duchamp's personal notes confirm that car trips with Picabia and Apollinaire, swiftly "conquering" the Paris-Jura route, prompted vanguard reflection on artistic production. Apollinaire announced World War I and bade farewell to the past in his poem "La petite auto" (The little car). He wrote that on August 31, 1914, he left Deauville a little before midnight in the little car that belonged to his friend Rouveyre. Counting the driver, there were three of them. They said good-bye to "an entire era," since furious giants were rising over Europe and eagles, waiting for the sun, were abandoning their nests. Voracious fish emerged from chasms, and the dead trembled with fear in their dark dwellings. In a race, they visited towns to know them better, while dogs barked in the direction of where borders once stood. They made three stops to change a tire that had blown out. When they reached Paris, as mobilization posters were being plastered on the walls, both understood that the small car had driven them into a new era and that the two—now mature men—had, however, just been born.

Avant-garde artists rebelled against the past by declaring they would not imitate nature. With typical vanguard pride, Duchamp and Picabia added the symbols of technology to art, just as the promiscuous Picabia, who drew many acquaintances (Marius de Zayas, Marie Laurencin, Albert Gleizes) as if they were parts of the automobile and who in *Le Saint des Saints* (The saint of saints) represented himself, ironically, as a phallic horn. "I will not serve you (Nature)," shouted Vicente Huidobro. In the modern era of mobility, one pursued freedom from the model of Nature. It was continually crossed by technical artifacts. Images in motion: locomotives, airplanes, ships, and automobiles were the privileged symbols. The vanguard poets threw open the door of the house to the infinite horizon to make mobility, circulation, and simultaneism their subject matter. Beyond the sun and the moon, the sky and the stars, there was an artificial nature where sheep ate flowers, the electric star smoked between one's fingers, the moon sounded like a clock, and God died between white pillows. It was art in movement that constructed the world and cut through it to the last edge possible:

We will soon reach
the last parallel
    The afternoon
My hand
Steers the automobile
Like an autopiano
    The silent plain
    80 horsepower
    The plain
To be crossing the earth
Someone has left their wings on the ground
And there are swallows in your chest[31]

It is the delight of the senses, the swift life of visual experiences. Guillermo de Torre appropriated futurist language in "Al volante" (At the wheel), a poem that appeared in *Hélices*:

At the wheel
all highways cavort
in the play of gears
the pedals
shuffle a kaleidoscope
of rolling perspectives
The car is a convex bow
that shoots
insatiable trajectories . . .

Leaps between the meshes of itineraries
Trepidations
The engine suffers from tachyarrhythmia
The little windows deplete the book of landscapes

The windshield multiplies our eyes
That sew evasive panoramas
And the wind liquefies sounds
In dynamic intoxication
the auto spreads
a trail
of winged cells.

In Brazil, Renato Almeida began his book *Velocidade* with a categorical statement: "If something could characterize civilization, something that transformed humanity, from the discovery of steam, it is speed."[32] The literature devoted to speed, Almeida declares, is synthetic and alters the form of writing. The incidental is exempted as useless, while the dressing of adjectives is abandoned for the dynamism of nouns.

But there are less glossy aspects of speed: anxiety, irritation, frustration. Speed left people nervous and grumbling. The phenomenon was particularly evident in big cities in the United States, to the extent that Paul Morand critically identified speed with "Americanism." It seemed to him that the notion that something produced quickly was something poorly made, an idea still rooted in the spirit of Europeans. The expression *"à l'américaine"* signified a combination of speed, lack of subtlety, and pantomime.[33]

As speed increased, symptoms of urban stress also increased. This particularly affected those groups whose relationship with technology spurred a growing dependence on the machine. There is little empirical proof of the psychological reaction of people faced with mechanical failures and accidents, but the machine-reliability relationship was an important element in the perception of the mechanical object. Psychological reactions such as impatience and irritation, so common today with the "slowness" of computers, were visible in the charges of the 1920s. The worker who ran, sweated, and was desperate to catch the bus; the lawyer who grew impatient in traffic; the millionaire who ordered the chauffeur to step on it and cut between pedestrians.

There is no question that the alteration in the rhythm of daily life, linked to the need to meet increasingly strict hours, produced anxiety. Even though urban congestion predated the automobile, the phenomenon was intensified in big motorized cities, and it gave people the jitters. The use of modern transport produced so-called technosis (a dependency on technological products). Without cars, electric streetcars, omnibuses, and taxis, life seemed impossible. Modern means of transportation went on to form part of the routine. However, not even those who loved mobilization could easily buy a car because of the high cost. The consequence was often, especially on the omnibus, that one rode with a blend of shame and resentment, brazenly observing the flashy cars and pretending not to see the occupants.

When Ezequiel Martínez Estrada examines aspects characteristic of Buenos Aires in *La cabeza de Goliat* (Goliath's head), he notes that speed is inherent to urban civilization. His position is critical, but it in no way alters the identification between city and speed:

> The city is converted into a racetrack of incessant hustle; machines and passengers are dragged like metallic particles by whirlwinds of electricity. This infinitely complicated and living mole is in perpetual agitation; men, vehicles, and even inanimate objects, it could be said, move because of an intrinsic need to move. . . . There is the same eagerness for speed in the driver, the pedestrian, the sales clerk behind the counter, the person on the phone, the guy waiting for his girlfriend, and the fellow drinking a cup of coffee determined not to do anything. . . . Speed is a tachycardia, not an activity. It springs from internal circulation more than from intense work, because we are channels, even those of us who might not be active. A city can be very agitated without being dynamic, like a man can be in bed with a pulse of a hundred beats per minute. Buenos Aires loves speed, which is not to say it is active, and perhaps it would mean the contrary if it had a sporting interest in fulfilling its obligations.[34]

The Lexicon of Automobility

Kinetic modernity invaded words, which had to recognize the imperative of movement. At the beginning of the twentieth century, there were demands for a new terminology to accompany the profound technological transformations. In 1905 Mario Morasso announced it would not be long before writers completely transformed the sonorous, grandiloquent terminology adopted at the culminating moments of narrative. Writers, continued Morasso, would have to abandon the old way of saying and imagining things, which ensured them great success in creating a disturbance, and they would be forced to renew their knowledge, updating their vocabulary of new inventions and progress, especially in physical science and chemistry.

The Italian writer suggested the replacement of the horse with the automobile and all of its derivatives, including "the automotive novel." He even offered an overview of the language of the future, which he regarded as both fascinating and strange, with its plethora of technical terms. The heroine falls in love with the driver—none of that falling in love at the riding competition, but instead on the racetrack, at high speed, breaking a record in the sporty red Panhard. And the dialogue between the lovers is peppered with automotive terms: She will say: "I want to be sure. Is it a Serpollet or a Mercedes? Is the *silencieux* [muffler] working properly?" He will respond: "60-HP Mercedes, as silent as a night bird. You'll see what blinding and sweet *démarrage* [acceleration]!"[35]

These are the very first attempts at using the lexicon of automobility. They are accompanied by a universal aspiration formerly reserved only for religious or political terminology. Their avant-garde tone leaves no room for doubt that total mobilization is on its way. The kinetic ethos ignored all boundaries and was prepared to sacrifice diversity to the common denominator of movement. It did not understand that the different regions of the planet had their distinctive histories and times. It would never understand it, and it would continue to mark the world in the image and likeness of mobility. In fact, throughout history linguistic loans arise as a function of cultural contacts between peoples. When it comes to cars, in Latin America such linguistic loan words basically came from French and English, although they were locally adapted within the phonological system that received them.

To convey the emerging situation, it is indispensable to have a command of today's material symbols. What matters less is the place of origin rather than the expressive needs of the historical situations. The writer who learned to deploy these words engendered primeval images with them. For Maurice Maeterlinck the automobile was an unknown animal, born recently, that possessed a hidden life. Its soul was the electric spark; its heart, the carburetor; its viscera, the pistons. This mechanical body demanded strange terminology, a metallic language capable of denoting the emergence of an unparalleled force. Where does the expression "advanced ignition" come from? From the factory. Later there would be common words such as "green light" (permission), "overaccelerated" (or hyper), and "needs fuel" (food).

The derivatives of automobility were, in fact, strange and confirm that it was meant to branch out. Car parts entered philosophical discussion. In no less than in *Being and Time*, by Martin Heidegger, the German philosopher examines the daily indifference of the *Dasein*, which refers to "mediocrity" and is used as a reference to the figure of the car instrument panel, in his reflection on the use and interpretation of the sign. Heidegger argues that automobiles have ultimately been given a movable red arrow whose position indicates, each time, for example, at an intersection, which road the car will take. The position of the arrow is regulated by the driver of the vehicle. This sign is useful both for the driver and for those who are not traveling in the car, favoring the pragmatic context of means of locomotion and traffic laws. The useful signaler is constituted by reference: it has the character of "for-something," the specific utility of signaling.[36] Obviously, Heidegger was not interested in the vehicle per se, but rather in the subject of "employability" of utensils. However, that is precisely what is interesting to highlight: the example of the utility of the sign was the recently introduced car dashboard. Philosophy makes use of the surrounding world to access the ontological being.

Similarly, in his brief essay "Experience and Poverty," Walter Benjamin refers to the example of the car engine to postulate the emergence of a new "constructive" culture opposed to an organic one. This constructive culture casts off the legacy of humanity to surrender to the present moment. From the figures by Paul Klee, who sought the support of engineers to develop his artistic language, it may be said that they were planned on the dashboard and that they obeyed "like a good car obeys the needs of the motor above all even in the body, above all the internal in the expression of its appearance. The internal more than the interiority: that is what barbarians do."[37] It is worth highlighting that with this oblique reference Benjamin expands the list of examples that are used to examine the relationship between art and technology—photography, cinema, journalism, industrial forms. His marked interest in nineteenth-century Paris, in that past world that left its material traces on the discontinuous reality of the present, led him to privilege the figure of the *flâneur* [idle stroller], instead of the *autoneur* [car rider]. On the other hand, it is understandable that on occasion Benjamin cast a dismal gaze on twentieth-century technology, as he expresses in "Eduard Fuchs: Collector and Historian." In this essay he states that in the contemporary world the speed of means of transportation or the capacity of apparatuses with which the word and writing are reproduced goes beyond human needs. The energies that technology develops beyond this threshold are destructive for Benjamin, because they favor the technology of war and its preparatory advertising or propaganda.

Part of the world transformed by the kinetic aesthetic is found in the poetry of Blaise Cendrars, who claimed to have deciphered all the confused texts dealing with wheels. Objects, especially the car and its upheaval of the human senses, dazzled this poet of violent beauty. Cendrars celebrates the bombing of urban stimuli in his poem "Hôtel Notre-Dame," in which the police commissioner's purple car is cut off by the fire chief's red

car, "magical and supple, wild and caressing, tigresses like shooting stars."
Coloring enchants modern vision. Throughout the nineteenth century a
clear separation of the senses was produced, especially of vision in relation
to the senses of touch, smell, and hearing. The sense of vision was freed by
new objects that were in circulation, such as mirrors, postcards, and photographs.[38] The city was the setting for the spectacle, and there the purple
automobile of the city official traveled.

The figure of the automobile also played a role in renovating the realm
of aromas. In this regard, Marcel Proust left us a magnificent portrait in
Contre Sainte-Beuve, in which he refers to the "fetid odor" of an automobile that at times wafts through his window. The importance of this stench
does not reside in its existence, but rather in the impression it evokes, for
the artist quickly transforms the unpleasant odor into the most intoxicating aroma of the summer countryside, associating the auto with the joy
of approaching a desired place. Even the perfume of pine trees does not
arouse more than a happiness in him that is to a certain degree immobile
and limited. However, the "delicious odor of petroleum," color of sky and
sun, represents the immensity of the countryside, the joy of going out, of
getting away surrounded by wildflowers, poppies, and violet trifoliolate
clover, and of knowing the desired destination will be reached, where our
beloved awaits. The fumes of the passing automobile filled the writer with
all of these pleasures and introduces new ones, the fragrance of summer,
power, freedom, nature, and love.[39]

Odors, which modernity combats like the plague, reserve a special
place in the individual's memory. It is the "fetid odor of the automobile"
that is associated with freedom, beloved people, and places. Automobiles,
summer, nature, and love have nothing to do with drainage pipes, tubes,
and sanitary disinfectants, which the city uses to purify it from unbearable
stenches. Proust is the one who most closely approximates the overall language of the journey, composed of sights and sounds. "Movement in con-
junction" is what Georges Poulet calls the relationship between the journey and the landscape that is established in Proust's work.[40] Distance is
not devoured, but rather magically suppressed. Poulet adds that for Proust
the ideal journey was the one that eliminated distances at one fell swoop,
situating two places side by side whose originality seemed to impose, for
all time, a distant existence on them without any possibility of communication. The Proustian automobile is a tool that brings dissimilar places
closer. It is the relationship between places, and not the distance between
them, that comes to the surface during the journey and is established in
memory as formerly imperceptible forms of proximity.

From literature to painting, the automobile links dissimilar spaces. Ramón Gómez de la Serna claims that Picasso "automobilized painting, he saw it run, introduce itself, crash, return in *panne* [a breakdown] to its hut, after having fixed its centuries-long damage, to undertake new catastrophes."[41] Pablo Picasso portrayed as a mechanic: his brushes are clean screwdrivers or electric screw guns; with his touch the motors that once seemed dead accelerate. We might have imagined Picasso in many ways, although only with difficulty as a mechanic.

Argentine critic and art historian Julio Payró synthesized the "state of the question." In the 1930s it was already possible for him to develop a parallel history of art based on means of locomotion. Payró told of the relationship between means of transport and artistic creation, pointing out that the airplane offered "a cartographic, futurist idea of the landscape," while the automobile annulled all vision, for it forced one to contemplate the "hypnotic road."

Once again the lexicon of automobility proclaimed its triumph through literary gesture and disconcerting expression. However, the "automobile literature" found it difficult to invent a new language within language. What Deleuze cited as the challenge of writing did not seem to be one of its virtues: remove language from the overused paths and make it *become delirious*. With the incorporation of the automobile, it could be said that the possibility of "drilling holes" in the language to see or hear "what was hidden behind it" was undermined. In this sense, it was a matter of impious power, which offered glossy surfaces, permeated by objects, places, people, desires, and even memories, which tended to fall apart as a succession of immediate realities or cinematographic flashes.

No system reveals cultural transformations as clearly as language. It is an infallible thermometer, because the process of the circulation of objects and ideas is externalized in it, often unconsciously. When drafts for laws intended to protect the national language from the use of foreign terms arise in different countries, we are seeing an example of the concern for identity. It is easy to perceive the use of foreign terms absorbed into a language. It is more difficult to understand that the language does not lose its characteristic features when foreign words are adapted into the corresponding phonological system.

Language was one of the preferred targets for Rafael Cansinos Assens, whether as an official declaration or in defense of nationalism. In the novel-essay *El Movimiento V. P.* (The V. P. movement), the character "Senectus Modernissimus"—perhaps a caricature of Valle-Inclán—writes with quill pens to avoid contaminating himself with the dangerous modernity of fountain pens "Made in England," and he is pathetic in his denial of Gallicisms and Anglicisms. He does not use certain foreign words lacking an equivalent in the Spanish language to avoid contradicting the richness of the sacrosanct Dictionary; he finds synonyms in his language such as "amasamiento" [kneading] for "massage," or he coins new words, such as "balompié" [from "balón-pie," literally, "ball-foot"] instead of using "football." When, surprisingly, he becomes modern and decides to stuff himself with Gallicisms and Anglicisms, saying *massage* and *factage, camouflage* and *football, garden party* and *foxtrot*, he is equally pathetic. He feels he is going to establish a new aesthetic and create a new lexicon by dusting off the old dirt and forgetting the classic Spanish *Diccionario de la Lengua*. A modern poet! Cansinos Assens, that peculiar anti-avant-gardist who backs the poetic production of the young and writes a vanguard book such as *El Movimiento V. P.*, mocking the literary scene in Madrid. It is a parody of both the hallowed Academia de la Lengua and the aesthetic principles of the radical avant-garde. These are the new times, declares the Poet of the Thousand Years, "that are not governed by those late clocks, but rather by these others: the automobile, the airplane, and the Wild West revolver."[42]

At the beginning of the twentieth century in Brazil, João do Rio recorded changes in the language and captured a particularly problematic dimension of motorization. Language became strange. In "A era do automóvel" (The age of the automobile), dialogue imposes a distance from traditional vocabulary. "Did you go to the A.C.B.? Yes. Factory brand? F.I.A.T. 60-H.P. I have to write to the A.C.O.T.U.K." Translated into vulgar language, the chronicler clarifies, it means that the gentleman has a 60-horsepower machine from the Italian automobile factory in Turin and he is going to write to the Aeroclub of the United Kingdom. This lexicon of the future is not only surprising, but, like all codes, it is restricted to a small group. A sublanguage of initials, it cuts down on time and space, it eliminates useless words, it imposes monosyllables, and it describes literature as a form of idleness. The language of action, speed, and simplification triumphs. How many times have we heard that the television and computer are responsible for deteriorating levels of reading and writing? Before that, it was the car. Or, according to João do Rio, the automobile was the great reformer of slow forms. However, the simplification of language, which the chronicler linked to the car, is part of a wide context of transformation. From 1880 to 1918 the technology of speed modified journalistic communication, in which the telephone and telegraph accelerated the ease of reporting. Given that economy of expression meant saving money, journalists cut down the number of words and avoided ambiguities.[43]

Technological motifs accompanied speed. Avant-garde poetry flooded writing of the period with technical vocabulary.[44] Kinetic terminology that was incorporated into writing was like an *experience* of modernization. People who wrote in this way usually collected their material from everyday urban life. They were subjected to the rapid, unbroken change in internal and external stimuli—the rise of nervous life that Georg Simmel detected as a psychological basis on which the metropolitan personality type of individualities arose. There was a sort of "death of literature" typical of the vanguard, which diminished the importance of grammatical purity and attempted to access what was real. What mattered was the experience of freedom and movement. In the tension between literature and life, the latter seemed to triumph, despite the fact that it dealt with literary formulations with a high degree of cerebral construction. Little was stated directly, but rather by means of selective mechanisms of refinement that simulated capturing reality itself. What a far cry from pre-Hispanic and colonial traditions! An overwhelming presence of the here and now.

On the other hand, the prestige of foreign languages diminished as a symbol of adaptation to the new times. The intellectuals who had taken control of the distinction granted by foreign languages, especially French, became representatives of a *traditional* current of modernity. When the refined use of foreign languages (a phenomenon distinct from the "proletarian" use by immigrants) clashed with technical vocabulary, it signaled knowledge out of sync with modern conditions.

There was a feeling of liberation in the appropriation of everyday brands of modernity, because the intelligentsia traditionally arises from another linguistic stock. It was a phenomenon of renovation relatively easy to perceive today, now that even children have incorporated terminology derived from information technology codes into their native idiom. This mixed vocabulary, which assimilated and reproduced words formerly controlled by technical know-how, developed during the first half of the twentieth century from the emblems of modernization: the automobile, airplane, streetcar, telephone, cinematographer, and radio. A contaminated vocabulary indeed, but marked by technology and movement. Updating language was rounded off with other forms of transculturation of the language, derived from psychoanalysis, music, Marxism, and sports. Mixture and hybridism gained in importance. The image of the Tower of Babel arose anew, although in truth it was not to such a degree. Language was adapted regionally to the process of modernization and communicated the ambivalent experiences of modernity. With greater or lesser aesthetic refinement, it was a vocabulary that produced "tainted" localisms.

Roberto Arlt was defined as the "radio and machine gun man," and he operated within this context in which migration was inseparable from machines. Some of his critics have pointed out this relationship between literature and machinism in Arlt, commenting that his technique is litera-ture of the humble, and that Arlt worked with an oblique language that appealed to forms of functioning and usage, but not the problem of inter-pretation and meaning.[45] In his texts, muscular writing operates based on the intersection of different literary registers, backed by the emblems of modernization. In addition to Arlt's hallucinatory Buenos Aires, where automobiles impregnated the air with the smell of burned rubber and gasoline fumes, São Paulo of the 1920s would be imaginatively converted into an industrial city, almost Metropolis. Luís Aranha spoke of streetcars, automobiles, speakers, factories, offices, clocks, airplanes, movie theaters, telephones, and electricity, of all the features of an extravagant city, a *Pau-licéia desvairada* that began to build its avant-garde identity anchored in the multiple images of technological modernization.

Generally it is the urban writers, with sophisticated knowledge of mod-ern literary techniques, who choose to represent the city from the perspec-tive of the outskirts. One of the most attractive examples of this model of writing is that of Mário de Andrade, in his classic book *Macunaíma*. The chapter "Carta pràs Icamiabas" is a parody of the sacred character of official language and is expressed in the language of the urban machine. Macunaíma tells the Amazon ladies of his arrival in São Paulo. We go into the interior of the great city: São Paulo will be a monster riddled with mechanical objects: "Not content with the dust stirred up by the feet of the pedestrians and by those roaring machine contraptions called auto-mobiles and electric trolley buses (also called 'cars' and 'trams,' barbarisms certainly coming from English), the diligent City Council charters some anthropoid hippocentaurs, dull blue in color, collectively called Public Sanitation."[46] Macunaíma, the hero without a character, defines urban as mechanized. The city is observed from the perspective of alienation, the eyes of the border, making free use of the aesthetics of innocence. "They were machines and everything in the city was a single machine"; "men were what machines were, and machines were what men were." The Machine, with a capital M, exterminates the men who build it. The land-scape is imaginatively urban, the resonance of speakers, radios, and tele-phones; the movement of elevators, automobiles, trucks, streetcars, and motorcycles, neon signs, clocks, factory smokestacks. Impersonal, asexual machines moved by electricity, fire, water, and wind, taking advantage of the power of nature. Machines without god, man-machines.

Of greater interest is the use of a mythological aura in writing about mechanical elements. The climax of such mythical utilization of the mechanical is precisely the chapter that narrates the genesis of the automobile: "In times gone by, my young friends, the motorcar was not the mechanical contraption it is today, but a golden-brown jaguar. His name was Palauá, and he lived in the great What's-its-name Forest" (chap. 14). This is an example of the creative response of Brazilian Modernism in the context of modernization. The mythical mimesis supposes formal experimentation and a parody at work, because the appropriation of an ethnological text—*Vom Roraima zum Orinoco*, by Theodor Koch-Grünberg—suggests some playful storytelling.

The technique of distancing impinges on the figure of the automobile, based on the assimilation and transformation of mythical into industrial language. The two great fireflies that Palauá the golden-brown jaguar swallows, during his escape from the tiger, become headlights. The jaguar Palauá also swallows an anvil, four forgotten wheels, and a motor; it ingests a purgative of oil and a can of gasoline; the *guazú* leaf is the hood. Swiftly, it is the new automotive machine:

> The jaguar never quite shook off the fright he had, and always kept close to him all those things that had helped him escape. Ever afterward he went around with wheels on his feet, a motor in his belly, a dose of oil in his gullet, water in his snout, gas up his backside, two fireflies in his mouth, and covered by a banana-leaf hood; all ready to roar off—bam bam!— in an instant. To begin with, he found himself in trouble with the great swarm of taxi ants he had trodden on. They found their way into his sleek pelt and bit his ear—wow!—and he howled to high heaven. After that, to disguise himself still further, he took a strange name; he called himself an automobile contraption.[47]

"They say that later on the jaguar produced an enormous number of children." Some were males and some females, Fords and Chevrolets.

One of the innovative powers of language is its double meaning. Unlike irony, which implicitly undermines what is said and denies the statement, in double meaning the context is less important than the common usage of words. In other words, these would not be understandable for the general public. In the case of car vocabulary it is included in the second meaning, which presupposed the literal statement. Words are transferred without difficulty to the horizon of courtship, as in "Fon-fon," the song by João de Barro and Alberto Ribeiro, in which the images of moving forward and acceleration, the speakers, the traffic signals and green eyes, the curves, mouth, and precipice are part of a journey by car that at the same time suggests the failed attempt to woo a woman: "Won't you make me yours to keep? / You won't hear me going beep beep beep!"

Malcolm Forest offers delicious Brazilian examples of automotive jargon:

Banco da sogra [Mother-in-law seat]: removable bench where one usually finds the car trunk. Also known as the mother-in-law-carrier, it was quite common in sports cars from the 1920s and 1930s. Barbeiro [Barber]: a bad driver. Banheira [Bathtub]: large automobile with rounded body, resembling a bathtub. Bicheira [Worm]: old car. It comes from bichado, having worms in the upholstery and wood. . . . Cabeça-de-cavalo [Horse-head]: a Chevrolet model from the 1920s. Caça-mulata [Mulatto-hunter]: a small auxiliary lamp next to the windshield used mainly to illuminate numbers on houses at night. Cristaleira [Display cabinet]: automobile from the first three decades of the twentieth century, whose body resembled a piece of furniture to keep objects made of crystal, a display cabinet. Ford com bigode [Ford with moustache]: a Model T from the 1910s and 1920s that had two small levers under the steering wheel, resembling a moustache.[48]

There were many nicknames for automobiles. However, the double meaning reached unexpected zones, such as the tradition of the medieval *exemplum*, in which the Catholic preacher had to rouse the attention of his public. Religious terminology was adapted to the new times and incorporated the fascination with technical novelties. The automobile served to go faster, because it was necessary to get to heaven more quickly. It demanded a careful, skilled driver, given the dangers of the terrestrial routes found on the path to the Lord: to know how to slow down, to avoid dangerous encounters, and to keep to the right (to fear God and to observe his commandments). Accidents arose from carelessness in the work of sanctification, and it was necessary to know how to pick up passengers, in other words, to help save others, not "wishing to go alone to heaven." Life is like the path of an arrow; there is no way back. Nevertheless, an authority that knows how to guide, a celestial *driver*, is necessary.[49]

5. MECHANICAL ACTORS

Desire for Consumption

Kinetic modernity is composed of promises. When the newspaper *O Globo* appeared in Brazil on July 29, 1925, the front page contained two articles related to the automobile. One was on Henry Ford, "the best known and the wealthiest capitalist in the world," and his plans to visit Belém do Pará in the Amazon region. The U.S. magnate hoped to examine the possibilities of reestablishing the former scale of rubber production in the region to combat the British monopoly over the raw material and to guarantee tire production for his cars.

The second article referred to the "amazing rise of cars" as an indicator of national progress: from 1922 to 1923 Brazil jumped from having 2,772 to 12,995 cars. In the drawing that represents 1922, a man looks at a diminutive car, from a respectable height and distance, through a large magnifying glass. The next year, the scene is reversed: the automobile dominates the image, and the man has become an insignificant being, dwarfed by the enormous machine.

The car was a reality of modern urban life. Like all promising technological inventions, it implied the possibility of new fortunes and social mobility. Booth Tarkington's *The Magnificent Ambersons*, a novel that won the Pulitzer Prize and that was taken to the silver screen by Orson Welles, portrays the decadence of a family fortune based on landed property, which is replaced in wealth and social status by the founder of a local car factory. In a series of socioeconomic shifts, it was impossible for Tarkington to predict what would become the course of spiritual civilization. Perhaps automobiles added little to the beauty of the world or to the human soul, but "they had arrived," bringing a much greater change than could ever be imagined. Tarkington's account, with its distinction between spiritual and material civilization, was typical of the contradictions of the era, when in the United States the automobile began to become the symbol par excellence of the nation's progress.

As the manufacturing techniques in the automotive industry evolved, greater attention was given to design. The trend toward utility, inherent in

all objects of technology, did not present any obstacles to the aestheticiza-
tion of the product. Fernand Léger recorded in "Esthétique de la machine"
(The machine aesthetic) that utility and beauty were not incompatible.
He used the example of the evolution of the car's shape; the more the
utilitarian functions of the machine were perfected, the more beautiful
it became. As long as the car was adapted to the natural aesthetic of the
horse—"horseless carriage"—the result was not particularly appealing.
However, when the car became lower and elongated, in response to the
aerodynamic requirements for greater speed, when horizontal lines bal-
anced by curves predominated, it became an entity logically organized for
its purposes. Although Léger did not conclude that the utilitarian appearance implied beauty by necessity, for him there was no question that the
automobile was beautiful, and it evolved as it distanced itself from the
natural model. Léger's assessment illustrates ambivalence when it came to
advertising and consumption. Technological beauty was not understood
as the triumph of alienation or capitalism's creation of false needs; creativ-
ity, good taste, and refinement were also valued. However, only with difficulty could Léger justify the need for an influential, extensive apparatus
aimed at converting the automobile brand into a commercial fetish.

To what extent did the car need to be more than a satisfactory tool for
transportation? Advertising began to enthrone the ideology of merchandise when the first ads proclaiming the automobile's wonders appeared
at the end of the nineteenth century. In the United States a significantly
named magazine was published, *The Horseless Age*, which presented the
virtues of a Racine, a 4-HP, 4-cylinder vehicle. The Racine combined
"Speed, Safety, Comfort and Economy." In England postcards were produced showing a white-gloved chauffeur inviting a traveler out for a drive
in the country: "If you will come to visit us we'll take you for a ride—for
we have a nice big auto and there's room for you inside."

The first edition of the *Michelin Guide*, published in 1900, is a valuable document from the period for observing the evolution of automotive
propaganda. Time and space are already subjugated to automobility in
this first edition of the French guide. In only a little more than ten years
after the commercial "birth" of the car, a book appeared specifically aimed
at guiding chauffeurs and velocipedists. Its objective was to provide all
information that could be useful for a driver traveling through France, to
supply his car, repair it, find food and lodging, and communicate by post,
telegraph, or telephone. The publication was free of charge.

Many car builders took advantage of the opportunity to offer their
products: Audibert & Lavirotte, Vermorel, Peugeot, Georges Richard, E. J.

Brierre, Brouhot, Rochet & Schneider, Tourand, Bébéli, Columbia, De Diétrich, Marot-Gardon, Panhard & Levassor, Gobron-Brillié, Delahaye, Renault. If anything draws our attention, it is the large number of builders in only one decade after the car's "birth." And each builder used a particular publicity strategy to attract potential consumers. To that end Peugeot simply listed its victories at races; E. J. Brierre promoted the elegance of its design; Rochet & Schneider described its product as "Robust, Simple, Comfortable, Elegant, Silent"; Bébéli automobiles were "the most beautiful in the World"; Marot-Gardon declared its model was a type intermediary between the regular *voiture* and the smaller *voiturette*, which had the advantages of the automobile—robustness, power, comfort—for the modest price of a small car, 6,700 francs. On the other hand, there were ads for a variety of accessories that accompanied the automotive object. Pages upon pages of Michelin tires; garages (initially also showrooms), such as that of Le Havre, with space for a hundred cars; gasoline stations; Grouvelle & Arquembourg radiators; and Blériot headlights and lamps.

The annual cost of automotive propaganda as a whole in the United States reached an astronomical one million dollars at the start of the century. By 1905 car producers in the United States were spending that sum on advertising annually, half of which was in twelve major magazines.[1]

Merchandise lost its innocence. It was necessary to charm. Objects of mobility appeared to be mechanical beings, elegant and vibrant, offering a new sensation of freedom. As a consequence, money invested in advertising increased at an accelerated pace because it was recognized for the decisive role it played in sales. In fact, advertising agencies, those "hidden persuaders," were proud of having created desire for the product and of associating it with the image of the triumphant consumer. Not only was the merchandise presented as beautiful, useful, and important, but a car buyer was also meant to feel part of the chain of success: a winner, the proprietor. For automotive publicity, devotion to facts was not enough. It began to exaggerate differences and to project an atmosphere of reverie, leaving the demand for sincerity by the wayside. Today it is still common to identify advertising with insincerity; automotive advertising and car salesmen contributed considerably to this perception.

Soon images of "classics" of U.S. automotive publicity began to appear. Thousands of reproductions showed the image of the Oldsmobile overtaking the train. The same was the case of advertising that showed a sporty Jordan outdoing a young woman on horseback, "Somewhere West of Laramie." The ad, aimed at university students and "flappers," earned its creator, Ned Jordan, thousands of letters from anonymous admirers.

Jordan captured the romantic spirit of the girl "trainer of colts who knows what I am talking about," because the model had been built "for her," for the girl "with her face tanned by the sun, when the day is composed of play, fun, and racing." There were also the "aristocratic" ads for Cadillac, Pierce-Arrow, and Duesenberg.

A Chevrolet ad had an unusual fate. It showed a happy, harmonious white family. The husband driving, his wife in the other seat, the two kids in the back, the doggie sticking his head out the window, the entire image one of magical beatitude. At the top it read, "World's Highest Standard of Living," and on the rural background, "There's no way like the American Way." Dorothea Lange used it in 1937 in her photograph *There Is No Way like the American Way*. The same year the "billboard" of the American Dream was made sadly famous in the photo by Margaret Bourke-White, *At the Time of the Louisville Flood*: the Chevrolet ad, with the beaming white family appears as the backdrop for the black victims of an Ohio River flood in line at a soup kitchen.

Fashion accompanied the development of automobility, above all in the United States. During the "infancy" of the automobile, clothing that permitted the driver to go out and fix the car at any moment was common. Leather and wool were preferred to withstand the cold. A journalist noted the triumph of the sporty stance over elegance and recommended that ladies give up any hope of preserving their delicate feminine appearance. Gradually an entire array of personal paraphernalia produced for automotive aesthetics began to appear—caps, scarves, sweaters, handbags, wallets, briefcases, flashlights, buttons, pencils.

Singers, poets, and film stars appeared standing beside their own car or in set-up shots: Ernesto Nazareth, Marinetti, Carmen Miranda, Jean Harlow, Carlos Gardel. Films took advantage of the prestige endowed by the automobile. It served as a new character. Wasn't it one of the keys to happiness and success in life? Rudolph Valentino stepped in and out of limousines to corroborate the glamour of the stars. Laurel and Hardy, in *Perfect Day*, kept bidding farewell, but could never actually get their car started. On the big screen, romantic heroes, seducers, passionate women, and criminals that the law did away with were associated with the car. It confronted animals. It raced against elephants, camels, and horses. In U.S. filmmaking from 1900 to 1920, the automobile was everywhere to be seen: the happy accident, the race for life, the agent of fortune, the "runaway" wedding.[2]

The cinematographic presence of the car is also visible in Latin America. It was a common figure in presidential parades, in scenes involving movement, in the social life of the elite, and in the transformation of urban physiognomy. I have already mentioned the 1919 Mexican gangster movie *El automóvil gris*, made by Enrique Rosas, and the 1928 Uruguayan film *Del pingo al volante*. When a group of gangsters came onto the scene, motifs of industrial technological modernity seemed obligatory: automobiles, trains, and telephones mixed up with machine guns, killings, escapes, and robberies. Gangster films demanded movement, speed, and drama.

A former Ford dealer was asked in the mid-1920s if Mr. Ford himself knew how much things had changed in recent years. The salesman had just finished reading Henry Ford's autobiography. In a passage from the book, Ford states that businesses grow with public demand, but never beyond it, because businesses cannot control or force demand. The salesman had no doubt that Ford was an exceptional man. Anyone worth a billion dollars had to be an intelligent man. In any case, when Mr. Ford said that business could not control or force demand, the former dealer thought it was a joke. Demand could be forced through advertising: you only needed to enter a Ford agency to prove it.[3]

It was even possible to determine different forms of publicity, depending on production stages. Claude Fischer points out that early advertising emphasized power, style, and the recreational uses of the automobile.[4] The distinction of the name was important, as in the limited production of the Santos Dumont model, made in the United States in 1903, which never reached Brazil. It sold for eighteen hundred dollars and was advertised as a car that flew and never failed.

Soon the subject of practical use as transportation was added to advertising. In this transition from luxury to need, and from limited editions to popular production, the Ford Model T played a preeminent role. Finally, publicity focused on the advantages of the brand for the consumer.

Another effective mechanism to augment sales was the credit line of financing for consumers. This mechanism consolidated the "compulsion for wheels." William Ashdown had been a highly restrained Puritan until he bought a car. Before that his greatest extravagance had been owning a bicycle. He waged battles with his conscience, but ultimately small-town social pressure defeated him. Perhaps what is most interesting in Ashdown's brief account, "Confessions of an Automobilist," published in June 1925 in *Atlantic Monthly*, is that the clear difference between owners and nonowners falls apart. At first sight, they seem to belong to two different classes of human beings. The purchase of a car forces one to use it and involves increasingly greater costs. Once he succumbed to temptation, there was no way back.

The well-known difficulty of letting go of a car is related to its role as a status symbol. A devastating psychological process begins for all car owners in which they are forced to successively incorporate mechanical innovations to keep the car up to date. Whatever is left over from the paycheck at the end of the month, instead of going to the bank as a nest egg, is destined for car expenses.

The ambition of owning a car was not restricted to the upper classes and those with substantial income; it also trickled down to office workers and individuals with low salaries. Many families lived on the threshold of ruin. They were "car-poor," because it was impossible for them to save anything. Future security was sacrificed for the pleasure of the moment, which was constantly mixed with anxiety over living beyond their economic means. The car was "another family" of expenses.

No matter the explanation of this compulsion for wheels, the result was the same: "debt, debt, debt, for a costly article that depreciates very rapidly and has an insatiable appetite for money. To be sure, the money goes out in small lots, but the toll is large if it be reckoned for a year, and the average man lacks the courage to face this; or, facing it, he lacks the courage to quit. He must keep his car."[5]

The automobile goes on to rival the house in terms of ambitions of ownership. The house, however, does not move, and few can see inside it. On the contrary, the circulation of the car in public places became an object of constant desire. Ashdown records with concern that the car has begun to win out over the home as an indicator of social status. And so it is inevitable that importance is conferred on the garage. A house without a garage loses much of its value and can be sold only with difficulty. The home in the suburbs, with a big garage beside it, almost another residence in itself to shelter the car, becomes a powerful element in the system of objects.

Who would sell a car if not out of sheer necessity or else to buy a better one? Losing the car was a calamity, and upgrading models generally implied a desire for betterment. With the principle of programmed obsolescence, the consumer became enslaved: the system of the yearly model, begun by General Motors in the 1920s, demanded change. The other companies had to adjust to the system of planned change, while a sector of consumers lived obsessed with exchanging what was new for something newer. In much of the planet, annually the greed for a "zero mile" auto and its ineffable "new car" smell was repeated, with all the publicity (displays, magazines, pamphlets, films, toy replicas, etc.) that accompanies brand-new models and with all the fantasies and problems that plague consumers.

The moralizing gaze of a philosopher such as Ortega y Gasset con-firmed that the car assumed a wide range of meanings. In his article "La moral del automóvil en España" (The morality of the automobile in Spain), which appeared in Madrid's *El Sol* on August 23, 1930, Ortega accuses the Spanish *señorito* (wealthy young man). At that time Spain had a large number of cars, considering the total number of inhabitants. And this disproportion between Spanish poverty and the number of automobiles was a paradigm of the *señorito*'s immorality. It was not that the philosopher rejected the car; on the contrary, his enthusiasm for the object was well known. He fervently supported the government policy of increasing tariffs for the entry of cars and their accessories to Spain for moral reasons, not political or economic ones. It was that the *señorito* did not buy the car to use it, and he had to pay such a high price for it. He would send a servant to wash it, polish it, shine it, and always leave it sparkling clean. What good did it do if it didn't facilitate the exercise of a profession? It was transformed into an instrument of social prestige, into a luxury object; it was not an article of essential need. The constant shine revealed the nation's underdevelopment. The car's prestige stemmed from the country's true lack of participation in the modern world. Unlike in France and Germany, countries with national industry, in Spain enthusi-asm for the modern machine expressed "Celtiberian backwardness" with regard to modernity. For Ortega y Gasset, the essence of what the auto-mobile meant for the Spaniard resided in the solitary character of the few highways that existed in Spain. It was not used to travel on business or to cross the territory, but rather to show off the vehicle. For the sake of van-ity, the poor Spanish nation made sacrifices and proportionally bought more cars from abroad than any other nation.

It was a lucid assessment of the technological consumption in periph-eral societies in the first decades of the twentieth century: the automobile as a luxury, polished to a luster by poor servants, while the consumer sank deeper into debt to acquire an object not even produced in the country. Several Latin American critics also expressed this idea of the car's ostenta-tion in peripheral societies. Clearly, the mechanical vehicle was indispens-able to modern nations such as France, Germany, and the United States, but was it equally indispensable for Latin America? The moral argument arose repeatedly in diverse contexts. Colombian Germán Arciniegas establishes clear-cut differences between Europe, the United States, and South America in "El automóvil," written in London and published in *La Antorcha* in August 1931. This brief text is a valuable document reflecting the sensibility of the times when it came to motorization by recognizing the fundamental importance of the car for the modern world as well as the problems caused by its introduction in South America. Never had any machine triggered such profound changes, according to Arciniegas. The new sensation of rubber wheels and motorism transformed customs. The automobile gave rise to divorce in homes, it freed women, it enslaved men, it multiplied the power of traffickers and bandits. Unexpected horizons opened up for industry, while roads grew longer, railroads came to a halt, savings were depleted, and a tribe of unsavory salespeople was created. In successive attacks, the transportation industry pushed ahead as it vanquished the horse, struggled against streetcars, and attacked railroads. The spirit of the new machine fit perfectly into the individualist, rebel, libertarian spirit of the time.

What can be said of the sensation of lording it over space and time? Pressing down on the accelerator and crossing plains with utter speed produced an exhilarating sense of satisfaction. It was the vertigo of speed. That vertigo was contagious among the humble; it led to burning hours and days, rejecting old ideas, giving up certain scruples, and casting aside incidentals of morality: overcoming time and devouring miles became all-important. To surrender to this motorized vertigo, youth sold its soul. In basements of U.S. universities walls were decorated with traffic signs taken from roads. The desire for the car undermined the moral foundation of youth. Anyone without a car was regarded as a wretch, abandoned, lacking, and somehow incomplete. Henry Ford's career served as a reminder that the world was nothing without a car.

Arciniegas reasoned by comparison. While in Europe and the United States the car fostered the advent of a new sensibility, in South America former vices were prolonged. It increased the debt of nations by making them dependent on international credit, while it abused public property for private ends. The deterioration of morality could be summed up in phrases like: "When you see a Rolls-Royce pass by, take off your hat: there goes a superior man." What is noteworthy is the description of the feeling of importance instilled in public officials when the Colombian government began to buy Lincolns and La Salles for the offices of the cabinet ministers. The ministers changed car models as if it were a humiliation to drive a 1927 model if the 1928 model was already out: "Then those pale-skinned clerks who had painstakingly scaled the rungs of intrigue to reach section heads in a ministry, pale little scribes, riddled with uncinariasis [hookworms] and playing at politics, saw the doors of the car swing open before them as if those of an enchanted palace, and they jumbled together in a corner of the upholstery that outlined them with sensual thrills, and they cruised the streets, surrounded by velvet and glass, on cushions of wind, as if princes, like nabobs" (quoted in John Skirius, *El ensayo hispanoamericano del siglo XX* [Mexico City: Fondo de Cultura Económica, 1994], 78). The chronicles that Miguel Ángel Asturias sent from Paris to Guatemala from 1924 to 1933 recorded different examples of the importance of technological imagination. Just as Ortega y Gasset, Arciniegas, and Martínez Estrada, Asturias perceived in the zeal for modern consumption—focused on the car bought on credit—a typical phenomenon of underdevelopment: luxury as a cause of social ills. In such a political-moral vision of consumption, the United States was converted into the invader that imposed luxury on lands of misery. Asturias's disapproval of car imports in Guatemala was a consequence of what he regarded as the "national reality." As a result, what was supposedly universal technology appeared as subordinated to regional use: "The car is not an element of progress well understood in a country that has had to go from the cart to airplane for want of roads, which lacks drivable streets, hygiene, everything, even the most elementary things. Its use, no matter how pleasant and modern, is less worthy of being condemned, because, as it is said, in Latin America we are not for frills."[6]

By analogy, Asturias denounces the abuse of official automobiles in Guatemala. Unlike other countries, where such vehicles are restricted to official use, in Guatemala the government car serves for morning drives with the family, for parties in the evening, or for chauffeur adventures (March 8, 1929). It should come as no surprise at this point that the issue of the improper use of official vehicles also arose in Brazil. Antonio de Alcântara Machado, in his short story "O patriota Washington" (from *Laranja da China*), points to the irony of Dr. Washington Coelho Penteado's patriotism, showing the contradictions between the democratic ideals of the republic and personal usage on the part of politicians. And the magazine *Fon-Fon!*—whose logo shows a speeding car—includes snippets of dialogues between pedestrians who refer to the corruption of the ministers of the Treasury, Transportation, Justice, and Defense Departments.

César Vallejo captured the contradictions of the "social kingdom of wheels" in exemplary fashion. In one of his chronicles, "Salón del Automóvil de París," sent from the French capital to Lima in October 1926, the Peruvian writer examines the significance of the *fiestas del motor*, or motor shows, which drew thousands of people from many continents. Vallejo notes that refined city life no longer begins with the vernissage of the Salon d'Automne (Autumn Salon), but instead with the opening of the Salon d'Automobile (Paris Motor Show): the car, no longer paintings or statues, dominates the scene. The city, battered by the fanatics of progress, has to put up with exhibitions of speed and the arrogance of drivers, who drove all over making "an obnoxious noise blowing their horns." Vallejo admits the truth of the discussion raised by Ernest Naef—the association between the new female eroticism and modern speed—but he points out they are "storylines of rich people," while the poor are left out of the festivities. Instead of industrial and scientific progress, the Peruvian poet emphasizes the importance of social justice. Without the fair distribution of earnings, "some sweethearts will continue kissing, sprawled out on the upholstery of a big Renault, while others are committing suicide over hunger, throwing themselves under the wheels of the perfect, shiny cars."[7]

On the other hand, car advertising served as the basis for rethinking forms of imagination. André Citroën put his name wherever he could: even on the Eiffel Tower. In 1925 Citroën rented the Eiffel Tower to publicize his car brand, paying a huge amount of money a month and illuminating his electric signs with some five hundred lights. Miguel Ángel Asturias refers in one of his columns from Paris to writers who speak of a "net to fish car headlights," a "great worm of light that goes on and off in the jungle of houses," a "woman's earring," and a "shaft of a Moorish dagger."[8]

Initially Citroën rejected the proposal made by Italian Jacopozzi to illuminate the Eiffel Tower with his name. However, when he found out that Henry Ford was interested in signing an exclusive contract for the illumination, he changed his mind. It seems that Ford was prepared to buy the entire Eiffel Tower and send it to the States.[9] From 1925 to 1934 the name Citroën illuminated many a Parisian night from the Eiffel Tower. The inaugural ceremony coincided with the 1925 opening of the Exhibition of Decorative and Industrial Arts. During the exposition painter-decorator Sonia Delaunay presented a Citroën B12, painted like a checkerboard and accompanied by models dressed in the same Art Deco design.

Auto consumption tended to trace a portrait in light. It meant liberty, options, purchasing power. This vision of happiness in consumption had little to do with the dramatization of daily life through art. Failure, loneliness, and alienation were common themes in the work of authors from Río de la Plata in the 1920s and 1930s. At no time were such themes found so directly connected to consumerism as in the story by Uruguayan writer Alberto Lasplaces, "El automóvil," from *El hombre que tuvo una idea* (The man who had an idea). This story about compensatory fantasy, about illusion and obsession, focuses on the tale of Anselmo Lopar, a man who lost his father when he was very young and who received little attention from his mother. Lopar is an honest and simple man. Unlike other individuals, attentive to myriad objects, his life has been reduced to a single ambition: to own a car. Celibacy pales in importance when compared to the right to feel passion for the machine, which dominates his existence and takes the place of marriage. Anselmo's fidelity to the car is his felicity. Anselmo Lopar spends years working with mounds of numbers, counting the earnings of others. He is sober in his conduct and active at work until the day his income surpasses his expenses. When he sees the opportunity to buy a car, the man is reborn. However, the obsessive determination for the object is simultaneously the beginning of a dialogue with the impossibility of being. In obsession there is a revelation that will never be fulfilled, for the object-sign is the enemy of the totality. It is always fugitive, slipping out of control, generating fissures, and producing interstitial spaces. The result is a story of anxiety, imperfection, and suffering.

Coming from or going to work, or on his long walks during holidays, Anselmo Lopar's joy is the contemplation of those vehicles that swiftly slip by on the asphalt. He knows the names of all the factories, the structure of the bodywork, the power of the engines, the composition of the tires, even the smell of the gasoline, blue or yellow label. He collects drawings of brands, which he contemplates in ecstasy at night in his extremely modest and dirty room in a boardinghouse. He is erudite when it comes to cars: warnings, information, races, records, and novelties, zealously hoarding the knowledge for himself. He never speaks of cars with anyone, only with himself, at night, while he carefully pastes clippings, drawings, and articles into a large, leather-bound book, which he has had made to store his treasure.

Describing this protagonist as heteronomous, who in fact was subjected to a strange power, would perhaps be an exaggeration. In the end, there are countless examples of obsessive people. However, Anselmo Lopar only manages to communicate through the vehicle and often he even engages in a dialogue with it: A and B discuss with great authority the range of a headlight, the force of the brake, the resistance of the tire, or the power of the cylinder system. At times there are passionate debates between A and B. The arrival of a small, elegant Rorth, a new brand for the country but one that Anselmo knows very well from his reading, leads him to contemplate it every day with amorous, almost lecherous, eyes, as if he is watching half-naked women at a peep show. There is something obscene in the maniacal contemplation of objects. Anselmo's adoration does not coincide with the fixations of other individuals, but it turns out that the car is not sold. It is replaced by another, ugly one, of a popular brand. The

Rorth's abandonment at the back of the showroom becomes a source of torment for the secret admirer. In general products lose their magical aura when they are displaced to an invisible corner; they cease to be desired objects and are transformed into a caricature of themselves. However, this is not the case of the Rorth for Anselmo Lopar, who after having a few drinks to steel his courage, enters the business and expresses his desire to buy it. He speaks haltingly, overcome by emotion. To his surprise, they not only sell him the car at a much lower price than originally quoted, but they also give him a generous credit plan, making it possible for him to pay for the rest in fairly low monthly installments.

First the object is transformed into the subject; then it seems to complete him. With the support of the car, his self-confidence and self-esteem blossom. Both, Anselmo Lopar and the Rorth, form an extraordinary, almost fabulous, entity: "Seated on the fine, soft cushioning that gave way under his weight with soft moans, he felt not like a man, but a God, and from that height, he envied absolutely no one. From the first instant he had the feeling that car was a living being, a very part of him that until then had not been complete." The object raises the subject, as does the driver's license, which Anselmo keeps carefully tucked away in the pocket of a vest, over his heart, as if it were the portrait of a beloved woman. In appearance the license authorizes control over the machine and the emotions. The overwhelming feeling of oceanic fusion with the machine produces moments of euphoria and gigantism. Any small positive detail disproportionately strengthens the sensitivity of someone in love while he sinks ever deeper into obsession. The car goes on to determine his physical and psychic space. It becomes a true fetish.

A salary raise allows him to rent a small garage, at the back of which is a small loft. From the miserable loft, his gaze is constantly vested on the object. He gazes at it again and again; sleep is dangerous, because he feels the incessant need to protect it. Better to caress it with tenderness. He engages in long dialogues with the Rorth. His colleagues at work, humiliated, cast him looks of envy or resentment. Ah, but are those looks directed at him or the car? The envy of others matters little to Anselmo.

His supreme happiness is Sunday. What pleasure Sundays bring him! He starts the day raising the hood to check the motor and clean the mechanical heart. Then he unscrews, oils, greases, and adjusts the pieces with meticulous care. Finally, he devotes himself to the "carrosserie" [body], applying wax to the metal, until it shines like a mirror. Before leaving, he climbs up to the loft, he changes his clothes to avoid sullying the jewel, and he pushes it with infinite care until it is outside the garage.

The greatest pleasure of life takes place at this precise moment, "launching his car at top speed on the straight roads like a dagger; making it swerve in harmonious and bold curves at the turns; throwing it like a lasso at the inclines and slopes; slipping in front of the heavier cars, which from afar seem to want to close off the horizon; cutting distances in unbelievable time, without witnesses or controllers, how profound, how immense, what indescribable voluptuousness!"

The character of Anselmo Lopar places us at one extreme of motorization. The few occasions when the Rorth owner invites a friend from the office to join on the ride, the companions feel attracted for reasons other than mechanical ones, such as the contemplation of nature. They entertain themselves admiring the changing landscapes, the streams, the solitary ranches, the violet, blue, and pink hills of the Sierra Carapé. They appreciate nature, which they describe as marvelous, but which is nonexistent for Anselmo. He has eyes only for the Rorth, the animated machine and the route along which it glides like a swift and immense insect. Even his companions are secondary to the throbbing sound of the motor, the wailing of the axles, and the proper functioning of the bands. The Rorth is not a cold, unresponsive machine, but rather a living, loving being, a body that the distrustful Anselmo knows right down to the smallest detail.

When the commercial establishment where he works suddenly goes bankrupt, he only has to tighten his budget to enjoy the first days of obligatory strike. The whole day for the Rorth. The joy of a long Sunday! At the start he manages to get some cans of gasoline and a tire credit. But once his resources are used up, Anselmo seems to awaken from a dream. He forgets his anguish by taking the Rorth for a ride. He who had always been such an early riser begins to go to sleep late and to reduce food to the minimum. When his credit runs out at all nearby businesses, needing gasoline, he dashes out into the street like a madman in search of work. He returns hungry, to find the owner of the garage threatening to throw him out. The few pesos that he manages to get are spent on the car. He eats practically nothing. He dreams up some fantastic businesses in addition to thinking about begging or stealing. Incapable of deciding, he spends day and night stretched out on his rickety cot, gazing sorrowfully at his beloved Rorth, completely immobile.

The owner of the garage utters the "immoral" question: Why don't you sell that car? What good is it? Obviously Anselmo cannot imagine the possibility of turning over his only property—the supreme reason for his existence—to some stranger. Only the struggle between life and death forces him to put the Rorth up "for sale." After he has violently thrown out the curious, speculators, and bargain hunters, when a buyer finally appears Anselmo weeps inconsolably. Like a man condemned to death, he deserves one last ride before selling the car. On the highway to Minas he speeds up. Cries and frightened faces make him realize that he might cause an accident. He tries to slow down by releasing the accelerator. It doesn't respond. Nor does the brake. Nothing like this has ever happened to him before. From the docile instrument submissive to commands, we shift suddenly to the machine out of control. Anselmo fearfully concludes that everything happens backward and that the car, possessed by a sort of insanity, is driving him. He understands his destiny:

> He was going to die, the two of them were going to die, before being sepa-
> rated, just as those lovers who refuse to be resigned to living one without
> the other prefer total annihilation. He was filled with a great tenderness,
> and it seemed that the two warm and perfumed arms, arms of a woman,
> held him in the seat, and that the arousing breath was caressing his face,
> and that an extremely sweet voice was calling him by name as he had
> never been called before. His agitated heart recovered the usual serenity
> of his normal heartbeat, a golden mist filled his pupils with ecstasy, and it
> seemed as if he were sinking, sinking into a softly yielding divan, a divan
> of clouds and rose petals, into a hot and inviting breast, where all traces of
> reality dispersed.[10]

"El automóvil" verifies that the sign eclipses the thing. There is no redemption of the object, according to Baudrillard, because in some place there lies a "remnant," which the subject never manages to appropriate.[11] Anselmo Lopar does not find the palliative in profusion. In fact, the accu-mulation simply multiplies the obstacles in the relationship. The car is his exclusive possession and his sole instrument of communication with the world. It is also the absence of the subject, melancholically displaced by the life of the object-sign.

Another dimension of the desire for consumption was the rise of new social types that literature swiftly began to parody. Spaniard Wenceslao Fernández Flórez, in *El hombre que compró un automóvil* (The man who bought a car), presents a gallery of individuals who organize their lives around the mechanical vehicle. One of them—the "car experimenter"—is the creator of the "Garcés system," so he test-drives all cars, but he never actually buys any of them. For this character, life consists of driving around in different expensive cars without spending a cent. Garcés believes that cars are modern man's feet and that to be someone, you have to have one.

Anyone who is not motorized is a pariah: even in the desire for consumption, modernity and mobility are combined.

Garcés spends his life continually driving around in magnificent automobiles without ever purchasing them. He turns up at showrooms ostensibly as a potential buyer who prefers to take the different models on a test-drive before making the purchase. First it is a "coupé," the next day a "roadster," after that a "seven-seater." When he has test-driven all the models in a showroom, he goes to the next one and carries out the same formula: "I want to buy one of your cars, let's go out for a test-drive." Of course, he takes advantage of the opportunity to visit different places in the city and to greet all of his acquaintances while happily shaking hands along the way. The salesmen, concerned with the business end, take him all over and even pay for aperitifs and invite him out to lunch. When he has finished with all the showrooms, Garcés plans to expand his system to include private parties who wish to sell their cars: he is an astute psychologist of the opportunities offered by the sale of merchandise.

Modern man finds the way to complete his persona through the car and through mobility. A battalion of opportunists survives on convincing indecisive and reluctant buyers that there is a stigma attached to walking. They are car salesmen, tenacious spies of alien desires, who go from house to house hoping to find a victim. "You were found," declares a salesman. From that moment on, peace vanishes. The sales agent is a middle-aged individual, dressed decently, with a tired expression, who begins by offering a variety of models. He insists on the prestige of the car, drastically slashes prices, and extends payment schedules. If the customer does not have enough money, he is willing to accept furniture, lamps, and typewriters. No matter what, the most important thing is that the deal cannot be lost, the reason for which this untiring shadow pulls out his cheese sandwich and lets the customer know that he should take his time and not worry about the vendor, who is capable of sleeping in any part of the house.

The world of cars produces "deformed" creatures, such as the members of the Club de los Automovilistas Conscientes (Conscious Drivers Club). Much earlier than *Crash*, the David Cronenberg film, Fernández Flórez invented a gallery of characters who gather to celebrate grotesque acts. For members on the society's lists, the car has a function other than that of devouring miles or admiring the mechanics of beauty. Mr. Revilla, a misanthrope who spits on passersby from the club windows, hits children with his car; Mr. Muñiz knocks down telephone and telegraph poles before severing both legs of a young woman who is quietly reading on the sidewalk outside her home and whom he marries because, in this way, he does not have to feed a whole body; Moyano pursues his father-in-law down the avenue and hits him with the car to hasten his inheritance; others drive cars to marry rich women; and there is the husband who is trying to free himself from his wife, discovers her with her lover, and transports them speedily to the port so that they will not miss the transatlantic ship bound for the United States. When they set sail, he thanks the car, hugs the hood, and kisses each headlight.

Fernández Flórez's parody is frankly unpleasant. Many of his characters are literally marked by deformity. Mouriz is mutilated: he is missing both legs, he has only one arm, a few fingers on his right hand, and a big scar on his forehead. Every so often he has himself run over to collect small indemnifications, until he is hired by the insurance agency as a doorman after he has already been severely deformed. "It is necessary to live," he confessed to the director. Mouriz, or at least what remains of him, gives new meaning to the slogan "Cherchez la femme" through "Cherchez l'auto." There is always a car in these stories.

Equally unhappy is the modest official who is forced to acquire a car to avoid being a social outcast. Like so many car drivers, he begins by purchasing a "second-hand" car. The expression "second-hand" is already an indication of the intimate relationship established between the organism and the machine. Learning to drive is equivalent to hurling an insult, hurtling the car into a crowd of people, and killing. In fact, the equivalence between the revolver and the car is a characteristic of the Fernández Flórez novel. Even worse is when the car disappears; this means disaster. Rewards, newspaper ads, trips to the police station, visits to embassies, all efforts undertaken to recover a car force the owner to give up smoking his English cigarettes, eliminate supper, cut back on outings, and pay taxes to the state. The world becomes filled with nightmares: literary figures are fiery-eyed automobiles, enraged and clamorous, impelled with a life of their own, and eager for human blood.

It is also difficult to buy a car and keep it in tip-top condition. It generally requires hiring a chauffeur, who also serves as a mechanic. Just protecting the leather hood is in itself a complicated task: "Take a liter of milk, boil it, let it cool, and add 50 grams of sulfuric acid. Shake it to mix the liquid and the casein precipitate from the milk; then add 25 grams of lavender essence and 25 grams of clove essence, a liter of vinegar, and an egg white that has been beaten on ice."[12]

A symbol of wealth, at the beginning perceived more as a sport than a means of transportation, the automobile often entered into contradiction with the ascetic world of the sacred. How could the ownership of the object be reconciled with priestly vows of poverty? Access to the vehicle was from the start the privilege of the ecclesiastical hierarchy, facilitating the visit of bishops, archbishops, and abbots to parishes. In contrast and especially for nuns or lower-level clergy, the car continued to be a luxury largely beyond their reach. When the archbishop of Montreal in 1922 lamented that the use of the automobile had become widespread among his clergy and he asked parish priests to use it "with the necessary discretion," a member of the church from the region of Redon complained in 1925 to the archbishop of Rennes that "many priests have cars, which makes a terrible impression."[13]

Another aspect of the emergence of the automobile was the adaptation of manuals of urbanity and good manners to the new means of motorized transport. A manual prepared in Venezuela by Manuel Antonio Carreño indicates the place of ladies when getting into a car driven by a chauffeur: in the back, the most distinguished ladies, and beside the driver, the younger ladies. In the case of ladies and gentlemen, the latter should take the seat beside the driver whenever all the seats in the back are occupied by ladies. The manual continues:

If the person driving the car is the lady or gentleman [who is the] owner of the vehicle, the seats will be distributed indiscriminately. If the gentleman who is driving the car is accompanied by a lady or if he invites a female friend of his same status to go out in the car, it should be insinuated that she should ride in the front seat if [the car] is for three people, [and] it is up to the latter to turn down this offer for the sake of general comfort. The owner of a car is the host of the people who ride with him and he is obliged to treat them with all due respect and consideration, avoiding sudden stops, excessive speed, and requesting the consent of his guests to open and close windows, turn on the radio, etc., asking the ladies if they are comfortable.[14]

While in the United States the art of car design stimulated a popular consumer economy, focused on stylistic diversity and the annual change in models in the automotive industry beginning in the late 1920s, there was nothing comparable in Europe and Latin America until well into the 1950s. It was only after World War II that a massive consumer culture based on multiple product options emerged outside the United States.[15] Indirect evidence of the new relationship between cars and mass consumption in the United States can be found in comic book characters. Even Grandma Duck visited the inventor Gyro Gearloose with her suitcase tied to the roof of a Ford Model T in Donald Duck comics.

In June 1938 an unusual hero first appeared in comic books: Superman. This "champion of the oppressed," this physical wonder who had sworn to devote his existence to helping those in need, did not yet fly. He ran very fast and he was an alien with superpowers, dedicated only to performing good deeds. However, on the cover of the first issue, he is shown furiously demolishing a car. The car belongs to the Butch Mason gang, whose leader had bullied Clark Kent at a nightclub and had abducted reporter Lois Lane. Superman chased the vehicle, rescued the woman reporter, and destroyed it: he smashed off the headlight and a wheel, shattered the windows, and rendered the engine useless. This scene would have been inconceivable prior to the rise of Fordism, when the car was still a handcrafted symbol of wealth and power. At the end of the 1930s, the destruction of the industrialized machine underscored the incomparable might of the superhuman hero, who was no longer concerned about protecting the vehicle.

Another comic book hero, Batman, was born in 1939. His first car, in which he sped down the dangerous streets of New York (Gotham City came later), was a great red Ford. Batman in a Ford! The Batmobile did not yet exist; it was invented in 1941 to singularize the figure of the bat hero. The Batmobile heralded that heroes who fought against evil could not be without special vehicles, and James Bond would have to divide his time between spectacular cars and dazzling women.

Love on Wheels

You might have to imagine it, because there is no empirical proof of the impact of the automobile on sexual practices during the first decades of the twentieth century. Claude Fischer warns against exaggerations resulting from cultural projections.[16] Phrases such as "the car has become a house of ill-repute on wheels," uttered by a judge in the state of Indiana in the 1920s, could be less a reflection of reality than a projection. Adults lost control over the activities of the young, and they imagined the vehicle was being used for promiscuous purposes.

On the other hand, there is no doubt that motorization stimulated the rise of romantic pursuit. In her history of courtship in the United States, Beth Bailey states that the automobile contributed to the dissemination of wooing as a nationwide practice.[17] Young people won mobility and privacy, especially those who lived in rural or suburban areas. Legitimate places emerged for amorous caresses and kisses. These were public at the same time as private spaces, where sexual practices were stimulated and controlled, such as the "besódromo" (kiss-o-drome). Some magazines even recommended the car as the best option for sexual privacy. Such changes in sexual practices formed part of a wider complex of modernization of the senses and the readjustment of modes of sociability.

Paul Morand recognized the shift in the speed of love in the machine age. In England and the United States, according to Morand, "love is made in cars."[18] Of course, the car was not the only means of transportation that stimulated sexual contact. Horses, bicycles, carriages, ships, and airplanes, trains and streetcars, all contributed to cutting distances and facilitating close contact. However, no means of transportation offered so many opportunities for sexuality as this motorized vehicle, which did away with the carriage, eliminated horses, and permitted displacement on land with a hitherto unimagined freedom. A combination of mobile room and bed, the car extended the scope of amorous conquest, placing itself at the disposal of outings, journeys, picnics, dances, parties, and bars. This was especially the case in the 1920s, when the majority of automobiles were closed, providing greater shelter for the occupants. One need only remember the scene of the seduction of the romantic heroine in the film *Titanic* in a car parked in the garage of the fabulous ship to understand the symbolic dimension of the four-wheeled mechanical vehicle as a sexual instrument.

There is certainly no lack of examples. The case of the United States, where this phenomenon is more visible, abounds in references to the connection between the car and sexuality. In 1899 the song "Love in an Automobile" showed how Daisy snubbed the offer of marriage of a young man in love. However, when the boy asked her how she would like to go on a honeymoon in a comfortable car, she quickly agreed to accept his proposal. There was also the character Johnny Miller, who at the slightest hint of rain raised the hood and closed the curtains, despite the—always mild—complaints of his female companion. From Tin Pan Alley, passion was combined with gasoline in songs like "In Our Little Love Mobile," "On the Back Seat of the Henry Ford," "I'm Going to Park Myself in Your Arms," "Fifteen Kisses on a Gallon of Gas," to tunes that warned girls to avoid men who had a car. All indications confirmed the impact of the car in the United States as a means of courtship, in amorous practices, and in sexual relations. David Lewis examines this subject and underscores the element of convenience.[19] Since young people lived with their parents, many couples made love in the car, because they simply had no other place to have sex. The automobile also provided a dose of fantasy and risk, because legislation had already been passed that prohibited indecent acts in public, and the private car infringed upon the public sphere.

The "sexmobile" took on different forms. From the "merry Oldsmo-bile" to the "pimpmobile," passing through the convertible, the limousine, the truck, trailer, and bus, the connection with sexuality was evident. Even the "drive-in theater," the architectural enclosure that accommodated the individual and the automobile—the first one opened in Camden, New Jersey, in 1933—was a variant of this movable, amorous geography. Plea-sure must certainly not have been the distinctive characteristic of sexual encounters, especially for women, a fact that a sculpture by Edward Kien-holz—*Back Seat Dodge '38* (1964)—represents with brutality. Many young women were surely the victims of situations that they were unable to con-trol. Obligated. Forced. Raped. It is said that Henry Ford limited the size of his Model T to inhibit sexuality. It seems that he failed in his attempt, because it takes the words of John Steinbeck in *Cannery Row* to remind us of the importance of the automobile in sex, when he states that the major-ity of the children in America were conceived in Model T Fords. The Ford was symptomatic of the preferred "hot rods," with their powerful, souped-up engines, especially the models from 1928 to 1935.

The automobile accentuated the feeling of intimacy and appeal, as well as the feeling of disgust and repulsion. Within the vehicle, freedom of movement was restricted, it seemed to alter the dimension of the bod-ies, and it was difficult to avoid being scraped.[20] The cultural transforma-tions, above all during the second half of the twentieth century, notably diminished the value of the car for amorous adventures. Nevertheless, vestiges of its importance are still visible, to the extent that depraved ver-sions appear in novels such as *Christine*, by Stephen King, and *Crash*, by James Ballard (both adapted for the big screen). Be that as it may, the perverse relationship between technology and sexuality is one of the sub-jects of Italian futurism, for instance, when Mario de Leone, in his poem "Fornication of Automobiles," personifies the car and identifies crashing with the act of copulation. The involuntary collision suggests the furious fornication of two cars; the clinch of two warriors, the syncopation of two "motor-hearts," shedding "blood-gasoline" and gasping like soon-to-die wounded.[21]

Trophies in the shape of women are no longer common for race win-ners. This reminds us that the car maintains an ambivalent, fluid rela-tion with gender. Apparently, technology does not establish a distinction based on sexual identity. In fact, there were always ways of distinguishing between the masculine and the feminine car. Smith reports that the first electric models were identified as "women's cars," while the more potent gasoline-fueled models were reserved for men.[22] Women had to make a much greater effort to be recognized as drivers with the same rights as men. It was regarded as suspicious if they left the house driving a car, at a time when they were occupied primarily in the domestic sphere. Although stereotypes have changed, it still draws attention to see a woman driving a bus or a taxi.

In *The Autobiography of Alice B. Toklas*, Gertrude Stein devotes a number of pages to French adventures in her Ford—which she fondly refers to as "Aunt Pauline." Apart from blocking Parisian traffic, since Stein was a horrible driver and she never managed to master driving in reverse, Aunt Pauline served as an ambulance to transport soldiers and a means of propaganda during World War I. Perhaps Virginia Scharff exaggerates when she claims that "thousands" of women in the United States and Europe were placed in the service of their country during the war as drivers,[23] but what is certain is that a large number of women were in control at the wheel, with their service making a contribution to modifying traditional notions of female passivity.

One of the figures associated with automobility that had a profound impact on popular imagery was the chauffeur. This was justified, because he was one of the most visible messengers of kinetic mobility. There were two types: the careful family chauffeur (for the head of the household usually did not know how to drive), and the proud government chauffeur. Early accounts highlight the importance of the chauffeur-mechanic-traveler, the irresistible seducer of servant girls from the countryside who took on mythical dimensions: a Don Juan in small towns. For Tristan Bernard, Mario Morasso, Octave Mirbeau, as well as Carlo Emilio Gadda, the chauffeur who drove and controlled the machine, dressed in a leather coat, thick goggles, gloves and cap, and boots lined in soft sheepskin, embodied modernity itself. He was a hybrid of driver and mechanic. The entire success of the trip hinged on his skill and knowledge.

This technical know-how put the chauffeur in a social situation clearly superior to that of the mere employee. Octave Mirbeau elevates him to a position of prominence in his book *La 628-E8*, devoting several pages to "Mon chauffeur." While the Victorian bourgeoisie was accompanied by servants who could not be described as "travelers" on their trips, the chauffeur-mechanic Charles-Louis-Eugène Brossette was enviably unique. He was the squire of the house on wheels, the Sancho Panza of kinetic modernity. We know where he was born, in Touraine, a small town near Amboise. That he moved to Paris to learn the new trade of car mechanic in a garage. That he traveled to the United States and returned disenchanted to France. We know of his liking for mechanics and his love for "the machine," which he compares to a beautiful woman. An excellent traveling companion, attentive without falling into servility, imperturbably level-headed, prudent, untiring, he had a sense of humor, but he was ugly. His back rounded and hunched, skinny legs, and a little knock-kneed, he did not inspire dreams of voluptuousness or glory.

However, Mirbeau verifies that mechanics exerted an almost irresistible prestige on the imagination of cooks and housemaids. This prestige arose from the profession, which was regarded as heroic, full of danger, and akin to war. A man continually launched through space, like a tempest or a cyclone, had to possess something of the supernatural. According to Attilio Brilli, the demiurgic and mysterious image of this figure of the chauffeur, the protagonist of grand communication routes and heroic seducer of cooks and servant girls, who frightened nymphs and satyrs of mythology, was based on the universe of automobile novels.[24] "Chauffeur" or "driver," the figure that Joan Miró symbolizes in *Portrait of Heriberto Casany (The Chauffeur)* is a Gallicism that no longer draws anyone's attention. However, the definition "mechanic who drives an automotive carriage" obscures the prestige of this other character from the time of its emergence as a social type. The modern literary figure of the chauffeur threatens the cast of Indian riders, Mexican charros, and Río de la Plata gauchos. And this character had an impact not only on cooks and servant girls, but also on men eager for homosexual adventures.

One famous writer who fell in love with his chauffeur was Marcel Proust. Another was Salvador Novo, who dedicated several poems and essays to chauffeurs, such as "Sonetos lubricantes." It is necessary to read the literary references to homosexuality in code based on the car, given the moral censure of the time. Therefore, a detailed study of the relationship between the automobile and homosexuality would be extremely useful.

In Latin America during the first decades the car was less the place for amorous encounters than a symbol of status and economic power. Rarely was it the specific place for sex, but rather a means of seduction. Antidemocratic, hierarchic, more seigniorial than perverse, it served at times as an instrument for licentiousness. Above all at night, in places where streetlights were dim, it was associated with young patricians and persons of notoriety, with "lost women," booze, abuse, immorality, scandal, "exchanging" favors, and libertine practices. An expression of wealth and the "good life," the car simplified conquest. It was more of an object of circulation and flirting than a hotbed of sexuality. In its interior, people exchanged kisses and fondling, but the sexual act was generally consummated in more appropriate spaces (such as the *garçonnière*, or bachelor pad). Above all, the car was about exteriority. Lots of image, surface, illusion: the plebeian fantasy of being "inside" luxury. A variety of chroniclers underscored the importance of the outer appearance of the vehicle and pointed to the difficulty of resisting a luxurious car. Young men who did not get excited about a suit, notes Ezequiel Martínez Estrada, "still got excited about a car. Good bodywork was an eloquent declaration of love, and dents in the fenders were the equivalent of stammering."[25]

Rio de Janeiro was a privileged center for the analysis of these urban-sentimental transformations. The capital of the Portuguese Empire beginning in 1808, when King João VI transferred the royal court to Brazil, Rio de Janeiro attracted a wide array of foreigners. Quickly it became one of the most important cities in nineteenth-century Latin America. Capital of the republic beginning in 1889, it underwent a profound urban transformation in the first decade of the twentieth century, with the reform carried forward by Mayor Pereira Passos. This explains in part the importance conferred on movement by writers such as João do Rio (the pseudonym of Paulo Barreto) and Lima Barreto. Although earlier Machado de Assis had recorded aspects of these urban transformations, João do Rio and Lima Barreto became the foremost writers on the early years of the automobile in Brazil.

As we have seen, the power of the car in sentimental relations was evident in João do Rio's work, especially in *Cinematographo* of 1909, *Psicologia urbana*, and *Vida vertiginosa*, the last two from 1911. In "A era do automóvel" (The automobile age) the vehicle undermines the resistance of any woman, from *cocottes* to difficult mothers-in-law. Women could resist all manner of male overtures: flowers, dresses, box seats, expensive dinners, but they could not resist the automobile. It was the mechanical lord of the day, the creator of a new life: "Enchanted Rider of urban transformation, Ulysses's Horse put into motion by Satan, unconscious Nature of our metamorphosis!"[26] Of course it was not merely a matter of the photographic record of the *flâneur*. Paris and London, as well as foreign readings, were projected on Rio de Janeiro, heralding the future.[27]

"Modern Girls" deals with the subject of the deterioration of customs based on the combination of riding in a car and economic misery. The two "Lolitas," with little-girl faces and red lips, drink whiskey and beer to the beat of *caxambu* before continuing on the ride in the rented vehicle with two vulgar young men. Although the girls' mother accompanies them, it is less a moral problem than one of the sheer pleasure of riding in the car and the desire to marry off her daughters. In the emerging life of the car, customs were degraded in speed, vice, and perversion: "Civilization created the supreme fury of precocity and appetites. There are no longer any children. There are men. Girls, who always were transformed into women more quickly than the men, follow the vertigo. The evil of civilizations, with vice, ennui, exhaustion, leads to perverted children."[28]

João do Rio explicitly links automobiles with women in his novel *A profissão de Jacques Pedreira* (Jacques Pedreira's profession), and he offers a panorama of the young dandy using his motorized vehicle to flirt. On occasion, the car followed the tradition of the luxurious carriages and was converted into an "amorous hideaway on wheels" and into the space of fast, unstable love.[29] Jacques and Alice begin their amorous relationship in the vehicle, driven by the chauffeur, surrounded by passersby:

> As novelists say, on wheels the world became alien, vague, and indecisive. She only wanted him. A sigh of attraction trembled in her flesh. Any word would be useless. With a fast movement, Jacques activated the stores, he blew, in the acoustic tube: slowly! He connected with the violence of his victorious adolescence. She managed to shake her head, fleeing the desired kiss. But he took her face between his two hands and sipped from Alice's wholesome, red mouth. "Naughty!" she said, "What took you so long!" And with tropical yearning, her lip sought his, and she sipped too, while their two bodies intertwined in the indescribable harmony of desire. And the slow car honked its horn in the streets, threatening passersby. It was half past six in the afternoon.[30]

Similarly, in exemplary form Lima Barreto sums up some of the sentimental and material changes of the great city. In his story "Um e outro" (One and the other) transportation and love blend the car and feminine submission. However, it does not deal with the well-known theme of the rich owner who captivates naïve young women, but rather with a former domestic employee who falls in love with a chauffeur. Lola, the woman from Spain whose beauty, even at the age of fifty, still draws attention, takes advantage of the money that a businessman paramour offers her to take on a second lover. José is coarse and vulgar, but he is the chauffeur of a "Pope." This marks the contrast between the car kept in a "garage" and the taxi as an expression of social prestige. José loses all of his charm, even assuming brutish traits, when he leaves his job as a chauffeur to drive a taxi. "He was not the same, the one who was there was no longer the demigod; he was someone else or else he was the same degraded, mutilated, horrendously mutilated man. Driving a *taxi* . . . My God!"[31]

These extremes in expectations formed part of a fundamental urban reconfiguration of novel spaces for the imagination. Just like the tram, the car expanded the circle of sentimental vehicles in an increasingly complex society. It promoted a conflictive relationship between desire, voyeurism, anonymity, and the right to privacy. On the way to the factory or to the office, on the way downtown or to the cinema, the proximity of bodies in mechanical vehicles favored dialogues, often imaginary ones. It was also the setting for irony or frustration, based on the vision of luxury vehicles that afforded comfort to transport the family, the head of the household, and even in some cases, his lover. Lima Barreto deals with these real and symbolic spaces and converts them into the stuff of fiction. This writer, a critic of the republican government, of intolerant ideologies, the press and science, of cosmopolitanism and symbols of distinction, moved in urban circles more full of vice than virtues.[32] In the streetcar that crosses the city, the character Lola feels passion for the chauffeur, while she feels powerful in the car, an extension of the machine of pleasure as well as death. Lola's excitement stems from the power of distinction. The lives of passersby depend, for her, on the will of her driver-lover, because with even the slightest of unexpected movements, even the Pope would be capable of mowing down unhappy mortals.

While the car consolidated the modality of fast love, mechanical transportation contributed to renewing urban awareness. References to the city began to form part of a fictional repertoire that used diverse urban spots as frames for social and emotional geography. As she rides the streetcar to meet her lover, Lola catches glimpses of recognizable landmarks in Rio de Janeiro. Her mind is consumed by her impending rendezvous with her lover, but we are informed of arrivals at different stops: Praça da Glória, Passeio Público, Teatro Municipal, and the street called Primeiro de Março. Nature and city, transport and leisure, work and love are all condensed in fiction to project urban signs.

Despite the complaints raised by chroniclers who desperately claimed to be witnessing what they regarded as the end of love, the mediation of the machine in matters of the heart did not fatally alter the romantic ingredient. It is true that the well-known phrase "Women want love, men, sex" is still recognizable in these texts, however, much less than expected. Compared with settings of traditional weddings, the character of Lola stands out for her sexual liberty. There is little that is religious or forced about her conduct. The principle of sexuality free from the purpose of reproduction predominates. The blurred line separating the car and the chauffeur/lover—one and the other—according to the story's title—is not merely aimed at emotional realization, but also at economic advantage.

They are relationships backed by external loyalties. Lola falls in love with the mobility of the illusion, of an "other," just as in Horacio Quiroga stories in which the characters fall in love with actresses on the silver screen. That "other" is not a distant or phantasmagoric figure, but rather a vulgar urban worker who poorly understands the phenomenon of the illusion to which Lola, this Madame Bovary from the tropics, surrenders with utter fervor. The machine and its movement, through the chauffeur who seems to hold sway over the life and death of pedestrians, serve here as a catalyst of sensations and emotions. Beyond expressing the beauty of form, the chauffeur records the beauty of dynamism, intensity, fashion, and the fetish. "The automobile, that magnificent machine that parades down the streets like a victor, was the beauty of the man who was driving it; and when he held her in his arms, it was not exactly he who was embracing her, it was the beauty of that machine that intoxicated her, the reverie and singular joy of speed."[33] Instead of two of them, woman and man, it is a *ménage à trois*, woman, man, and machine. And it is not the pressure of the supposed feminine role that affects the ideal of romantic love; it is the subtle perception of descent from the pedestal of lover, now a lowly taxi driver, in lieu of the Pope.

There is none of that plenitude that one expects from loving relations. However, if the forms of love suggest inevitable disenchantment, movement triumphs as a constituent element of modern society. It forms part of the democratization of amorous feelings and sexual desires, to the extent that Lola's "adultery," in deceiving her protector Freitas, lacks importance. Her conduct could be classified as indecent, but it is inspired by the idea of passion as the supreme value in life.

What does Lola love about the chauffeur? His impeccably white uniform, the coordinated movement of his arms, his erect torso guiding the gleaming car, the image of power, the control over life and death. What makes this amorous connection melancholy is not the lack of intimacy but of reciprocity. Desires go back and forth without touching; there are only bodies that intersect for disparate reasons. Love is degraded in an instant; after six months of the affair, the rivalry of objects takes center stage. These become the true characters in the amorous plot, bringing about the swift fall of the demigod to the mutilated driver, apart from any sincerity or authenticity.

Lola does not see things more "clearly" when she perceives José as a mutilated horror. Both the demigod and its opposite are projections of the female desire for the object of mobility. Neither blindness nor justice: the lover is fatally composed of extreme visions. One extreme produces absolute surrender; the other, absolute rejection. Glorification is followed by demonization. The image is loved, the image is hated. The car, through the intermediary of the chauffeur, assumes the form of Cupid and his arrow. It is no longer clear if she is dying of love for the car or for the chauffeur. In both cases, it is an ill-fated love that reveals the impossibility of communication.

It was common to speak of enthusiasm for change, as well as the disenchantment it brought about. Like all new technologies within popular reach, the automobile both opened and shut the door to job opportunities. Being a chauffeur was a new occupation (we should not forget that the first cars almost always required a mechanic), and Lola falls in love with that rustic character, an Olympian dressed in white. The distinction disappears when José abandons the Pope and the chauffeur's uniform. In a taxi, dressed like any other man, the romantic aura that surrounded him vanishes; the lack of distinction is his ruin.

The chauffeur's allure did not go unnoticed by Horacio Quiroga. In the story "Su chauffeur" (His chauffeur), published in *La Nación* in April 1925, Quiroga deals with the figure of the opportunist, the *pícaro*, or rogue, in the Río de la Plata version of "the Creole spirit." It is not the story of a migrant worker, but rather of a Lothario from the lower class attempting to conquer upper-class women. Whoever lacks direct access to elite young women has to pursue them indirectly: by entering into their service to seduce them. This is the opportunist's reasoning. The car is not what matters, but rather the job as chauffeur as a mechanism facilitating proximity. The driver who takes the exam before a committee is the same "psychologist" of women who embraces a temporary subordinate position in order to climb the social ladder. It begins with the frivolity of the girls, who discuss fashionable writers and feel curious about the stranger who serves them. This chauffeur not only learns to drive and repair the car, his bearing is that of a professional, dressed in a uniform, worthy of the wheel. All of it is part of a strategy that consists of repressing any conduct improper to the function, to then, at a prudent moment, offer hints of the contradiction between the job and the man. It is a matter of creating a mystique surrounding his character. Thus, the chauffeur, with his impeccable conduct, amidst a cluster of chattering girls, quickly slips in the name of Proust.

The story that unfolds around that of the eldest daughter's curiosity is the persona behind the chauffeur. Constant provocations and mockery are interspersed with passionate kisses and the plan's ultimate failure. The handsome chauffeur is not highly desired as a man, and his plans crumble when he leaves the job to seduce her as an independent suitor. His biggest obstacle remains his social class. He cannot escape from it, no matter how hard he tries. He confesses to his friend: "By God, never do foolish things beyond your powers, no matter how grand they might be. I think mine were immense, and I'm ruined. I am me now, do you understand? The one who would give his life for a kiss . . . I don't know what else to do now but this: blow up all cars and chauffeurs with a single bomb!"[34] Meanwhile, to be able to continue kissing her, at least sometimes, there is no other solution but to return to the family's service and to his condition as chauffeur.

Quiroga explores a relatively well known theme in American films from the first decades of the century: the story of an apparently impossible love between a poor driver and a rich young woman. In the American version, however, that felicity of yore triumphs to please public sentiment. In *The Girl and the Chauffeur*, the driver rises for his practical skills to a position of wealth as a garage owner and he even manages to save his father-in-law from financial ruin in the Wall Street panic. Other movies show young rich people who pretend to be mechanics, traffic cops, taxi drivers, or ambulance drivers to get close to the loved one. It is disinterested love that conquers all obstacles by oblique means. However, in Horacio Quiroga, it is different. In Quiroga there is a disenchanted realism when it comes to the difficulty of upward social and literary mobility impelled by one's own means. The extremely narrow-minded elite permanently destroys the ambition to overcome poverty. If the young people of a lower class hope to spend part of the day close to the rich girl, they will have to continue as chauffeurs. There's no happy ending, not even in literature.

Diverse chroniclers record the impact of material culture on sentimental relations in language, in symbols, in ways of courtship. Two Latin American writers living in Paris, César Vallejo and Miguel Ángel Asturias, witnessed the importance of the car in wooing women in the 1920s. Vallejo cites Ernest Naef, for whom the boy who is looking for a girl but does not have a car is irremediably lost. Naef even ingeniously links love on asphalt roads to the birth rate in towns: "A kiss is given on a swerve and God knows in what garage the baby will be born. All countries complain of the low rise in birth rate. Could it be there aren't enough cars? . . . In our times, gas rules above all. Give a little gasoline to the couple and leave them in a good car and you'll see how the population will grow."[35] What twenty-year-old would be seriously interested in a young man without a car? How many of them wouldn't trade in their pedestrian loves for a sentimental high-speed adventure? How could a fifteen-year-old think that "mister" wasn't a wretch when, by merely seeing him drive a car, she envisioned him as a seducer of queens and film stars capable of great loves? These are questions that Miguel Ángel Asturias, frightened by the influence of the automobile, raises in a provocative article, "Itinerarios-flirt: El automóvil y las mujeres" (Itineraries-flirt: The car and women), published on July 13, 1929. Asturias points to the intercession of four wheels in the amorous relations between a man and a woman, to the extent that "many twentieth-century Juliets are more enamored with their cars than with their lovers."

The vertigo of speed corresponds to the vertigo of love: in cars, women surrender. It is the century of the machine, and many marriages fail or triumph depending on the possession of such technological objects. Asturias contrasts the "life of gasoline and the steering wheel" with "interest in one's nation" and the need for freedom. Speed is conceived from the model of "freedom of" as distinct from "freedom for." In Guatemala, imported cars, which might potentially offer freedom, become forms of amorous slavery: "I do not think this recent relationship between love and the machine, as they say in Havana, has anything objectionable, generally speaking, but from our particular perspective, very much in spite of the tone that we have given to this article and without filling the note with immoral moralists, we believe that our beautiful compatriots should reflect a little, accepting for the good of the homeland the sacrifice of falling in love with men without cars, perhaps owning a horse or carriage, to teach them to love above all things: freedom."

Similarly, the Brazilian chronicler and caricaturist Belmonte (pen name of Benedito Bastos Barros), who wrote about São Paulo in the 1920s and 1930s, paradoxically, associates love, cars, and machines in *Meu amor! Adoro-te* (My love! I adore you): "Oh! Little one! How about going out for a ride, eh? And this is how the conquests begin . . . Dynamic, in the century of futurism. The car has an ir . . . radiating [a pun on radiator and irradiating] prestige, for those 'steering wheel' loves. Isn't love also born from an 'explosion'? And isn't it also a matter of 'internal combustion'"?[36]

The car is expected to preserve its position as a status symbol, to be everything except an instrument for work. Pure entertainment. Natalia is a modern girl who falls in love with the main character in the novel by Spanish writer Fernández Flórez, *El hombre que compró un automóvil* (The man who bought an automobile). This fellow does not have a car, so Natalia rejects him. Kinetic modernity manages to impose the burden of the guilty conscience: the man without freedom of mobility feels inferior and unhappy. Our literary character is an incomplete being who thinks with bitterness of all of the adventures that his friends owe to the automobile: those of Ramírez, who conquers the hard heart of Atanasia while driving an eight-cylinder model, with his hands beautifully protected by cream-colored gloves; those of González, who every afternoon takes dressmakers for a ride; those of Gutiérrez, who kisses beautiful girls at dusk. Here the car includes and excludes. Possession and free access to mobility ensure conquest, surrender, and limited movement, envy. Decades later McLuhan made the claim that the "mechanical bride" broke the ties of family life, it separated work and home, it leveled physical and social spaces, it fragmented the city into dozens of suburbs, it built an asphalt jungle, it did away with the countryside, and it created new modes of life on highways.

An example of the use of the car for artistic purposes is the painting by Tamara de Lempicka, *Self-Portrait* (also known as *Woman in the Green Bugatti*) of 1925. It was initially the cover of a German fashion magazine, *Die Dame*, and it quickly went on to become the symbol of the independent woman. The impact of that cover (the small painting was only exhibited as an autonomous work of art several decades later) attests to the importance of the car as a symbol of liberation. The representation was an act of challenge that overlooked natural references and appropriated metallic forms.

Curiously, Tamara de Lempicka did not own a green Bugatti at all, but rather a simple, although garish, yellow and black Renault. She coordinated her clothing with the color of the car: a bright yellow pullover, a black skirt, and hat. She dressed like the car. This Art Deco artist, a chorus girl from the period between the wars, when she was known as the "belle Polonaise," became the paradigm of the modern woman in Paris in the 1920s. The *New York Times* defined her as "the beauty with eyes of steel, the diva of the automobile age." Gilles Néret studied the life of the painter and wondered where the woman-car began and where the car-woman ended: the car as her double.[37]

A symbiotic relationship was established between the driver and the object. To reach this point, an adaptation of the feminine image to modern technology was necessary. There were more than a few at the beginning of the century who questioned the possibility that women could drive a car: their "naturally hysterical" temperament seemed incompatible with the control of a powerful machine. The car was associated with masculinity, not with femininity. But motorization could not be stopped before gender. Its fate was proliferation. In the shift of image, advertising played a preponderant role, destined to modify the guidelines of consumption. Women also had to be incorporated into the market and to purchase transportation technologies. This was evident in the appearance of serialized novels aimed at girls and adolescents, entitled *Automobile Girls*, *Motor Girls,* and

Motor Maids.[38] It opened up a world of infinite adventures, that of women drivers. Female Tintins. Fame and fortune awaited them.

Not only was it important that women maintain their femininity when driving a powerful vehicle; in addition, the machine should enhance her figure. At the wheel of the Bugatti, Tamara de Lempicka seemed to dominate the world. She was a woman confident in her control of the symbol of power. She was the defiant vamp, red lips, insinuating and mysterious gaze. Aristocratic. Independent. Sovereign. Diva. A military cap, the wide scarf enveloping her, the left glove calmly poised on the wheel. The woman-car was a machine to be admired. Its static character indicated that kinetic modernity no longer needed to represent movement to colonize the imagination. The mere sight of a part of the car sufficed to ignite the feeling of adventure. A steering wheel, a tire, a brand hood ornament, everything metonymically announced the world of movement and seduction.

In the 1920s photography began to make explicit use of the car in the representation of eroticism. It went beyond erotic photos of interiors, individuals, or couples, of seminaked odalisques in a harem setting, near the pool, with a satyr bust in the background. In photos combining the woman and the car, the naked figure and the importance of the sexual position were retained, but the novel juxtaposition was subordinated by the idea of displacement. The coupling of "woman and car" was highly photogenic. One and the other, female and machine, were fused into one as objects of masculine desire. The message was clear, perhaps a bit crude for modern tastes, but not substantially different: the woman and the car went together. Both belonged to the same world of objects. There was no incompatibility between the eroticism of industrial and corporeal products. Although on occasion the desire arising from the automobile seemed to compete with the feminine image, as in conversations between men about cars, in erotic photos the vehicle appeared to be a "romantic" background. All it took to consummate the sexual act in one's imagination was to climb into the car, generally through the back door.

The photos are clear in this respect. A classic is the "female mechanic": stretched out on a tarp, dress lifted to the waist, surrounded by screws, gently fixing a defect in the car with pliers. Or else seated on the hood of a Renault, playfully smiling, with her skirt open. She is the one shown touching her vagina or her breasts in front of the open back door of the car.

While some photos are directly pornographic, others are almost subtle. A variant of the "female mechanic" displays a young woman seen from the back, her head stuck in the motor, her skirt raised to the waist, stockings with garter belt, her back end facing outward, and her foot propped provocatively in the air.

The photos that show two or more women have similar particularities. They suggest lesbianism, such as in the example of two women on the verge of a kiss or in an embrace and entering the backseat of a car. Completely naked except for their shoes. There is almost always the detail of the stilettos. Very few of the photos include men, and invariably the presence of the man indicates the imminence of sex, whether for the effusive kiss or the "romantic" mood.

Thus, as photos juxtapose women and cars, avant-garde language tends to link the woman and machine fundamentally from the male perspective. Carl Sandburg explicitly associates the car and woman in the poem "Portrait of a Motor Car" (from *Cornhuskers*), inventing the driver Danny, who fantasizes about the car when he sees women dressed in a skirt and red stockings in his dreams. Often the human and the mechanical are blurred, to the extent that we ask ourselves if love is directed at the woman or the machine. The ambiguity of (sexual) initiation in the car is a central element of the notable poem by E. E. Cummings, "she being Brand" (from *is 5*). It is one of the characteristic poems of the young Cummings—concise syntax, experimental typographic composition with marked erotic content, dislocated and twisted words, innovative use of prefixes and suffixes, surprising use of spatial structures with upper and lower case. All of the images in "she being Brand" converge toward a humanized machine that serves eroticism by means of movement. Therefore it is difficult to accept that it is above all a patriarchal poem concerned with male control of the female, which tends to "de-romanticize" sex.[39] Get into the car and drive, arrive, put in gas, oil the joints, turn the corners, combine body and machine, accelerate and brake until the dead point suggests on the contrary an imaginative extension of poetic figurations of love, which undoubtedly include passion (very American) for the machine and movement.

The avant-garde language of Latin America reinforces this connection between love and mobility. "Love exists. But go by car! There are no more lakes for the Lamartines of the twentieth century! . . . And the poet recalls the last time he saw the small one, no longer beside the sweet water, but rather disputing the cup between Palestra and Paulistano," declares Mário de Andrade in *A escrava que não é Isaura* (The slave who is not Isaura). Even the telephone can inspire love. And if the leisurely romantic language of the nineteenth century disappeared in the century of the automobile and the airplane, the figure of the poet of love does not fade away. He continues to dedicate "electric" poems to the beloved and writes of images based on speed. In *Cocktails* Luis Aranha composed verses in which the car forms the erotic background of women transformed into enormous flowers: "I am a poet / and women are the charm of the Triangle, / Limousines glide on Persian rugs . . . / The tenuous Light nests in the interior of luxury cars / Women are big bouquets / of flowers / that I yearn to hold in my arms! Silk dresses on elastic bodies."

Uruguayan poet and journalist Alfredo Mario Ferreiro deals with the subject of urban transformations with humor in *El hombre que se comió un autobus: Poemas con olor a nafta* (The man who ate a bus: Poems that smell of gasoline). Parts of the car and bus become actual characters in his bold lyrical poetry full of scientific motifs: "Radiator," "Differential," "Carburetor," "Spare tire," and "Toolbox." On the other hand, the structure of many of these poems "that smell of gasoline" is based on the speed and movement of urban means of transportation, as in "Poema sin obstáculos del tránsito ligero" (Poem without light-transit obstacles) "Los amores monstruosos" (Monstrous loves), "El ballet del agente de tránsito" (The ballet of the traffic cop), "El dolor de ser Ford" (The pain of being a Ford), "Poema de los trolleys prensados" (Poem of pressed trolleys), "La balada de los frenos" (The ballad of the brakes), "Loa en acción de gracias para mi voiturette 'Buick', 13-331, Modelo 1927" (Praise in thanksgiving for my *voiturette* 'Buick', 13-331, Model 1927).

Remains of this shared identification in the 1920s, when women and cars were equated as a result of their high cost and because they came in different models, still survive today in TV advertising, the parlance of the young, and car repair shop calendars. Woman personified as the human machine, the accelerator driving the man, the electric starter, the garage ornament, the sporty little *voiturette* of the species. A pretty woman resembled a Packard, and her breasts were equivalent to bumpers.

At other times the car is portrayed in avant-garde poetics as a woman's rival, given the reliability of the machine in comparison to the fickle temperament associated with women. In an extension of the tone of European futurism in the Río de la Plata, Alfredo Mario Ferreiro condenses the changing relationship between man, woman, and the machine in "Loa en acción de gracias para mi voiturette "Buick," 13-331, Modelo 1927." It is a straightforward poem about a man who gets home late, parks his Buick outside the door, and leaves the next morning. What is curious about this simple poem is that the machine takes on the virtues of a woman beloved for her reliability and dedication to the owner. Forgotten, "she" stands alone waiting with her fear and her shame. In the morning the owner finds her silent and benign. After a night abandoned outside, the machine is ready to serve her master. Quickly, she shows him how glad she is to see him, shaking her tailpipe and offering three or four explosions. This is enough to make the poet explain: "Beloved Voiturette! / The only constant woman that I know!" and both set off elegantly "on the golden streets / of this city of mine."

A different form of sexual rivalry is expressed in "Los amores monstruosos":

> The bus desires, with all its axle and all its differential the pretty *voiturette* with harmonious lines.
>
> Little by little it manages to approach her side to lull her with the moderation of the powerful motor.
>
> The *voiturette*, startled by that din, takes a true leap of an agile female and flees.
>
> From afar, she waves farewell with the little blue kerchief of the tailpipe.
>
> The bus sets off in immediate pursuit. In its clumsiness of lustful pachyderm it barely avoids the obstacles of the nervous and minute street traffic.
>
> Grotesque pursuit. The monstrous behind the winged.
>
> The bus devours the pretty *voiturette* with the eyes of all of its eager windows.
>
> The *voiturette* stretches with her long arms of speed.
>
> Suddenly, it stops short next to the line of the pavement. When all is said and done, the female in it has become excited by the bus's persevering pursuit.
>
> The bus sees her stop. It approaches all sweaty, boiling drool dripping from the radiator cap; all the windows vibrating; the windshield moist; the fender trembling; the eyes of the headlights bulging.
>
> It is going to stop. But—the demands of work—the clutch makes it go on by. The norm! The bus is for work and not for falling in love with *voiturettes* in the streets.
>
> Then the poor monster suffers rabid anguish. A rage that is condensed in the looks of red hatred cast by the taillights.

Machines personified and in movement, the bus and the *voiturette* (a little car whose motor developed from 10 to 14 CV [*cheval vapeur*]) are part of a growing motorization trend that left its mark on literature. The virile component of size and scoping gaze are set off by the small, passive, harmonious element. However, the masculine demands of work and sweat also arise in contrast to feminine entertainment and idleness. The realization of proletariat erotic desire is impossible, since the weapon of popular masculinity consists of work, not of seduction. And lechery gives rise to social resentment. An ironic, humoristic, and scientific language runs through these examples, adapting the parts of the car and of the bus to the emancipatory gesture of the avant-garde and the imperative of movement.

The Killer Machine

At the start of the twentieth century, Battles of the Flowers were competitions featuring cars bedecked with fresh flowers that were paraded down the street. For Malcolm Forest, they are "a clear demonstration that the growing industrialization of the car did not rend the ties that bound man to Nature."[40] Forest reports that such contests, held mainly in France and England before car shows, triggered great popular interest and were an excellent means of promotion. In the first "battle," held in Nice in 1902, a French Panhard richly adorned with flowers won. Less than a decade later, at a competition in São Paulo, the Matarazzo family car was so laden with flowers that it was difficult to identify the make of the vehicle.[41] However, it was not an elegy to nature, but rather to artifice. The artificial predominated in the car: it came to replace nature. The flowers were already subordinate to the machine, regarded as the mechanical son.

This mechanical son had been born in 1885. Karl Benz, inventor of the automobile propelled by an internal-combustion motor, recounted in his memoirs the tale of the unusual birth of technology. Extracted from thought and placed in the world of reality, the baby-machine arose in the factory patio. The vehicle's structure was simple and based on the principle of bicycle construction: lightweight, with three large wheels with fine spokes (one up front and two in the rear). But it moved by itself, without the need for a horse, making a strange noise, "töff, töff, töff." It is the kiss of a new era, Benz explains, the first toot of the command of the earth.[42]

The people in the street gaped in amazement. How did it work? A coach without horses, moving supremely down the streets? The driver was like a king, he waved like a king, had the proud bearing of a king. The pride soon faded: the strange car came to a stop and ceased to function. Now the people mocked the useless toy. Some people pointed to the absurdity of using a noisy, unsafe mechanical crate when there were plenty of horses and carriages in the world. Poor man, others thought, he will ruin his business with that crazy idea. But Benz decided to patent the machine, anticipating its utility and the worldwide triumph of automobilism. A few years later, Henri de Toulouse-Lautrec produced the lithograph *The Motorist* (1896), in which the driver, protected by goggles, a cap, and a thick leather coat, passes by triumphantly in his machine, overtaking a slow pedestrian with a diminutive dog.

The *Michelin Guide de France* of 1900 offered unequivocal confirmation that travel was becoming increasingly dependent on automobility. Clearly, economic interests were at play. Ultimately, the inflatable Michelin tires that appeared on the market in 1895 became an integral part of the car. But these changes transcended the marketing dimension because they were a sign of changes in the very organization of time and space. The entire system was organized around mobility: distances between cities; duration of travel; post, telegraph, and telephone offices; hotels; mechanics; gasoline stations; hospitals; cathedrals; churches; tram lines; train stations; pharmacies; physicians; and carports. The one who recommended the best restaurants and hotels was the Automobile Club of France; members of the Touring Club got a 10 percent discount.

In the *Michelin Guide* of 1900 there is practical advice specifically for people traveling by car. This new social type, unlike the traditional traveler, had to display self-confidence and express himself loudly and clearly. In the hotel he deserved to be accommodated in well-appointed rooms. Given that it was not customary to charge for taking care of horse-drawn carriages, the same should apply to cars. The formulation here was bold: it was an emerging need of general interest, for which he requested "colleagues" to always refuse to pay for taking care of the car. If the hotel insisted, the proprietor of the vehicle would provide his name and address, would pay the rest of the account, and would propose that the amount charged for taking care of the car be recovered in legal proceedings. *General interest, colleagues*, and *legal system* were words that denoted how movement imposed its own rules and created its interest groups.

Automobilism intensified awareness of the alterations in the landscape. It did not produce change, because the perception of modifications of nature is an element that the car shared with the train, horse, and carriage. By analogy to what had occurred with train passengers, people riding in automobiles recorded the change in perspective as a novelty. Photographing cars in movement became a passion for the young Jacques-Henri Lartigue and his aesthetics of the instantaneous. The greater the speed, the greater the change in perception. Maurice Maeterlinck speaks to us of the trees that for many an unhurried year lived peacefully along roadsides and that now shrank in fear of disaster. From the perspective of the car at high speed, trees seemed to be closer to each other, and as a group they discussed how to prohibit this strange apparition from the road.

A few hours of traveling offered a varied spectacle: countryside, small towns, and cities. Prior to his controversial manifesto on futurism, F. T. Marinetti extolled the mechanical sensibility in the poem "All'Automobile da corsa" (1905), in which the car surpasses earthly nature. In the "crazed monster" the driver crosses mountains, rivers, and plains to reach the stars. He lacks any desire for greater contact with the "filthy world." Finally he departs from it and flies serenely through the luminous plenitude of the stars that flicker on their great blue background. Marinetti celebrated the rise of the mechanical landscape in a variety of texts. He greeted it with well-studied cries, denying the demands of beauty and the verbal symphony. There was no need to be understood, but rather to liberate the words.

Violent words: it was necessary to spit every day on the altar of Art, to annihilate the "I," to destroy syntax, to use the verb in the infinitive, to abolish the adverb and punctuation. Power and brutal sounds. Dead in space and time, they had to express the simultaneity of states of mind in the work of art. The life of steel, pride, fever, and speed had to be transformed into literary and visual elements; the tick-tock and hands on the clock; the movement of the piston of a cylinder; the furious turbine of a propeller. The opening and closing of a valve created a rhythm as beautiful as the blink of an animal's eyes, but infinitely newer. Long live the engine and the mechanical man! After the animal kingdom came the mechanical kingdom, Marinetti declares in the *Technical Manifesto of Futurist Literature*.

In contrast to Marinetti's claims, the death of the "mechanical man with interchangeable parts" from car accidents rose considerably. Accidents were the bane of kinetic modernity. They were sometimes mentioned, but poorly received, and drama stalked them like a shadow. Everything was designed to stimulate the fluidity of the system, to guarantee permanent circulation. The less one thought, the more automatic the movement, the better it worked. It is worth considering the "perverse" effects here, because the mobility projects entailed unexpected consequences. When technicians are called to resolve unforeseen problems, the phantasm of "technology out of control" pursues us. An important current of thought from Freud to Virilio took control of expressing the impossibility of self-correction of technology. It produced symptoms that it attempted to correct, trapped in a vicious cycle, to present remedies for the ills that it made possible. Others, such as Ballard, were more exaggerated. An undeniable fascination and excitement hid behind the horror of car crashes. Nevertheless, the means of modern transportation—electric tram, motorcycle, car, airplane—contributed to the excitement of feelings and so-called hyperstimulation.

It was difficult to conceive of the influence of the car in the history of death at the end of the nineteenth century. The first urban fatality took place in London on August 17, 1896. It was precisely the year when the British Red Flag Act was revoked, which had obligated a man to walk in front of the car with a red flag to alert passersby. A lady was struck by a car moving at only seven kilometers per hour in the vicinity of the Crystal Palace. It seems that the driver called out to the lady to stop and sounded his horn several times, apparently without success.

Initially, the press reported with an abundance of details on the accidents and problems associated with automobilism. Although from the start they were machines notorious for their victims, their novelty and distinction amply overcame the danger. As the number of accidents increased, diverse voices were raised against the "lethal weapon." Those who were getting rich, according to the ironic commentary in a newspaper from the time, were the makers of crutches. In 1934 more than 240,000 traffic accidents were recorded in England and more than 880,000 in the United States. Painting reminds us of that landscape of anguish in works by Grant Wood, *Death on the Ridge Road* (1935) and by Alfonso Ponce de León, *The Accident* (1936), at the same time as history does not deny this version of the car as a criminal. Pierre Curie, Nathanael West, James Dean, Albert Camus, Jackson Pollock, Roland Barthes, Grace Kelly, Vilém Flusser, W. G. Sebald, Ayrton Senna, and Princess Diana are among millions of men and women, children, young and old, who have died in car accidents, in addition to thousands of dogs, chickens, horses, cows, sheep, and migrant turtles who nested on beaches while drivers tested the power of their machines on the sand.

Journalist and antimonarchic activist José de Patrocínio was the first person to drive a car around Rio de Janeiro. He was often in the company of Olavo Bilac. There the two figures could be seen: the sacred poet (Bilac) and the spokesman of abolitionism, the son of a freed slave (Patrocínio). However, what really sparked the curiosity of children, adolescents, and adults was the vehicle. In one chronicler's opinion, it was "ugly, yellow, it bounced about on uneven roads and let out an unbearable stench of petroleum." Often it had to be pushed. Mário da Silva Brito pointed out that Olavo Bilac, the prince of Parnassian poets, had to find out that the car symbolically represented the great enemy who struck down the winged Pegasus and would give rise to Brazilian Modernism.[43]

Patrocínio's car came to a not-very-glorious end. It had been the source of scandalous attention when it first appeared, and people stopped to gape at it as if they were seeing a creature from Mars or an apparatus of fulminating death. A few days later, the abolitionist speaker and some friends, who thought they were flying a few miles per hour, crashed the machine into some trees on Rua da Passagem. Olavo Bilac had been at the wheel trying to learn how to drive.

It was difficult to anticipate the influence of the car given that broken-down, useless machine. Nevertheless, as João do Rio underscored, the car "needed and accentuated an era purely its own, the era of the fury to live, ride, and enjoy, because deep down, we are all moral chauffeurs, tied to the motor of the apparatus aiming at the greed for status and satisfaction, at full speed, without any concern for the guardians of traffic, accidents, pedestrians, without giving any thought to the idea that the bronze could melt in the out-of-control race toward the fierce triumph!" ("A era do automóvel"). The car had been transformed into "He," an autonomous character, while movement took on the characteristic of self-propulsion.

On the one hand, speed intensified the feeling of pleasure; on the other, it emphasized the dangers of modern life. Aviator and inventor Santos Dumont commanded his vehicle without paying any attention to speed limits. He refused to accept controls or fines. When they finally arrested him, he thought revealing his identity would suffice to exonerate him. But with the spread of the car, together with the rise in accidents, this brand of individuality did not serve as an excuse.

Regulating traffic and controlling accidents through laws became a necessity. These prescriptions were made known in varied media. They were published in the *Diario Oficial* [akin to the Federal Register] and were inserted in the *Boletín de Leyes* (Bulletin of Laws). The first edition of the *Michelin Guide de France* in 1900 also included a decree from the president of the republic regulating the circulation of cars. Safety measures to prevent explosions and fires appeared as did instructions to avoid frightening horses or spreading annoying odors. The maneuvering tools had to be grouped in such a way that the driver could activate them without taking his eyes from the road; the vehicle had to obey the steering wheel, turn with ease on tight curves, and have two braking systems. The speed was not supposed to exceed 30 kilometers (18 miles) per hour in the countryside and 20 kilometers (12 miles) in population centers.

Each vehicle had to clearly display the name of the builder, the model, the order number, the name and address of the proprietor. It could not be driven without a certificate of ability granted by a local official. To obtain this certificate, it was necessary to take a practical exam with an inspector. The latter had to assess the candidate's prudence, level-headedness, and "presence of spirit," the precision of his gaze, the safety of his driving, his skill of adaptation to circumstances, and the speed with which he activated, when necessary, the braking systems. There were guards and traffic signals, laws and fines, speed limits and warnings, qualification exams and inspectors, safety belts. Restrictions against the odor, noise, and weight of the car multiplied, against exhaust emissions and the dust it raised. However, accidents did not decrease. What also increased was the number of insurance companies. In the first decades there were problems arising from schism between the car's traction and the engine's power. The poor quality of tires and roads further aggravated dangers for drivers and passengers, as well as pedestrians.

"Epileptic machine" was the expression coined by Georges Duhamel in *Scènes de la vie future* (Scenes from life in the future), an account based on his trip to the United States shortly after World War I. Not only did it take its toll in victims, it converted the human being into a beast. The streets of Chicago were infested with troglodytes with a human visage in the fearful mechanical horse, intimidating their fellow creatures. Would individual freedom in the modern world survive? Could that everyday war be called "civilization"? Duhamel put the American car at the defendant's table and declared it guilty: it aggrandized our vices without exalting our virtues. The car brought out some curious traits, which generally were not a distinction, arising from the depths of people. It transformed sensible beings into nervous ones and nervous ones into demented creatures. It made strong men into brutes and brutes into beasts, offering unimaginable occasions for rejection, treachery, and cowardice. The car made it possible to be rude and a coward with impunity.[44]

Duhamel recognized in the car the American triumph of materialism. The triumph of matter and money. A heartless object, the car. In *Scènes de la vie future*, Duhamel writes that "the car arrived" and it changed everything. It brought an end to hypocrisy, it made masks fall away, it gave rein to the free play of nature and passions. It might be said that this French surgeon and writer was a romantic reader of the Communist Manifesto: the car put everyone in their place, reinstating the kingdom of the power of money, the only thing that ultimately mattered, the only thing that could triumph.[45] In a chapter symptomatically called "Automobile ou les lois de la jungle" (Car or rules of the jungle), he expresses his doubts concerning the value of material progress by describing a car cemetery on the outskirts of Chicago. A car graveyard! The first the Frenchman had ever set eyes on in his life. The vision of this funereal sight struck Duhamel as supremely sad, almost apocalyptic. The barren field, dominated by useless iron, blended with the city and lost its physiognomy. Instead of wooden crosses or marble tombs, it was filled with useless parts of old cars. What a terrible vision, that great wasteland full of old, broken-down, dismantled, and destroyed cars. Several hundred, of all makes and models, were taken to the "cemetery" like old horses that were no longer useful, not even for their hide or their innards. They were piled up at the bottom of a pit, amidst a cloud of dust. Car ossuaries and scrap metal cemeteries: the revenge of technology over nature and culture.

Duhamel was part of the line of French scholars who mobilized humanism against Americanism. Philippe Roger undertook a detailed study of the genealogy of French anti-Americanism and stated that from Duhamel to Bernanos and from Mounier to Garaudy, the cause seemed understood: anti-Americanism was a brand of humanism.[46] For Duhamel the consumer machine was an abstract curse, a method of manipulating needs and of transforming the individual into a standardized consumer. "The Defense of man!" was the motto of these French technophobes, who, in the lapse between the wars, perceived the destructive potential of machines; they rejected the idea of standardization and they denounced the standardization of individuals in the United States, identified as a technical, social, and cultural complex that destroyed the human being.[47]

This is not the way Gertrude Stein saw things when she drove her car around Chicago. On the contrary, she was fascinated by the organization of urban circulation. She was even surprised by the slowness of traffic compared to that of France, where people seemed to believe there would be no accidents no matter what the speed. The American writer thought that people drove very slowly in the United States, forty-five miles per hour. Drivers stopped at traffic signals when they should and they never passed another car while driving uphill or on a curve. Therefore, the number of accidents on the streets of Chicago was an enigma.[48] Stein's observation merits attention: there was a "civilizing process" as part of the phenomenon of mobilization. Traffic served as a school of learning of sorts, despite the fact that it often worked in perverse ways.

Identifying traffic problems was easier than recognizing its positive aspects. Thousands of miles from Chicago, in Buenos Aires, Ezequiel Martínez Estrada trained his gaze on the car and its occupant while raising the same critique that Duhamel leveled against the Americans: the car mania of the port city personified an overt form of antisocial conflict. The dividing line between casual accidents and those that responded to criminal tendencies that tended to arise from car use was a tenuous one. In a somewhat confusing way, Martínez Estrada insinuated that the car was the extension of the house. In other words, it extended the values of private space. Everything in its surroundings, in public space, was converted into a means to a personal end, with the resulting danger.

The fact that the drivers of collective forms of transport displayed antisocial inclinations on the streets of Buenos Aires is well known. They drove at a speed inconceivable in the middle of traffic, placing the life of passersby at risk. However, according to Martínez Estrada, accidents were less the result of the clumsiness or temerity of drivers than of the lack of attention paid by pedestrians. While drivers had to contend with the eventualities of traffic and anticipate the movement of bodies, pedestrians disassociated themselves from the traffic system. Their lack of attention was the fundamental cause of their perdition. It was the foreign machine against the worker: "I think that the driver's skill and the pedestrian's anger obey a subconscious—or an ancestral and collective I—of fencers or bullfighters. The pleasure of escaping unharmed in each move confirms the worker's belief that the machine's attack is utterly useless gringo fury against him."[49]

The argument that the car is an inconvenience is an old one. Martínez Estrada alleges in *Radiografía de la Pampa* (X-ray of the Pampa) that using the car is a problem, especially in rural areas, because it does not resolve transportation conflicts. Again it is the image of the car adapted to ostentation: roads for tourism and not for heavy traffic. The capital finds its expression in machines as tools adjusted to "mechanical and not organic reality, multiplier and not creator, material and not spiritual." For Martínez Estrada, it is the arrival of a system of destruction underlying its apparent rationality, because Argentina lacked solid social support against the invasion of foreign machinery.

Martínez Estrada expands the analysis of the meaning of the automobile in *La cabeza de Goliat* (Goliath's head), in which he examines a variety of urban spaces, such as railway stations, schools, monuments, streets, cemeteries, and tailors' shops. His displeasure is all too evident when he points out that the car is the principal machine transporting people in the port city, because he believes that we are witnessing an irreversible reality. The use of that prestigious mechanical being displaced the horse and contributed to the loss of respect and love for the past. Although Martínez Estrada observes without compassion the brutal treatment that deliverymen inflict on their beasts of burden, it is because "the former fondness for the horse had been wholly transferred to the car." However, both the car and the horse represent, for the Argentine essayist, a form of display: the Spaniard, who considered it beneath him to set foot on miserable Creole lands, projected his former equestrian pride on the automobile. Therefore, just like riding horseback—which was superior to walking—he rode in a car for the same unconscious reasons.

In the past, as today, car makes and models boast of the owner's social status. Whoever went down the street in a luxurious car displayed his economic well-being, because the auto served as a symbol of distinction. Martínez Estrada politicizes the denunciation of the brand of prestige: it reveals the cozy ties between the proprietor and those in power. The official license plate took on special significance in Latin America, because "contact with those cars tended to be prophetic because they are loaded with *manna*." Such administrative heraldry translated into prerogatives and immunity and fueled all sorts of power imagery, derived from the possibility of abusing the assigned functions. In short, for Martínez Estrada the use of the car represents a return to the primitive. Even the cultivated man, once at the wheel, becomes a rude being because of the power he holds over the life and death of the passerby.

Beside the control of the motorized vehicle emerged "a dark side of resentment and coarseness." The car was equivalent to the thermometer of the ancestral, unleashing pulsations of rage. Léon Bloy took this argument to an extreme: he imagined a voluntary intention of running over his fellow man with the car. The opposite of the cardinal virtues of humility, prudence, and charity proposed to Christians. Such a male fantasy of hurtling the car into an unprotected crowd unable to move was not uncommon in big cities; it was a reminder of the automobile's deadly potential. It was the bull that entered the ring ridden by another beast with a human face.

The pleasure of unleashing a machine against pedestrians predates the car. Whenever the possibility existed of expressing social difference against the defenseless, some snobs always took advantage of the opportunity. In mid-nineteenth-century Rio de Janeiro, a city renowned for its excesses in speed, men were on display in their carriages cutting a swift path among plebeians on foot. Slaves or blacks elevated to the status of coachmen, crowned with a top hat, careening at breakneck speeds, also became overbearing toward pedestrians and passersby.[50]

The car intensified the tendency to proclaim oneself superior to the pedestrian. Chroniclers are clear on this point. Leopoldo Thévenin, a well-known Uruguayan physician who wrote accounts documenting customs under the pseudonym Monsieur Perrichon at the start of the twentieth century, in his brief article "Automóviles" mocks the fact that it never would have occurred to him that regulations longer than Lent would be necessary to avoid street traffic victims. The solution seems simple to the good doctor. The idea of going slowly and making people remember that cars were on the street had to be inculcated in the minds of chauffeurs. In matters of cars, Thévenin was radical: "The pedestrian and the car are, for me, two completely unequal forces. Given the machine's power, man does not exist. I never forget this."[51]

However, many did forget. Rubén Darío wrote from Paris that in the attempt to suppress space and time, the "runaway homicidal contraption" continued to consume the poor devils of pedestrians who had the misfortune to be in the street or on a royal road. In the case of the "super-chauffeur, the poor wretch who had the bad luck to be flattened by the car did not matter at all." However, in sum, this fearful driver was at the same time a victim of the horrible violence of business:

> The super-chauffeur is the representative of human energy and the omnipotence of industry and capital: the poor wretch who happens to stand in his path! It turns out that he too, the super-chauffeur, crashed the person into a tree trunk or into a ravine. Everything is perfect. The boss needs his factory to triumph, that industrial power increase, that Moloch eat his Spanish omelette, and to eat a tortilla, you have to break the eggs. . . . The human being has never been less charming; it has never been a wild beast. And the same with cars, with wireless telegraph, with the cinema, with the omnipotence of the machine in industry and gold in everything.[52]

Cartoons from the first decades of the twentieth century offer a picture of people being run over by cars and other car-related deaths with the appearance of the automobile. There was virtually no difference between pedestrians and chickens: they were both miserably run over. Representations of accidents in newspapers and magazines in Rio de Janeiro were routine. There are cartoonists such as K. Lixto, J. Carlos, Julião Machado, Angelo Agostini in magazines like *Fon-Fon!* and *Careta*, in newspapers such as *O País, O Malho,* and *Gazeta de Notícias.* The black humor of the cartoons deals in particular with the subject of the "poor chauffeurs" and the egoism of the owners. In one cartoon a corpse rises from beneath the car, blood spills on the ground, while the chauffeur gets out of the car exclaiming his bad luck because it is the seventh time it has happened to him that day. Similarly, the vehicle's passenger responds that he is the one with the bad luck, because it is already the tenth car he has ridden in that day and in all the others, the same thing happened.

Herman Lima offers numerous examples of political cartoons from the time that attest to the danger of this new scourge. And the subject of egoism of owners and chauffeurs given the defenseless pedestrian finds magnificent irony in a 1912 political cartoon by J. Guerreiro: a car has just run over a pedestrian. Inside the vehicle, a gentleman shouts. A woman, on the sidewalk, also laments seeing the car spattered with blood:

> Oh, what a shame, a car painted just two days ago and now [it's] all dirty . . . You have to spend so much money on a car . . .
> *The husband*: You can't go out for a ride without some fellow coming along and blocking the road.[53]

The ambivalence between the car as symbol of progress and criminality is clear in an article by Juan José Churión, "La influencia del automóvil," published in *El Cojo Ilustrado* on August 15, 1912:

> Hail, car, you who erases borders! Hail, car, coefficient of progress! Hail, hail, hail! Hail thrice to you, oh beautiful mechanical monster! Great benefactor and ally of science!
> I love you and admire you when your traction is applied to pulling heavy loads. Then you are useful, you are a harbinger of work. Thus and only in this way could I forgive you if you smashed my brain, like Curie. But that some idiots who speed after having had a few drinks, whose little birdbrains are less brilliant than mine, make me as flat as a tortilla, no. Not that.

Death was lying in wait. Or as an insurance company advertised, "Death is watching you." Highways in poor condition, carelessness, high speed, horses that bolted in front of the mechanical monster, dogs that crossed the vehicle's path, tires that blew out, brakes that failed—an ample array of factors explained accidents. There were collisions with other cars, the cart drawn by oxen, the train and highway killers that Churión disparagingly referred to as "idiots." The fact that the Civil Code imposed on the pedestrian involved in the accident, or that individual's representatives, the burden of proof of the driver's guilt did little to help diminish the number of accidents.

Chronicles recorded the way the car "made its entrance" onto the scene once it left the garage. Enrique Amorim formulated it in terms of the car that sneezed when it went out on the street because the engine was cold and it suddenly "made its entrance in the world." The period of transition was short and swift, but quickly it was integrated into action and public space. Soon the car was driving in the present continuum of movement.

The ingenious typologies in diverse chronicles reflect the flexibility of classificatory systems. Those luxury cars that awaited their lady owners outside movie theaters resembled "zealous goalkeepers." Cars were "disguised," for man's craftiness took charge of transfiguring them, placing an expensive ornament of a different brand over the radiator to deceive the gullible. The car that had just crashed, with dented fenders, front wheels bent out of shape, and cross-eyed headlights brought to mind a person who could not utter a word, a sort of stutterer in metal. There is a blink-of-an-eye transition between the impeccable and the wreck after an accident, which radically metamorphoses the object. The car that has just crashed is, for Amorim, equivalent to a normal being who is transformed into a monstrous being in a second. Other cars awaken curiosity only once in a lifetime: the day they crash into a pole.[54]

Perhaps the practice of the collective blessing of cars is related to accidents, because in the early years ambulances were blessed in the diocese of Lucca, Italy. However, the car was also inscribed in the religious sphere following the tradition that arose in praise of the train. Michel Lagrée reports that in all periods, the blessing of an object was accompanied by the selection of a patron saint, linked to its activity or its inherent risk, and therefore, a celestial protector was found for motorists.[55] The Old Testament offers the image of the prophet Elijah's chariot of fire and the New Testament, the story of the deacon Philip, who rode a chariot driven by an Ethiopian high official whom he had converted and baptized. Neither Elijah nor Philip reappears in popular imagery, however, since in 1908 the custom was introduced of placing Saint Christopher medallions in cars, the saint traditionally associated with protection from storms and accidents on voyages.[56] The emblems that adorn the rearview mirror in taxis, cars, and trucks in Brazil—religious images, ribbons of the Lord of Bomfim, and Our Lady of Aparecida, protective talismans of diverse kinds—remind us of the indirect, but powerful, importance of accidents in modern transport.

While accidents appear as an unexpected misfortune, races were the official setting for risk. Triumph in racing was still the best publicity for carmakers. The fascination with speed was combined with economic interests and with the lack of safety measures. Builders, not countries, competed against each other. French and German companies dominated the scene. But the glorification of speed left its mark on race car drivers, symbols of manhood, and also on spectators, because initially there were no means to protect the spectators, who were crowded together along the edge of dirt roads without any awareness of the potential danger. These naïve witnesses of tests of speed virtually became suicides. The first leg of the Paris-Madrid race of 1903 was for Rubén Darío a display of irrationality. Seven dead and countless injured, beyond the victims found on the roads and gutted by the "speedy and heavy iron and rubber cockroach."

Risk, especially when it came to the public, diminished with the modernization of racing circuits. However, this was not the case for the race car drivers. Engines burst. Gas tanks exploded. Brakes gave out. Dust accumulated in the air. Tires were punctured. "Macoco" Alzaga Unzué's description of the San Sebastián Race is illustrative of the dangers:

The day of the race it had rained a little and the surface was treacherously slippery. There was a straightaway that ended in a sharp curve where the car could reach up to 140 miles per hour. I was going at the maximum speed possible, which was some 110 miles per hour, considering the slippery surface; but when I approached the curve, I touched the brake and felt something strange. I looked and saw that one of those small pulleys of the brake cables had come loose. I didn't have brakes! I tried to enter the curve anyway, but the car skidded sideways. I straightened it out, but it went to the other side and hit a signpost. We were practically flying in the air. My mechanic fell on a wire fence, and they had to operate on his stomach and intestines. He lost part of his intestine. The car fell on top of me and, the gas cap, which had been in the back, cut me behind the ear, where I still have the scar.[57]

All of this justifies the severe criticism that Lewis Mumford aimed in the 1930s at the capitalist "machine" and at the car in particular, a new type of deadly locomotion, by claiming that if someone would have asked in sangfroid whether this new form of transport merited the annual sacrifice of 30,000 lives in the United States alone, not including the injured and mutilated, "the answer would have been, without doubt: No."[58]

FINAL REMARKS

Kinetic Modernity and the Automobile

The automobile heralded the advent of a new era. Karl Benz defined it as the representative of the "era of engines." The human being abandoned his position as slave to space to rise up as its master and dominator. Italian futurism in particular exalted the rupture: it glorified lordship over time and space. The Manifesto of Futurism made the racing car sublime, adorned with huge serpentlike pipes, with explosive respiration, the muse of speed and dynamism. It seemed to run like gunpowder, more beautiful than the Winged Victory of Samothrace.

It was initially perceived as a luxury item, a toy for millionaires, a symbol of distinction, power, freedom, and emotion. Much of its worship involved the hobby aspect and little had to do with work. When it passed, driven by an impeccably attired chauffeur, it served as a luxury version of the private horse-drawn carriage.

It renewed the spirit of travel. Many accounts tell the story of the first adventures by car: Otto Julius Bierbaum, *Eine empfindsame Reise im Automobil von Berlin nach Sorrento* (1903); A. B. Filson Young, *The Complete Motorist* (1904); Eugène Demolder, *L'Espagne en auto: Impressions de voyage* (1905); Winthrop Scarritt, *Three Men in a Car* (1906); Octave Mirbeau, *La 628-E8* (with illustrations by Pierre Bonnard, 1908); Carlo Placci, *In automobile* (1908); Edith Wharton, *A Motor-Flight through France* (1909); Henry James, *Italian Hours* (1909); Harriet White Fisher, *A Woman's World Tour in a Motor Car* (1911); Paul Konody, *Through the Alps to the Apennines* (1911); Effie Gladding, *Across the Continent by the Lincoln Highway* (1915); Beatrice Massey, *It Might Have Been Worse: A Motor Trip from Coast to Coast* (1920). Typical of this feeling of the expansion of the kinetic experience is Octave Mirbeau's warning to readers in *La 628-E8*, when he states that the car trip through France, Belgium, The Netherlands, and Germany was also a bit of a journey through his own persona. So great was his gratitude to "la merveilleuse automobile" that he dedicated the account of the trip to Fernand Charron, a car builder.

The horse was placed in counterpoint to the train. Advertising especially showcased the car's advantages. Instead of traditional pursuit of the train by bandits on horseback, advertising emphasized the "horsepower" of the automobile and the freedom it offered from schedules. It was the "machine in the country," which, unlike the train, permitted intimate contact with nature at the same time it offered the advantages of modern transport.

European in origin, the automobile became popularized in the United States, where it was accused of promoting immorality, causing accidents, keeping people away from church, and inciting them to break the law. However, its triumph was overwhelming. It represented mobility and the epic poetry of the road, if not individual freedom itself. It was celebrated in music, literature, film, and painting. It was associated with the hero, the inventor, the millionaire, the gangster, the young man, the salesman, the beatnik, and most of all with sexuality. Black men were identified with their enormous automobiles, to the extent that the possibility was discussed that the peculiar history of dispossession and material privation inclined American black men to make disproportionate investments in particular forms of ownership and status that were publicly visible.[1] The Nick Gomez film *New Jersey Drive*, through the subject of stealing cars, denounces racial conflicts between black adolescents from Newark and the predominantly white police force.

The automobile contributed to the development of characteristics that became blurred with the "American way of life": individualism, pragmatism, consumerism, comfort, and a blend of high and low culture. A marked emphasis was placed on private property and on the effort of the machine more than that of the body. To be modern, a car was a necessity.

From the United States, it spread throughout the world, proclaiming the victory of Fordism, motorization, and kinetic modernity. At the end of the 1920s, Mexican writer Salvador Novo captured this change perfectly: "But in Europe they had a lamentable notion of industry and mechanics! Cars were almost solemn; each piece was expensive and they didn't even know how to put *huaraches* [rubber-soled sandals] on wheels. What's more, chauffeurs were slow, uniformed, and they bowed as they opened the doors. That's why Henry Ford was born, and he flooded the streets of the universe with ants."[2]

The automobile crossed the first half of the twentieth century in multiple forms. It was referred to in many ways: "mechanical saurian," "magical beast," "fabulous unicorn," "house on wheels," "epileptic machine." An extremely wide panorama of cultural production embraced it as an object of reference and examined its environments, people, languages, and symbols. It was portrayed from diverse angles: moral, family, individual, psychological, political, legal, and economic. It was an outstanding element in capitalism and socialism, in Fascism and in Nazism, with its specific characteristics in each sociopolitical context. A modern political system was inconceivable without the project of the massive distribution of the car. Russian poet Mayakovsky came to write a film script, "Benz number 22," of which only a passage from the prologue has survived, in which he regards the automobile as a revolutionary protagonist. In this prologue, the car begins at a distant point, when it was dominated by omnibuses, streetcars, and wagons, and it begins to grow until it occupies the entire canvas.

This trust in motorization was a unifying element of diverse modern projects, although it never came to hide profound political divergences. In the 1930s, for example, it was common to establish differences in relation to the national technological approach: technocratic mechanization of American liberal democracy, the forced technical advance of the Soviet collectivist system, Germanic romantic spiritualism, and French rationalism. The car in Latin America was a symbol of distinction: an "automobile-jewel," a sort of luxury item of clothing or calling card. It was not necessary to possess the creamy green Rolls-Royce of Jay Gatsby to transmit the image of a winner. It did not even aspire to imitate the Canadian model, which set out to sell, to a consumer with high purchasing power, a more elaborate version of the American original. The irony in Latin America during the first decades of the twentieth century was the arrival of the popular American car, with the characteristics of European distinction.

There were, of course, significant differences between brands. After all was said and done, the fetish of the brand mattered. Oswald de Andrade's Cadillac was not the same as Alfredo Mario Ferreiro's poetic Ford. In Argentina and Brazil, thousands of Ford Model Ts were sold in the 1920s and 1930s, as synthesized in the magazine *El Hogar* in 1933: "Today the democracy of the car has changed the concept, and if it is true that it still remains a sign of elegance, things are acquiring the tone that gives them resonance. Who today doesn't have a car? Who today doesn't drive a car?"[3]

Literature with political aspirations perceived in the car a material expression of social inequalities. There was nothing of the great equalizer. A book like *Parque industrial*, by Mara Lobo, mentions the car to criticize the socioeconomic disparity between capitalists and the proletariat.[4] Each time the text refers to the automobile, it is to censure the exploitation of the proletariat by the bourgeoisie. On the other hand, the memoirs and chronicles tend to record shifts in the family and urban context. Érico Veríssimo incorporated the car into the field of biography when he recalled that his father bought a Ford Model T and decided to take the whole family out on a terrifying ride through the city. When Cecília Meireles commented that the car formed part of the family and was loved as if a living being, she pointed to the democratizing element of technology. The extension of the technological object into everyday life and the feminine world is what marks the transition from male pioneering and the luxury apparatus to the horizon of utility and enjoyment, independent of technological knowledge.

A trained animal was ranked equally with a humanized machine that obeyed the driver's will. However, the vehicle could be a nightmare. It depended on the driver, who did not always manage to control the mobile object, which seemed to possess a sort of "metallic manna" and was capable of producing legitimate forms of schizophrenia at high speed (a fundamentally male neurosis, the obsession for the car and speed). Even the most noble of Englishmen could turn into a monster under the car's command. For others, the speed experience could only be compared to a mystical experience. In any event, the words of Dettelbach continue to be valid: "Behind the wheel of a car, every man is like Gulliver, seemingly stronger, more powerful, and more capable of success than his non-motorized or less mobile brothers."[5]

And then there were accidents. Violent deaths. The fascination for the automobile could only in part be explained by its utility. The double capacity to render service and inflict damage without doubt contributed to making it an awe-inspiring figure. Although the identification of the car with a loyal servant predominated (for some people it was more obsequious and powerful than Aladdin's genie), it inspired terror. More than true and false, the car was useful and potentially threatening.

The car was a private object that affected public space. Consequently it was an ongoing source of polemics. The reactions to automobility varied from the most fervent enthusiasm to skepticism and severe criticism. More in thought than in practice, questioning the utility of the automobile was common. And there were those individuals who resisted experimenting with the new technology less from a fear of innovation than from insecurity or from fear of fully participating in an experience in which they did not trust. However, it was not a matter of ignorance. The car circulated showily and noisily through a public urban space still unsuited to travel on four wheels. Not even the blind and deaf could ignore it. Automobiles were insolent. Their owners were arrogant. Chauffeurs were haughty.

It was a mass-produced product reproduced mechanically that conferred on consumers the illusion of individualization. In addition to "my kingdom for a car," it was a matter of my machine and I. My totem. An object of worship, understood according to the meaning of Roland Barthes when referring to the new Citroën: "the best messenger of a world above that of nature: one can easily see in an object at once a perfection and an absence of origin, a closure and a brilliance, a transformation of life into matter (matter is much more magical than life), and in a word a *silence* which belongs to the realm of fairy-tales."[6] To bring to mind the magical dimension of objects, it is enough to recall the scene from Clara Law's movie, *The Goddess of 1967*, in which the young Japanese man weeps when he gets into the French Citroën manufactured in the 1950s (the "goddess") that he had set off on a quest to buy in Australia.

The automobile clearly expressed the function of fashion: to distance and to approach. It functioned as a consumption of signs and as a daily practice of hierarchies. Therefore, symbolic rivalries, feelings of self-confidence or shame, connections with sexuality, expectations, and fantasies persisted in its materiality.

Like the purloined letter in the story by Edgar Allan Poe, today the automobile appears in excess and tends to fade from awareness. Julio Cortázar expresses that obviousness literally in "Las babas del diablo" (The devil's drool): "I would have liked to know what the man in the gray hat seated at the wheel of the car on the pier that leads to the walkway was thinking, and who was reading the newspaper or sleeping. I had just discovered him, for the people in a stopped car almost disappear, lost in that wretched cage deprived of the beauty stemming from movement and danger. And yet, the car had been there all the time, forming part (or deforming that part) of the island. A car: like saying a streetlight, a park bench."[7] Despite its massive presence, it never reached the extreme of becoming a "neutral" object, like the household telephone.

Despite the evident risks and perverse effects of proliferation, kinetic modernity intensified its promise of freedom of movement. Hundreds of weekly magazines and advertising flyers, TV ads, glamorous halls, world championships, rallies, toy cars, prototype cars—moved by hydrogen, ecological, silent, with sensor systems and electronic commands—stolen cars, armored cars, car bombs, old cars, zero-mile cars, and 800 million used cars, many in pieces, if not rusted out. Cars everywhere, in front and behind, ever proclaiming the grandeur and misery of kinetic modernity.

NOTES

Preface

1. See Ruth Schwartz Cowan, *A Social History of American Technology* (New York: Oxford University Press, 1997).

2. See Claude Fischer, *America Calling: A Social History of the Telephone to 1940* (Berkeley and Los Angeles: University of California Press, 1992).

3. R. Kline and T. Pinch, "Users as Agents of Technological Change: The Social Construction of the Automobile in the Rural United States," *Technology and Culture*, 37, no. 4 (October 1996): 763–795.

4. Mentioned by Paul Virilio, *The Aesthetics of Disappearance,* trans. Philip Beitchman (Los Angeles: Semiotext, 2009).

5. Eric Hobsbawm, *The Age of Extremes: A History of the World, 1914–1991* (New York: Pantheon, 1994).

6. See Peter Sloterdijk, *Eurotaoismus: Zur Kritik der politischen Kinetik* (Frankfurt: Suhrkamp, 1989).

7. Ibid., 42.

8. Jean Baudrillard, *Passwords*, trans. Chris Turner (London, New York: Verso, 2003).

9. J. Schnapp, "Two Drivers," unpublished, 1997.

10. Karl Benz, *Lebensfahrt eines deutschen Erfinders: Meine Erinnerungen* (Munich: Kochler and Amelang, 2001), 105.

11. Alfred P. Sloan, *My Years with General Motors* (New York: Doubleday, 1990), xvii.

12. See Norbert Elias, *The Civilizing Process: Sociogenetic and Psychogenetic Investigations,* trans. Edmund Jephcott (Oxford: Blackwell, 2000).

13. The phenomenon of shrinking contrasts worldwide, together with the increase in local variety, was studied in the 1930s by Norbert Elias in his classic *The Civilizing Process.* Elias points out the progressive reduction of contrasts thanks to the processes of interpenetration and mixing. Processes of interpenetration would be responsible for the reorganization of power relations, generating a new unit with a peculiar character in non-European countries, but one in which the values of Western civilization were clearly imposed. In the course of resignifications, in Marc Augé's opinion, the superhighway became a privileged example of a "non-place." Superhighways for Augé are a manifestation of the solitude typical of "super-modernity." They express the triumph of mobile homes and uprootedness, the freedom of the traveler, the overabundance of happenings, the excess of space,

and the individualization of the references. See Augé, *Non-places: Introduction to an Anthropology of Supermodernity*, trans. John Howe (London: Verso, 1995).

14. See Pauline Garvey, "Driving, Drinking and Daring in Norway," in Daniel Miller (ed.), *Car Cultures* (Oxford: Berg, 2001).

15. Igor Kopytoff, "The Cultural Biography of Things: Commoditization as Process," in Arjun Appadurai (ed.), *The Social Life of Things: Commodities in Cultural Perspective* (Cambridge: Cambridge University Press, 1986).

16. Ibid., 67.

17. Fredric Jameson, *Postmodernism, or, The Cultural Logic of Late Capitalism* (Durham: Duke University Press, 1991), 36.

18. Jorge J. Okubaro, *O automóvel, um condenado?* (São Paulo: Senac, 2001).

19. See Daniel Miller, ed., *Car Cultures* (Oxford: Berg, 2001).

20. See John Urry, *Sociology beyond Societies: Mobilities for the Twenty-first Century* (London: Routledge, 2000); and idem, "Inhabiting the Car," in *Collective Imagination: Limits and Beyond* (Rio de Janeiro: UNESCO, 2001).

21. Urry, *Sociology beyond Societies*, 57–58.

22. The bibliography about the automobile is immense in the United States and considerable in Europe. In Latin America, the bibliography relating to the cultural dimension of the automobile is minimal. Granted its transnational features, there has been research into the presence and function of the automobile in different cultures. See Attilio Brilli, *La vita che corre: Mitologia dell'automobile* (Bologna: Il Mulino, 1999); Ronald Primeau, *Romance of the Road: The Literature of the American Highway* (Bowling Green: Bowling Green State University, 1997); Gerald Silk, *Automobile and Culture* (New York: Abrams, 1984). Of interest for the cultural effects of the automobile in Latin America are the studies on "peripherical automobility"; see Donald F. Davis, "Dependent Motorization: Canada and the Automobile to the 1930s," *Journal of Canadian Studies* 21 (Fall 1986): 106–136; B. A. Brownell, "A Symbol of Modernity: Attitudes toward the Automobile in Southern Cities in the 1920s," *American Quarterly* 24(March 1972): 20–44; Miller, *Car Cultures*.

23. Renato Ortiz defines "international popular memory" as the creation of globalized cultural references inside a consumer society. Its people, images, and situations, driven by advertising, comic books, television, and movies, are in the lower reaches of this memory, common to all. The international popular memory, according to Ortiz, functions as a communication system that guarantees the intelligibility of the message, distinct from the domestic memory comprising the language, the school, and the state; see Renato Ortiz, *Mundialização e cultura* (São Paulo: Brasiliense, 1994), 126.

1. Henry Ford: From Popular Inventor to Legend

1. *Jornal do Brasil* (October 18, 1931).

2. See Walter Burkert, *Mito e mitologia*, trans. Maria Helena da Rocha Pereira

(Lisbon: Edições 70, 1991); Antonio Gramsci, *Maquiavel, a política e o estado moderno*, trans. Carlos Coutinho (Rio de Janeiro: Civilização Brasileira, 1989).

3. See Umberto Eco, *Apocalípticos e integrados*, trans. Andrés Boglar (Barcelona: Lumen, 1981).

4. Siegfried Giedion, *Modernization Takes Command: A Contribution to Anonymous History* (New York: Oxford University Press, 1955), 116.

5. Witold Rybczynski, "The Ceaseless Machina," in *Our Times* (Atlanta: Turner Publishing, 1995), 80.

6. See David Harvey, *The Condition of Postmodernity: An Enquiry into the Origins of Cultural Change* (Cambridge: Blackwell, 2000).

7. Quoted in David Hounshell, *From the American System to Mass Production, 1800–1932: The Development of Manufacturing Technology in the United States* (Baltimore: Johns Hopkins University Press, 1985), 217.

8. Ibid., 252.

9. Keith Sward, *The Legend of Henry Ford* (New York: Atheneum, 1972).

10. Quoted in David Lewis, *The Public Image of Henry Ford: An American Folk Hero and His Company* (Detroit: Wayne State University Press, 1976), 214.

11. Quoted in Allan Nevins and Frank Ernest Hill, *Ford: Expansion and Challenge, 1915–1933* (New York: Charles Scribner's Sons, 1957), 600.

12. J. Flink, *The Car Culture* (Cambridge: MIT Press, 1975), 68.

13. Ibid., 73.

14. Thomas Hughes, *American Genesis: A Century of Invention and Technological Enthusiasm* (New York: Penguin, 1989).

15. Susan Buck-Morss, *Dreamworld and Catastrophe: The Passing of Mass Utopia in East and West* (Cambridge: MIT Press, 2000), 105.

16. Richard Stites, *Revolutionary Dreams: Utopian Vision and Experimental Life in the Russian Revolution* (New York: Oxford University Press, 1989), 148.

17. Quoted in ibid., 149.

18. *Argentina, Periódico de Arte y Crítica* 1, no. 1 (November 1930).

19. Sloan, *My Years with General Motors*, 1.

20. Ibid., 162–163.

21. Ibid., 163.

22. Henry Ford, *My Life and Work* (New York: Garden City Publishing, 1922), 2.

23. Ibid., 120.

24. Ibid., 212.

25. Ibid., 249.

26. Ibid., 10.

27. Jean Baudrillard, *The System of Objects*, trans. James Benedict (London, New York: Verso, 2005).

28. Ford, *My Life and Work*, 27–28.

29. See Ortiz, *Mundialização e cultura*.

30. Rudi Volti, "A Century of Automobility," *Society for the History of Technology* 37, no. 4 (1996): 663–685.

31. Ford, *My Life and Work*, 90.
32. Ibid., 113.
33. Sloan, *My Years with General Motors*, 163.
34. Ford, *My Life and Work*, 33.
35. Ibid., 153.
36. Ibid., 192.

2. Fordism and Cultural Circulation

1. C. P. Russell, "The Pneumatic Hegira," in George Mowry (ed.), *The Twenties: Fords, Flappers & Fanatics* (Englewood Cliffs: Prentice-Hall, 1965), 53.
2. David Lewis and Laurence Goldstein (eds.), *The Automobile and American Culture* (Ann Arbor: University of Michigan Press, 1983), 224.
3. See Nevins and Hill, *Ford: Expansion and Challenge*.
4. See Frank E. Hill and Mira Wilkins, *American Business Abroad: Ford on Six Continents* (Detroit: Wayne State University Press, 1964).
5. Quoted in John Skirius, *El ensayo hispanoamericano del siglo XX* (Mexico City: Fondo de Cultura Económica, 1994), 229.
6. Mário de Andrade, "Manuel Bandeira," *Revista do Brasil* 9, no. 107 (November 1924): 217.
7. Edgar Cavalheiro, *Monteiro Lobato*, 2 vols. (São Paulo: Brasiliense, 1962), I: 205 and 290.
8. Monteiro Lobato, *Revista do Brasil* (1926): 348–349.
9. Henry Ford, *Minha vida e minha obra*, trans. Monteiro Lobato (São Paulo: Companhia Editora Nacional, 1926), viii.
10. Cavalheiro, *Monteiro Lobato*, I: 292.
11. Ibid., 293.
12. Ibid., 296.
13. Hill and Wilkins, *American Business Abroad*, 149.
14. William L. Stidger, *Henry Ford: The Man and His Motives* (New York: George H. Doran, [c1923]).
15. Quoted in David E. Nye, *American Technological Sublime* (Cambridge: MIT Press, 1999), 131.
16. See Nevins and Hill, *Ford: Expansion and Challenge*.
17. Quoted in ibid., 288.
18. José María Delgado, *Por las tres Américas* (Montevideo: N.p., 1928), 83.
19. Ibid.
20. Barbara Haskell, *The American Century: Art & Culture 1900–1950* (New York: W. W. Norton, 1999), 154.
21. Mary Jane Jacob, "The Rouge in 1927: Photographs and Paintings by Charles Sheeler," in Linda Downs and M. J. Jacob (eds.), *The Rouge: The Image of Industry in the Art of Charles Sheeler and Diego Rivera* (Detroit: Detroit Institute of Arts, 1978).

22. See Andrea Kettenmann, *Frida Kahlo* (Cologne: Taschen, 1994).

23. See Linda Downs, "The Rouge in 1932: The *Detroit Industry* Frescoes by Diego Rivera," in Linda Downs and Mary Jane Jacob (eds.), *The Rouge: The Image of Industry in the Art of Charles Sheeler and Diego Rivera* (Detroit: Detroit Institute of Arts, 1978).

24. See Andrea Kettenmann, *Diego Rivera* (Cologne: Taschen, 1997); Downs, "The Rouge in 1932."

25. See Downs and Jacob (eds.), *The Rouge.*

26. See Michel Foucault, *Discipline and Punish: The Birth of the Prison,* trans. Alan Sheridan (New York: Vintage Books, 1977).

27. Charles Madison, "My Seven Years of Automotive Servitude," in David Lewis and Laurence Goldstein (eds.), *The Automobile and American Culture* (Ann Arbor: University of Michigan Press, 1983), 18.

28. Quoted in Flink, *The Car Culture,* 103–104.

29. Louis-Ferdinand Céline, *Journey to the End of the Night,* trans. Ralph Manheim (New York: New Directions, 1983), 193–194.

30. Ibid., 194.

31. See Jerome Meckier, "Debunking Our Ford: *My Life and Work* and *Brave New World,*" *South Atlantic Quarterly* 78 (1979): 448–459.

32. Theodor Adorno, *Prisms,* trans. Samuel and Shierry Weber (Cambridge: MIT Press, 1981), 114.

33. Miguel de Castro Vicente, *Historia del automóvil: Enciclopedia del automóvil* (Barcelona: Ediciones CEAC, 1990), 730.

34. In *Unsafe at Any Speed* (New York: Grossman, 1965), Ralph Nader dynamites the glorious image of the American automotive industry, especially General Motors.

35. Edward T. Hall, *The Hidden Dimension* (New York: Anchor Books, 1990), 175.

36. Marshall McLuhan, *Understanding Media: The Extensions of Man* (Boston: MIT Press, 1994), 221.

37. See Baudrillard, *The System of Objects.*

38. See Henri Lefebvre, *Everyday Life in the Modern World,* trans. Sacha Rabinovitch (London: Allen Lane, 1971), 77.

39. Harvey, *The Condition of Postmodernity,* 139.

40. Quoted in Roger N. Casey, *Textual Vehicles: The Automobile in American Literature* (New York: Garland Publishing, 1997), 25.

41. John Dos Passos, *U.S.A.* (London: Penguin, 1988), 774.

42. Ibid., 775.

43. Quoted in Hounshell, *From the American System,* 321.

44. Italo Calvino, *Numbers in the Dark: And Other Stories,* trans. Tim Parks (New York: Pantheon Books), 1995.

45. See Casey, *Textual Vehicles*; Jean-François Bayart, *The Illusion of Cultural Identity,* trans. Steven Rendall (Chicago: University of Chicago Press, 2005).

3. The Transnational Object

1. Mario Morasso, *La nuova arma: La macchina* (Turin: Bocca, 1905), 61; Silk, *Automobile and Culture*, 66.

2. Vergniaud Calazans Gonçalves, *A primeira corrida na América do Sul* (São Paulo: Empresa das Artes, 1988), 24.

3. Ibid., 31.

4. Clara Stinnes, *En auto a través de los continentes* (Barcelona: Juventud, 1930), 229.

5. John Reynolds, *André Citroën: The Man and the Motor Cars* (New York: St. Martin's Press, 1997), 63.

6. Diana Young, "The Life and Death of Cars: Private Vehicles on the Pitjantjatara Lands, South Australia," in Daniel Miller (ed.), *Car Cultures* (Oxford: Berg, 2001), 52.

7. Miguel Ángel Asturias, "Navidad: La derrota de los soldados de plomo," *Billetes de París* (January 7, 1927).

8. Ilya Ehrenburg, *The Life of the Automobile*, trans. J. Neugroschel (London: Pluto Press, 1985), 130.

9. Ibid., 23.

10. Ibid., 129.

11. See Reynolds, *André Citroën*, 63.

12. Ibid., 102.

13. Haardt and Audoin Dubreuil, *The Black Journey*, 22.

14. Ibid., 28

15. Ibid., 364

16. See James Clifford, *The Predicament of Culture: Twentieth-century Ethnography, Literature and Art* (Cambridge: Harvard University Press, 1988).

17. Gonçalves, *A primeira corrida*, 41.

18. Quoted in ibid., 38.

19. See Álvaro Casal Tatlock, *El automóvil en América del Sur. Orígenes, Argentina, Brasil, Paraguay, Uruguay* (Montevideo: Ediciones de la Banda Oriental, 1996).

20. Raúl García Heras, *Automotores norteamericanos, caminos y modernización urbana en la Argentina, 1918–1939* (Buenos Aires: Libros de Hispanoamérica, 1985), 11.

21. Ibid., 16.

22. Raúl García Heras, *Transportes, negocios y política: La compañía Anglo Argentina de Tranvías, 1876–1981* (Buenos Aires: Sudamericana, 1994), 55, 128.

23. Quoted in Anahí Ballent, "La 'cruzada por la obra caminera': Estado, política y sociedad en la obra pública de los años treinta," *Jornadas del Programa de Historia de las Relaciones entre Estado, Economía y Sociedad en Argentina* (Bernal: Universidad Nacional de Quilmes, 2000), 4.

24. Anahí Ballent and Adrián Gorelik, "País urbano o país rural: La modernización territorial y su crisis," in Alejandro Cattaruzza (ed.), *Nueva historia argentina*, vol. 7 (Buenos Aires: Sudamericana, 2000), 157–159.

25. Ibid., 162.

26. See Ballent, "La 'cruzada por la obra caminera.'"

27. See Gonzalo Aguilar, "El uso vanguardista de la tecnología en *Martín Fierro* y la *Revista de Antropofagia*," in M. A. Pereira and E. L. Reis (orgs.), *Literatura e estudos culturais* (Belo Horizonte: Faculdade de Letras–UFMG, 2000), 159–174.

28. Jorge Luis Borges, "Otra vez la metáfora," in *El idioma de los argentinos* (Buenos Aires: Manuel Gleizer, 1928), 55.

29. See Kevin Heterington, "Second Handedness: Consumption, Disposal and Absent Presence," unpublished, 2002.

30. Roberto Arlt, *Obras. Tomo II. Aguafuertes* (Buenos Aires: Losada, 1998), 251 ("El paraíso de los inventores," January 28, 1931).

31. Ibid.

32. Quoted in Gonçalves, *A primeira corrida*, 14.

33. Paulo Barreto (João do Rio), *Vida vertiginosa* (Rio de Janeiro: Garnier, 1911).

34. Quoted in *Automóveis de São Paulo: Memória fotográfica de pessoas, automóveis e localidades do Estado de São Paulo* (São Paulo: State Archives, 2002), 125.

35. Oswald de Andrade, *Pau-Brasil*, 1925.

36. Mário de Andrade, "Louvação da tarde," in *Poesias completas* (Belo Horizonte: Itatiaia, 1987).

37. Antonio Candido, *O discurso e a cidade* (São Paulo: Duas Cidades, 1993), 257.

38. Ibid., 277.

39. Mário de Andrade, *Amar, verbo intransitivo: Idílio* (Belo Horizonte: Itatiaia, 1982), 118.

40. J. C. Barros Rodrigues, *O automóvel em Portugal* (Lisbon: CTT Correios de Portugal, 1995), 26.

41. Álvaro Casal Tatlock, *El automóvil en Uruguay: Los años heroicos 1900–1930* (Montevideo: Ediciones de la Banda Oriental, 1981), 62.

42. See Linda Hutcheon, *A Theory of Parody: The Teachings of Twentieth-Century Art Forms* (New York: Routledge, 1991).

43. Jorge Luis Borges, *Textos recobrados: 1919–1929* (Barcelona: Emecé, 1997), 321.

44. Quoted in Pablo Rocca, "Alfredo Mario Ferreiro: Un poeta a toda máquina" (*El País Cultural*, Montevideo, November 21, 1997).

45. See Guillermo Zapiola, "El cine mudo en Uruguay," in Héctor García Mesa (coord.), *Cine latinoamericano: 1896–1930* (Caracas: Consejo Nacional de la Cultura, 1992).

46. See Ramón Giovanni, *Carros: El automóvil en Colombia* (Bogotá: Villegas Editores, 1995).

47. Ibid.

48. Quoted in Edgar Vásquez Benítez, *Historia de Cali en el siglo 20: Sociedad, economía, cultura y espacio* (Cali: Universidad del Valle, 2001), 178.

49. Guillermo José Schael, *Apuntes para la historia: El automóvil en Venezuela* (Caracas: Gráficas Edición de Arte, 1969), 17.

50. Ibid., 31.

51. Ibid.

52. Nicanor Navarro, *Margarita bajo ruedas* (Mérida: Universidad de los Andes, 1995), 85.

53. See Abigail Aguirre, "A Cultural History of American Cars in Cuba," MA thesis, Reed College, 2001.

54. Louis A. Pérez, *On Becoming Cuban: Identity, Nationality and Culture* (New York: Ecco Press, 1999), 336.

55. Ibid., 320.

56. Rubén Martínez Villena, "En automóvil," in Alberto Garrandés (ed.), *Aire de luz: Cuentos cubanos del siglo XX* (Havana: Letras Cubanas, 2004), 626.

57. Pérez, *On Becoming Cuban*, 341.

58. Ibid., 340.

59. See Emilio Huyke, *Historia de la transportación en Puerto Rico* (San Juan: Editorial Cordillera, 1973).

60. Ibid., 76.

61. Quoted in Merlin H. Forster, *Los contemporáneos 1920–1932: Perfil de un experimento vanguardista mexicano*, Colección Studium, no. 46 (Mexico City: Ediciones de Andrea, 1964), 101.

62. Moisés Viñas, *Historia del cine mexicano* (Mexico City: Universidad Nacional de México, 1987), 57.

63. Ibid., 58.

64. Quoted in Aurelio Reyes, "El cine en México," in García Mesa, *Cine latinoamericano*, 258.

4. Contradictions of Mobility

1. See Warren J. Belasco, *Americans on the Road: From Autocamp to Motel, 1910–1945* (Baltimore: Johns Hopkins University Press, 1997).

2. See Nancy West, *Kodak and the Lens of Nostalgia* (Charlottesville: University Press of Virginia, 2000).

3. Malcolm Cowley, *Exile's Return: A Literary Odyssey of the 1920's* (New York: Viking Press, 1951), 213.

4. Felipe Arocena, *De Quilmes a Hyde Park: Las fronteras culturales en la vida y la obra de W. H. Hudson* (Montevideo: Ediciones de la Banda Oriental, 2000), 109.

5. Urry, *Sociology beyond Societies*, 51

6. Hans Ulrich Gumbrecht, *In 1926: Living at the Edge of Time* (Cambridge: Harvard University Press, 1997), 27–29.

7. John Wain, *Motopolis: Les ouvriers de la MG. Oxford 1919–1939. Un cruset intellectuel ou les métamorphoses d'une génération* (Paris: Autrement, 1991), 159–176.

8. See Gilberto Freyre, *Tempo de aprendiz*, 2 vols. (São Paulo: IBRASA, 1979).

9. Casal Tatlock, *El automóvil en América del Sur*, 86.

10. Skirius, *El ensayo hispanoamericano del siglo XX*, 157.

11. Ibid., 97.

12. Casal Tatlock, *El automóvil en el Uruguay*, 17.

13. See Juan Carlos Ghiano, "Los grotescos de Armando Discépolo," in Armando Discépolo, *Tres grotescos* (Buenos Aires: Losange, 1958).

14. Armando Discépolo, *Tres grotescos* (Buenos Aires: Losange, 1958), 34.

15. Ibid., 32.

16. José Bento Monteiro Lobato, *América* (São Paulo: Editora Brasiliense, 1957), 68–69.

17. See Maurice Maeterlinck, "In an Automobile," *The Double Garden* (New York: Dodd, Mead, 1926).

18. See Virilio, *Estética de la desaparición*; Jeffrey Schnapp, "Crash: Uma antropologia da velocidade ou por que ocorrem acidentes ao longo da estrada de Damasco," *Lugar Comum*, no. 8 (1999): 21–61.

19. Gilberto Freyre, *Sobrados e mucambos*, 2 vols. (Rio de Janeiro: José Olympio, 1985), I:535.

20. See Schnapp, "Crash: Uma antropologia."

21. Gilberto Freyre, *Pessoas, coisas & animais* (Porto Alegre: Globo, 1981), 392.

22. Stephen Kern, *The Culture of Time and Space, 1880–1918* (Cambridge: Harvard University Press, 1983), 130.

23. See Rubén Darío, *Parisiana* (Madrid: Mundo Latino, 1907).

24. Spanish cited in Herschel B. Chipp, *Teorías del arte contemporáneo: Fuentes artísticas y opiniones críticas*, trans. Julio Rodríguez Puértolas (Madrid: Akal, 1995), 309; English from Web site: http://www.italianfuturism.org/manifestos/foundingmanifesto/. English translation copyright ©1973 Thames and Hudson Ltd, London.

25. Silk, *Automobile and Culture*, 58.

26. Marie Holzer, "Das Automobil," *Die Aktion* 2, no. 34 (August 21, 1912): 1072–1073.

27. See Alberto Hidalgo, *Panoplia lírica* (Lima: Imprenta Víctor Fajardo, 1917).

28. Paul Virilio, *Un paisaje de acontecimientos*, trans. Marcos Mayer (Buenos Aires: Paidós, 1997), 89.

29. See Davis, "Dependent Motorization."

30. Cited in Michel Lagrée, *Religião e tecnologia: A benção de Prometeu*, trans. Viviane Ribeiro (Bauru: Edusc, 2002), 325.

31. Vicente Huidobro, "HP," in *Arctic Poems*, trans. Ian Barnett, consulted at Web site: http://www.saltana.org/1/inv/arctic_poems.pdf .

32. Renato Almeida, *Velocidade* (Rio de Janeiro: Schmidt, 1932), 52.

33. Paul Morand, "De la vitesse," *Papiers d'Identité* (Paris: Grasset, 1931), 279.

34. Ezequiel Martínez Estrada, *La cabeza de Goliat: Microscopía de Buenos Aires* (Buenos Aires: Nova, 1957), 34.

35. Morasso, *La nuova arma*, 185.

36. Martin Heidegger, *Sein und Zeit* (Tübingen: Niemeyer, 1986), 78; Gumbrecht, *In 1926*, 26.

37. Walter Benjamin, *Discursos interrumpidos*, vol. I, trans. J. Aguirre (Buenos Aires: Taurus, 1989), 169.

38. Urry, *Sociology beyond Societies*, 83.

39. Marcel Proust, *Contre Sainte-Beuve* (Paris: Gallimard, 1994), 73–75.

40. See Georges Poulet, *O espaço proustiano*, trans. Ana Luiza Costa (Rio de Janeiro: Imago, 1992).

41. Ramón Gómez de la Serna, *Ismos* (Buenos Aires: Posición, 1943), 82.

42. Rafael Cansinos Assens, *El Movimiento V. P.* (Madrid: Hiparión, 1978), 22.

43. Kern, *The Culture of Time and Space*, 115.

44. See Jorge Schwartz, *Las vanguardias latinoamericanas: Textos programáticos y críticos* (Madrid: Cátedra, 1991).

45. Beatriz Sarlo, *Una modernidad periférica: Buenos Aires 1920 y 1930* (Buenos Aires: Nueva Visión, 1999), 57; Alan Pauls, "Arlt: La máquina literaria," in Saul Sosnowski (org.), *Lectura crítica de la literatura americana: Vanguardias y tomas de posesión* (Caracas: Ayacucho, 1997), 243.

46. See Mário de Andrade, *Macunaíma,* trans. E. A. Goodland (New York: Random House, 1984), 75.

47. See Mário de Andrade, *Macunaíma,* chap. 14, in *Obra escogida: Novela-ensayo-epistolario* (Caracas: Biblioteca Ayacucho, 1979).

48. Malcolm Forest, *Automóveis de São Paulo: Memória fotográfica de pessoas, automóveis e localidades do Estado de São Paulo* (São Paulo: Arquivo do Estado, 2002), 177.

49. Lagrée, *Religião e tecnologia*, 332.

5. Mechanical Actors

1. See David Lewis and Bill Rauhauser, *The Car and the Camera: The Detroit School of Automotive Photography* (Detroit: The Detroit Institute of Arts, 1996).

2. See Julian Smith, "A Runaway Match: The Automobile in the American Film, 1900–1920," in David Lewis and Laurence Goldstein (eds.), *The Automobile and American Culture* (Ann Arbor: University of Michigan Press, 1983).

3. Jesse Rainsford Sprague, "Confessions of a Ford Dealer," in George Mowry (ed.), *The Twenties: Fords, Flappers & Fanatics* (Englewood Cliffs: Prentice-Hall, 1965), 27.

4. See Fischer, *America Calling*.

5. William Ashdown, "Confessions of an Automobilist," cited in George Mowry

(ed.), *The Twenties: Fords, Flappers & Fanatics* (Englewood Cliffs: Prentice-Hall, 1965), 50.

6. Miguel Ángel Asturias, chronicle of September 10, 1929, in *París 1924–1933: Periodismo y creación literaria* (Paris: ALLCA-UNESCO, 1993).

7. César Vallejo, *Crónicas. Tomo 1: 1915–1926* (Mexico City: Universidad Nacional Autónoma de México, 1984), 398.

8. Asturias, *París 1924–1933*, 48.

9. Reynolds, *André Citroën*, 76.

10. Alberto Lasplaces, *El hombre que tuvo una idea (cuentos)* (Montevideo: La Cruz del Sur, 1927), 128.

11. See Baudrillard, *Passwords*.

12. Casal Tatlock, *El automóvil en el Uruguay*, 36.

13. Cited in Lagrée, *Religião e tecnologia*, 324–328.

14. Cited in Schael, *Apuntes para la historia*, 110.

15. See David Gartman, "Postmodernism; or, The Cultural Logic of Post-Fordism?" *Sociological Quarterly* 39, no. 1 (1998): 119–137.

16. See Fischer, *America Calling*.

17. See Beth L. Bailey, *From Front Porch to Back Seat: Courtship in Twentieth-century America* (Baltimore: Johns Hopkins University Press, 1989).

18. See Morand, "De la vitesse."

19. Lewis and Goldstein, *The Automobile and American Culture*, 124.

20. Brilli, *La vita che corre*, 54.

21. Silk, *Automobile and Culture*, 68.

22. See Sidonie Smith, *Moving Lives: Twentieth-century Women's Travel Writing* (Minneapolis: University of Minnesota Press, 2001).

23. Virginia Scharff, *Taking the Wheel: Women and the Coming of the Motor Age* (New York: The Free Press, 1991), 89.

24. See Brilli, *La vita che corre*.

25. Martínez Estrada, *La cabeza de Goliat*, 42.

26. P. Barreto, *Vida vertiginosa*, 11.

27. Orna Messer Levin, *As figurações do dândi: Um estudo sobre a obra de João do Rio* (São Paulo: Editora da Unicamp, 1996), 144.

28. See Paulo Barreto (João do Rio), *Alma encantadora das ruas* (Rio de Janeiro: Garnier, 1908), 42.

29. Flora Süssekind, "O cronista & o secreta amador," in Paulo Barreto (João do Rio), *A profissão de Jacques Pedreira* (São Paulo: Scipione, 1992), xxvii; also see Schnapp, "Crash: Uma antropología."

30. Paulo Barreto (João do Rio), *A profissão de Jacques Pedreira* (São Paulo: Scipione, 1992), 44.

31. Afonso Henrique de Lima Barreto, *Um e outro: Clara dos Anjos* (Rio de Janeiro: Mérito, 1948), 263.

32. See Nicolau Sevcenko, *Literatura como missão: Tensões sociais e criação cultural na Primeira República* (São Paulo: Brasiliense, 1983).

33. L. Barreto, *Um e outro*, 256.

34. Horacio Quiroga, *Todos los cuentos* (Madrid: Scipione Cultural, 1997), 1045.

35. Vallejo, *Crónicas*, 397.

36. Cited in Elias Thomé Saliba, "A dimensão cômica da vida privada na república," *História da vida privada no Brasil. República: Da Belle Époque à era do rádio* (São Paulo: Companhia das Letras, 1998), 334.

37. See Gilles Néret, *Lempicka* (Cologne: Taschen, 1999).

38. Sherrie Inness, "On the Road and in the Air: Gender and Technology in Girls' Automobile and Airplane Serials, 1909–1932," *Journal of Popular Culture* 30 (Fall 1996): 47.

39. Karen Alkalay-Gut, "Sex and the Single Engine: E. E. Cummings' Experience in Metaphoric Equation," *Journal of Modern Literature* 20 (1996): 254.

40. Forest, *Automóveis de São Paulo*, 117.

41. Ibid.

42. Benz, *Lebensfahrt eines deutschen Erfinders*, 64.

43. Mário da Silva Brito, *História do modernismo brasileiro*. Vol. I, *Antecedentes da Semana de Arte Moderna* (São Paulo: Saraiva, 1958), 24.

44. Georges Duhamel, *Scènes de la vie future* (Paris: Mercure de France, 1930), 98.

45. Ibid., 96.

46. See Philippe Roger, *L'Ennemi américaine: Généalogie de l'antinorteaméricanisme français* (Paris: Éditions du Seuil, 2002).

47. Ibid., 481–490.

48. See Gertrude Stein, *Everybody's Autobiography* (New York: Random House, 1937).

49. Martínez Estrada, *La cabeza de Goliat*, 36.

50. Freyre, *Sobrados e mucambos*, vol. II.

51. Leopoldo Thévenin, "Automóviles," in Pablo Rocca (comp.), *De la Patria Vieja al Centenario: La vida social y las costumbres* (Montevideo: Ediciones de la Banda Oriental, 1992), 52.

52. Darío, *Parisiana*, 178–179.

53. Cited in Herman Lima, *História da caricatura no Brasil* (Rio de Janeiro: J. Olympio Editora, 1963), 455.

54. Enrique Amorim, *Buenos Aires y sus aspectos* (Buenos Aires: Galerna, 1967), 61–65.

55. Lagrée, *Religião e tecnologia*, 323.

56. Ibid.

57. Cited in Casal Tatlock, *El automóvil en América del Sur*, 54.

58. Lewis Mumford, *Technics and Civilization* (New York: Harcourt, Brace & World, 1963 [1934]), 237.

Final Remarks: Kinetic Modernity and the Automobile

1. Paul Gilroy, "Driving while Back," in Daniel Miller (ed.), *Car Cultures* (Oxford: Berg, 2001), 84.

2. Salvador Novo, "El joven," *La Novela Mexicana* 1, no. 2 (1928): 6.

3. Cited in Ballent, "La 'cruzada por la obra caminera,'" 5.

4. See Mara Lobo (Patrícia Galvão), *Parque industrial* (São Paulo: Alternativa, n.d.).

5. Cynthia G. Dettelbach, *In the Driver's Seat: The Automobile in American Literature and Popular Culture* (Westport: Greenwood Press, 1976), 6.

6. Roland Barthes, *Mythologies*, trans. A. Lavers (New York: Hill and Wang, 1980), 88.

7. Julio Cortázar, "Las babas del diablo," in *Las armas secretas* (Buenos Aires: Sudamericana, 1976), 87.

BIBLIOGRAPHY

Adair, Daryl. "Spectacles of Speed and Endurance: The Formative Years of Motor Racing in Europe." In *The Motor Car and Popular Culture in the 20th Century*, edited by Tim Claydon et al. Aldershot: Ashgate, 1998.

Adorno, Theodor. *Prismas: La crítica de la cultura y la sociedad*. Translated by Manuel Sacristán. Barcelona: Ariel, 1962.

———. *Prisms*. Translated by Samuel and Shierry Weber. Cambridge: MIT Press, 1981.

Aguilar, Gonzalo. "El uso vanguardista de la tecnología en *Martín Fierro* y la *Revista de Antropofagia*." In *Literatura e estudos culturais*, organized by M. A. Pereira and E. L. Reis, 159–174. Belo Horizonte: Faculdade de Letras–UFMG, 2000.

Aguirre, Abigail. "A Cultural History of American Cars in Cuba." MA thesis, Reed College, 2001.

Alkalay-Gut, Karen. "Sex and the Single Engine: E. E. Cummings' Experiment in Metaphoric Equation." *Journal of Modern Literature* 20 (1996): 254–258.

Allen, F. R. "The Automobile." In *Technology and Social Change*, edited by F. R. Allen et al., 107–132 New York: Appleton-Century Crofts, 1957.

Almeida, Renato. *Velocidade*. Rio de Janeiro: Schmidt, 1932.

Amorim, Enrique. *Buenos Aires y sus aspectos*. Buenos Aires: Galerna, 1967.

Andrade, Mário de. *Amar, verbo intransitivo: Idílio*. Belo Horizonte: Itatiaia, 1982.

———. *A escrava que não é Isaura: Discurso sobre algumas tendências da poesia modernista*. São Paulo: N.p., 1925.

———. "Louvação da tarde." *Poesias completas*. Belo Horizonte: Itatiaia, 1987.

———. *Macunaíma: O herói sem nenhum caráter*. Madrid: ALLCA, 1997.

———. *Macunaíma*. Translated by E. A. Goodland. New York: Random House, 1984.

———. "Manuel Bandeira." *Revista do Brasil* 9, no. 107 (November 1924): 214–224.

———. *Obra escogida: Novela-cuento-ensayo-epistolario*. Caracas: Biblioteca Ayacucho, 1979.

Appadurai, Arjun, ed. *The Social Life of Things*. Cambridge: Cambridge University Press, 1986.

Aragon, Louis. *Le paysan de Paris*. Paris: Gallimard, 1953.

Araújo, Rosa Maria Barboza de. *A vocação do prazer: A cidade e a família no Rio de Janeiro republicano*. Rio de Janeiro: Rocco, 1993.

Arlt, Roberto. *Obras.* Vol. II: *Aguafuertes.* Buenos Aires: Losada, 1998.

———. *Los siete locos: Los lanzallamas.* Madrid: ALLCA, 2000.

Arnold, H. L., and F. L. Faurote. *Ford Methods and the Ford Shops.* New York: Engineering Magazine Company, 1915.

Arocena, Felipe. *De Quilmes a Hyde Park: Las fronteras culturales en la vida y la obra de W. H. Hudson.* Montevideo: Ediciones de la Banda Oriental, 2000.

Ashdown, William. "Confessions of an Automobilist." In *The Twenties: Fords, Flappers & Fanatics,* edited by George Mowry. Englewood Cliffs: Prentice-Hall, 1965.

Asturias, Miguel Ángel. *París 1924–1933: Periodismo y creación literaria.* Paris: ALLCA-UNESCO, 1993.

Augé, Marc. *Los "no lugares": Una antropología de la sobremodernidad.* Translated by M. Mizraji. Barcelona: Gedisa, 1996.

———. *Non-places: Introduction to an Anthropology of Supermodernity.* Translated by John Howe. London: Verso, 1995.

Automóveis de São Paulo: Memória fotográfica de pessoas, automóveis e localidades do Estado de São Paulo. São Paulo: State Archives, 2002.

Bailey, Beth L. *From Front Porch to Back Seat: Courtship in Twentieth-century America.* Baltimore: Johns Hopkins University Press, 1989.

Ballard, J. G. "Project for a Glossary of the Twentieth Century." In *Zone 6, Incorporations,* edited by Jonathon Crary and Sanford Kwinter. New York: Urzone, 1992.

———. "Proyecto para un glosario del siglo XX." In *Incorporaciones,* edited by Jonathan Crary and Sanford Kwinter, translated by José Casas. Madrid: Cátedra, 1996.

Ballent, Anahí. "La 'casa para todos': Grandeza y miseria de la vivienda masiva." In *Historia de la vida privada en la Argentina,* edited by F. Devoto and M. Madero. Vol. 3. Buenos Aires: Taurus, 1999.

———. "La 'cruzada por la obra caminera': Estado, política y sociedad en la obra pública de los años treinta." *Jornadas del Programa de Historia de las Relaciones entre Estado, Economía y Sociedad en Argentina.* Bernal: Universidad Nacional de Quilmes, 2000.

———, and Adrián Gorelik. "País urbano o país rural: La modernización territorial y su crisis." In *Nueva historia argentina,* edited by A. Cattaruzza. Vol. 7. Buenos Aires: Sudamericana, 2000.

Barreto, Afonso Henrique de Lima. *Um e outro: Clara dos Anjos.* Rio de Janeiro: Mérito, 1948.

Barreto, Paulo [João do Rio, pseud.]. *Alma encantadora das ruas.* Rio de Janeiro: Garnier, 1908.

———. "Modern girls." In *João do Rio: Uma antologia,* edited by Luís Martins. Rio de Janeiro: Sabiá, 1987.

———. *A profissão de Jacques Pedreira.* São Paulo: Scipione, 1992.

———. *Vida vertiginosa.* Rio de Janeiro: Garnier, 1911.

Barros Rodrigues, J. C. *O automóvel em Portugal*. Lisbon: CTT Correios de Portugal, 1995.

Barthes, Roland. *Mythologies*. Translated by A. Lavers. New York: Hill and Wang, 1980.

Baudrillard, Jean. *Passwords*. Translated by Chris Turner. London: Verso, 2003.

———. *O sistema dos objetos*. Translated by Zulmira Ribeiro Tavares. São Paulo: Perspectiva, 1989.

——— *The System of Objects*. Translated by James Benedict. London: Verso, 2005.

———. *Senhas*. Translated by Maria Helena Künher. Rio de Janeiro: Bertrand Brasil, 2001.

Bayart, Jean-François. *L'illusion identitaire*. Paris: Fayard, 1996.

———. *The Illusion of Cultural Identity*. Translated by Steven Rendall. Chicago: University of Chicago Press, 2005.

Belasco, Warren J. *Americans on the Road: From Autocamp to Motel, 1910–1945*. Baltimore: Johns Hopkins University Press, 1997.

Benjamin, Walter. *Discursos interrumpidos*. Vol. 1. Translated by J. Aguirre. Buenos Aires: Taurus, 1989.

Bentham, Jeremy. *O Panóptico*. Translated by Tomaz T. da Silva. Belo Horizonte: Autêntica, 2000.

Benz, Karl. *Lebensfahrt eines deutschen Erfinders: Meine Erinnerungen*. Munich: Koehler and Amelang, 2001.

Borges, Jorge Luis. *El idioma de los argentinos*. Buenos Aires: Manuel Gleizer, 1928.

———. *Textos recobrados: 1919–1929*. Barcelona: Emecé, 1997.

Brilli, Attilio. *La vita che corre: Mitologia dell' automobile*. Bologna: Il Mulino, 1999.

Brito, Mário da Silva. *História do modernismo brasileiro*. Vol. 1: *Antecedentes da Semana de Arte Moderna*. São Paulo: Saraiva, 1958.

Brownell, B. A. "A Symbol of Modernity: Attitudes toward the Automobile in Southern Cities in the 1920s." *American Quarterly* 24 (March 1972): 20–44.

Buck-Morss, Susan. *Dreamworld and Catastrophe: The Passing of Mass Utopia in East and West*. Cambridge: MIT Press, 2000.

Burkert, Walter. *Mito e mitologia*. Translated by Maria Helena da Rocha Pereira. Lisbon: Edições 70, 1991.

Calvino, Italo. *Henry Ford: Um general na biblioteca*. Translated by Rosa Freire D'Aguiar. São Paulo: Companhia das Letras, 2001.

———. *Numbers in the Dark: And Other Stories*. Translated by Tim Parks. New York: Pantheon Books, 1995.

Candido, Antonio. *O discurso e a cidade*. São Paulo: Duas Cidades, 1993.

Cansinos Assens, Rafael. *El Movimiento V. P.* Madrid: Hiperión, 1978.

Carlos, J. *O Rio de J. Carlos*. Organized by Cássio Loredano, text by Zuenir Ventura Rio de Janeiro: Lacerda, 1998.

Carpentier, Alejo. "Problemática del tiempo y del idioma en la moderna novela latinoamericana." In *Lectura crítica de la literatura americana*, compiled by Saúl Sosnowski. Caracas: Biblioteca Ayacucho, 1997.

Carvalho, Ronald de. *Itinerário: Antilhas, Estados Unidos, México*. São Paulo: Companhia Editora Nacional, 1935.

Casal Tatlock, Álvaro. *El automóvil en América del Sur. Orígenes, Argentina, Brasil, Paraguay, Uruguay*. Montevideo: Ediciones de la Banda Oriental, 1996.

———. *El automóvil en el Uruguay: Los años heróicos 1900–1930*. Montevideo: Ediciones de la Banda Oriental, 1981.

Casey, Roger N. *Textual Vehicles: The Automobile in American Literature*. New York: Garland Publishing, 1997.

Castro Vicente, Miguel de. *Historia del automóvil: Enciclopedia del automóvil*. Barcelona: Ediciones CEAC, 1990.

Cavalheiro, Edgard. *Monteiro Lobato*. 2 vols. São Paulo: Brasiliense, 1962.

Céline, Louis-Ferdinand. *Journey to the End of the Night*. Translated by Ralph Manheim. New York: New Directions, 1983.

———. *Viagem ao fim da noite*. Translated by Rosa Freire D'Aguiar. São Paulo: Companhia das Letras, 1995.

Chipp, Herschel B. *Teorías del arte contemporáneo: Fuentes artísticas y opiniones críticas*. Translated by Julio Rodríguez Puértolas. Madrid: Akal, 1995.

Claridge, Laura. *Tamara de Lempicka: A Life of Deco and Decadence*. New York: Clarkson Potter, 1999.

Clifford, James. *A experiência etnográfica: Antropologia e literatura no século XX*. Translated by Patrícia Farias. Rio de Janeiro: Universidade Federal do Rio de Janeiro, 1998.

———. *The Predicament of Culture: Twentieth-century Ethnography, Literature and Art*. Cambridge: Harvard University Press, 1988.

———. *Routes: Travel and Translation in the Late Twentieth Century*. Cambridge: Harvard University Press, 1997.

Cortázar, Julio. "Las babas del diablo." *Las armas secretas*. Buenos Aires: Sudamericana, 1976.

Courteville, M. Roger. *La première traversée de l'Amérique du Sud en automobile, de Rio de Janeiro a La Paz et Lima*. Paris: Plon, 1930.

Cowan, Ruth Schwartz. *A Social History of American Technology*. New York: Oxford University Press, 1997.

Cowley, Malcolm. *Exile's Return: A Literary Odyssey of the 1920's*. New York: Viking Press, 1951.

Crary, Jonathan, and Sanford Kwinter. "Project for a Glossary of the Twentieth Century." In *Zone 6, Incorporations*, edited by Jonathan Crary and Sanford Kwinter. New York: Urzone 1992.

Cummings, E. E. *Complete Poems, 1913–1962*. New York: Harcourt, 1980.

Darío, Rubén. *Parisiana*. Madrid: Mundo Latino, 1907.

Davis, Donald F. "Dependent Motorization: Canada and the Automobile to the 1930s." *Journal of Canadian Studies* 21 (Fall 1986): 106–136.

Deleuze, Gilles. *Crítica y clínica*. Translated by Thomas Kauf. Barcelona: Anagrama, 1996.

Delgado, José María. *Por las tres Américas*. Montevideo: N.p., 1928.

Dettelbach, Cynthia G. *In the Driver's Seat: The Automobile in American Literature and Popular Culture*. Westport: Greenwood Press, 1976.

Discépolo, Armando. *Tres grotescos*. Buenos Aires: Losange, 1958.

Doctorow, E. L. *Ragtime*. New York: Random House, 1975.

Dos Passos, John. *U.S.A.* London: Penguin, 1988.

Downs, Linda. "The Rouge in 1932: The *Detroit Industry* Frescoes by Diego Rivera." In *The Rouge: The Image of Industry in the Art of Charles Sheeler and Diego Rivera*, edited by Linda Downs and Mary Jane Jacob. Detroit: Detroit Institute of Arts, 1978.

———, and Mary Jane Jacob, eds. *The Rouge: The Image of Industry in the Art of Charles Sheeler and Diego Rivera*. Detroit: Detroit Institute of Arts, 1978.

Duhamel, Georges. *Scènes de la vie future*. Paris: Mercure de France, 1930.

Eco, Umberto. *Apocalípticos e integrados*. Translated by Andrés Boglar. Barcelona: Lumen, 1981.

Ehrenburg, Ilya. *The Life of the Automobile*. Translated by Joachim Neugroschel. London: Pluto Press, 1985.

Elias, Norbert. *El proceso de la civilización: Investigaciones sociogenéticas y psicogenéticas*. Translated by Ramón García Cotarelo. Mexico City: Fondo de Cultura Económica, 1987.

———. *The Civilizing Process: Sociogenetic and Psychogenetic Investigations*. Translated by Edmund Jephcott. Oxford: Blackwell, 2000.

Eulalio, Alexandre. *A aventura brasileira de Blaise Cendrars*. São Paulo: Editora da Universidade de São Paulo, 2001.

Fabris, Annateresa. *Futurismo: Uma poética da modernidade*. São Paulo: Perspectiva, 1987.

———. *O futurismo paulista: Hipóteses para o estudo da chegada da vanguarda ao Brasil*. São Paulo: Perspectiva, 1994.

Fernández Christlieb, Federico. *Las modernas ruedas de la destrucción: El automóvil en la Ciudad de México*. Mexico City: Ediciones El Caballito, 1992.

Fernández Flórez, Wenceslao. *O homem que comprou um automóvel*. Translated by A. Ogando. Porto: Livraria Civilização, n.d.

Ferreiro, Alfredo Mario. *El hombre que se comió un autobús: Poemas con olor a nafta*. Edited, with prologue and notes, by Pablo Rocca. Montevideo: Ediciones de la Banda Oriental, 1998.

Fischer, Claude. *America Calling: A Social History of the Telephone to 1940*. Berkeley and Los Angeles: University of California Press, 1992.

Flink, J. *The Automobile Age*. Cambridge: MIT Press, 1988.

———. *The Car Culture*. Cambridge: MIT Press, 1975.

Ford, Henry. *My Life and Work*. New York: Garden City Publishing, 1922.

———. *Minha vida e minha obra*. Translated by Monteiro Lobato. São Paulo: Companhia Editora Nacional, 1926.

Forest, Malcolm. *Automóveis de São Paulo: Memória fotográfica de pessoas, automóveis e localidades do Estado de São Paulo*. São Paulo: Arquivo do Estado, 2002.

Forster, Merlin H. *Los contemporáneos 1920–1932: Perfil de un experimento vanguardista mexicano*. Mexico City: Ediciones de Andrea, 1964.

Foucault, Michel. *Discipline and Punish: The Birth of the Prison*. Translated by Alan Sheridan. New York: Vintage Books, 1977.

———. *Vigiar e punir: Nascimento da prisão*. Translated by Lígia M. Pondé Vassallo. Petrópolis: Vozes, 1991.

Freyre, Gilberto. *Pessoas, coisas & animais*. Porto Alegre: Globo, 1981.

———. *Sobrados e mucambos*. 2 vols. Rio de Janeiro: José Olympio, 1985.

———. *Tempo de aprendiz*. 2 vols. São Paulo: IBRASA, 1979.

Frugoni, Emilio. *La epopeya de la ciudad*. Montevideo: Maximino García, 1927.

———. *Poemas montevideanos*. Montevideo: Maximino García, 1923.

Galvão, Patrícia. *See* Lobo, Mara.

García Heras, Raúl. *Automotores norteamericanos, caminos y modernización urbana en la Argentina, 1918–1939*. Buenos Aires: Libros de Hispanoamérica, 1985.

———. *Transportes, negocios y política: La compañía Anglo Argentina de Tranvías, 1876–1981*. Buenos Aires: Sudamericana, 1994.

García Mesa, Héctor, coord. *Cine latinoamericano: 1896–1930*. Caracas: Consejo Nacional de la Cultura, 1992.

Gartman, David. "Postmodernism; or, the Cultural Logic of Post-Fordism?" *Sociological Quarterly* 39, no. 1 (1998): 119–137.

Garvey, Pauline. "Driving, Drinking and Daring in Norway." In *Car Cultures*, edited by Daniel Miller. Oxford: Berg, 2001.

Ghiano, Juan Carlos. "Los grotescos de Armando Discépolo." In *Tres grotescos*, by Armando Discépolo. Buenos Aires: Losange, 1958.

Giedion, Siegfried. *Mechanization Takes Command: A Contribution to Anonymous History*. New York: Oxford University Press, 1955.

Gilroy, Paul. "Driving while Black." In *Car Cultures*, edited by Daniel Miller. Oxford: Berg, 2001.

Giovanni, Ramón. *Carros: El automóvil en Colombia*. Bogotá: Villegas Editores, 1995.

Gómez de la Serna, Ramón. *Ismos*. Buenos Aires: Poseidón, 1943.

Gonçalves, Vergniaud Calazans. *Automóvel no Brasil 1893–1966*. São Paulo: Editora do Automóvel, 1966.

———. *A primeira corrida na América do Sul*. São Paulo: Empresa das Artes, 1988.

González Casanova, Manuel. "Crónica del cine silente en México." In *Cine latinoamericano: 1896–1930*, coordinated by Héctor García Mesa. Caracas: Consejo Nacional de la Cultura, 1992.

Gorelik, Adrián. "Peregrinazioni del moderno: Antonio Vilar e la rete di stazioni di servizio in Argentina, 1938–1943." *Casabella* 65 (2001): 695–696.

Gounet, Thomas. *Fordismo e Toyotismo na civilização do automóvel*. Translated by Bernardo Joffily. São Paulo: Boitempo, 1999.

Gramsci, Antonio. *Maquiavel, a política e o estado moderno*. Translated by Carlos Coutinho. Rio de Janeiro: Civilização Brasileira, 1989.

Gumbrecht, Hans Ulrich. *In 1926: Living at the Edge of Time*. Cambridge: Harvard University Press, 1997.

Haardt, Georges-Marie, and Louis Audouin-Dubreuil. *The Black Journey: Across Central Africa with the Citroen Expedition*. New York: Cosmopolitan Book Corporation, 1927.

———. *A través del Continente Negro: Expedición Citroën al centro de África*. Translated by A. Bom. Barcelona: Ediciones Iberia, 1929.

Hall, Edward T. *La dimensión oculta*. Translated by Félix Blanco. Mexico City: Siglo XXI, 1972.

———. *The Hidden Dimension*. New York: Anchor Books, 1990. (Originally published in 1966 by Doubleday.)

Harvey, David. *A condição pós-moderna*. Translated by Adail Sobral. São Paulo: Loyola, 1993.

———. *The Condition of Postmodernity: An Enquiry into the Origins of Cultural Change*. Cambridge: Blackwell, 2000.

Haskell, Barbara. *The American Century: Art & Culture 1900–1950*. New York: W. W. Norton, 1999.

Heidegger, Martin. *Sein und Zeit*. Tübingen: Niemeyer, 1986.

Herf, Jeffrey. *Reactionary Modernism: Technology, Culture, and Politics in Weimar and the Third Reich*. Cambridge: Cambridge University Press, 1984.

Herrera, Hayden. *Frida: Una biografía de Frida Kahlo*. Mexico City: Diana, 1988.

Heterington, Kevin. *New Age Travellers: Vanloads of Uproarious Humanity*. London: Cassel, 2000.

———. "Second Handedness: Consumption, Disposal and Absent Presence." Unpublished, 2002.

Hidalgo, Alberto. *Panoplia lírica*. Lima: Imprenta Víctor Fajardo, 1917.

Hill, Frank E., and Mira Wilkins. *American Business Abroad: Ford on Six Continents*. Detroit: Wayne State University Press, 1964.

Hobsbawm, Eric. *The Age of Extremes: A History of the World, 1914–1991*. New York: Pantheon, 1994.

———. *Historia del siglo xx, 1914–1991*. Translated by J. Faci. Barcelona: Grijalbo, 1998.

Holzer, Marie. "Das Automobil." *Die Aktion* 2, no. 34 (August 21, 1912): 1072–1073.

Hönscheidt, Walter, and Uwe Scheid. *Wheels and Curves: Erotic Photographs of the Twenties.* Translated by Roger Warner. Cologne: Taschen, 1994.

Hounshell, David. *From the American System to Mass Production, 1800–1932: The Development of Manufacturing Technology in the United States.* Baltimore: Johns Hopkins University Press, 1985.

Hughes, Thomas P. *American Genesis: A Century of Invention and Technological Enthusiasm.* New York: Penguin, 1989.

Huidobro, Vicente. "HP." In *Arctic Poems.* Translated by Ian Barnett; http://www .saltana.org/1/inv/arctic_poems.pdf .

———. *Obras completas.* Santiago: Zig-Zag, 1964.

Hutcheon, Linda. *A Theory of Parody: The Teachings of Twentieth-century Art Forms.* New York: Routledge, 1991.

Huxley, Aldous. *Brave New World.* Stockholm: Zephyr Books, 1944.

Huyke, Emilio E. *Historia de la transportación en Puerto Rico.* San Juan, Puerto Rico: Editorial Cordillera, 1973.

Inness, Sherrie. "On the Road and in the Air: Gender and Technology in Girls' Automobile and Airplane Serials, 1909–1932." *Journal of Popular Culture* 30 (Fall 1996): 47–60.

Jacob, Mary Jane. "The Rouge in 1927: Photographs and Paintings by Charles Sheeler." In *The Rouge: The Image of Industry in the Art of Charles Sheeler and Diego Rivera,* edited by Linda Downs and Mary Jane Jacob. Detroit: Detroit Institute of Arts, 1978.

Jameson, Fredric. *Postmodernism, or, the Cultural Logic of Late Capitalism.* Durham: Duke University Press, 1991.

Kern, Stephen. *The Culture of Time and Space, 1880–1918.* Cambridge: Harvard University Press, 1983.

Kettenmann, Andrea. *Diego Rivera.* Cologne: Taschen, 1997.

———. *Frida Kahlo.* Cologne: Taschen, 1994.

Kline, R., and T. Pinch. "Users as Agents of Technological Change: The Social Construction of the Automobile in the Rural United States." *Technology and Culture* 37, no. 4 (October 1996): 763–795.

Kopytoff, Igor. "The Cultural Biography of Things: Commoditization as Process." In *The Social Life of Things,* edited by Arjun Appadurai. Cambridge: Cambridge University Press, 1986.

Lacey, Robert. *Ford, the Men, and the Machine.* Boston: Little, Brown, 1986.

Lackey, Kris. *RoadFrames: The American Highway Narrative.* Lincoln: University of Nebraska Press/Bison Books, 1999.

Lagrée, Michel. *Religião e tecnologia: A benção de Prometeu.* Translated by Viviane Ribeiro. Bauru: EDUSC, 2002.

Lasplaces, Alberto. *El hombre que tuvo una idea (cuentos).* Montevideo: La Cruz del Sur, 1927.

Lawton, Anna, and Herbert Eagle. *Russian Futurism through Its Manifestoes, 1912–1928.* Ithaca: Cornell University Press, 1980.

Leblanc, Georgette. *Mi vida con Maeterlinck.* Translated by B. L. Vidal. Madrid: Ediciones Literarias, 1931.

Le Corbusier. *Cuando las catedrales eran blancas.* Translated by Julio Payró. Buenos Aires: Poseidón, 1948.

Lee, Ou-Fan Leo. *Shanghai Modern: The Flowering of a New Urban Culture in China, 1930–1945.* Cambridge: Harvard University Press, 1999.

Lefebvre, Henri. *Everyday Life in the Modern World.* Translated by Sacha Rabinovitch. London: Allen Lane, 1971.

———. *La vida cotidiana en el mundo moderno.* Translated by Alberto Escudero. Madrid: Alianza, 1972.

Léger, Fernand. *Fonctions de la peinture.* Utrecht: Gonthier, 1965.

Lempicka, Tamara de. *Tamara de Lempicka, 1898–1980.* Cologne: Taschen, 1999.

Leonard, Jonathan Norton. *The Tragedy of Henry Ford.* New York: G. P. Putnam's Sons, 1932.

Lévi-Strauss, Claude. *Saudades do Brasil.* São Paulo: Companhia das Letras, 1994.

Levin, Orna Messer. *As figurações do dândi: Um estudo sobre a obra de João do Rio.* São Paulo: Editora da Unicamp, 1996.

Lewis, David. *The Public Image of Henry Ford: An American Folk Hero and His Company.* Detroit: Wayne State University Press, 1976.

———, and Laurence Goldstein, eds. *The Automobile and American Culture.* Ann Arbor: University of Michigan Press, 1983.

Lewis, David, and Bill Rauhauser. *The Car and the Camera: The Detroit School of Automotive Photography.* Detroit: Detroit Institute of Arts, 1996.

Lima, Herman. *História da caricatura no Brasil.* Rio de Janeiro: J. Olympio Editôra, 1963.

Lobo, Mara [Patrícia Galvão]. *Parque industrial.* São Paulo: Alternativa, n.d.

Löfgren, Orvar. "In Transit: On the Social and Cultural Organization of Mobility." Unpublished, 1996.

Luhmann, Niklas. *O amor como paixão.* Translated by Fernando Ribeiro. Lisbon: Difel, 1991.

Lynd, Robert, and Helen Merrell Lynd. *Middletown: A Study in Contemporary American Culture.* New York: Harcourt, Brace, 1929.

Madison, Charles. "My Seven Years of Automotive Servitude." In *The Automobile and American Culture,* edited by David Lewis and Laurence Goldstein. Ann Arbor: University of Michigan Press, 1983.

Maeterlinck, Maurice. "In an Automobile." *The Double Garden.* Translated by A. Y. de Mattos. New York: Dodd, Mead, 1926.

Martínez Estrada, Ezequiel. *La cabeza de Goliat: Microscopía de Buenos Aires.* Buenos Aires: Nova, 1957.

———. *Radiografía de la Pampa.* Mexico City: Consejo Nacional para la Cultura y las Artes, 1993.

Martínez Villena, Rubén. "En automóvil." In *Aire de Luz: Cuentos cubanos del siglo XX*, edited by Alberto Garrandés. Havana: Letras Cubanas, 2004.

Mathiesen, Thomas. "A sociedade espectadora: O 'Panóptico' de Michel Foucault revisitado." In *Margem 8: Tecnologia, cultura*, 77–95. São Paulo: EDUC, 1998.

McLuhan, Marshall. *Os meios de comunicação como extensões do homem*. Translated by Décio Pignatari. São Paulo: Cultrix, 1979.

———. *Understanding Media: The Extensions of Man*. Boston: MIT Press, 1994.

Meckier, Jerome. "Debunking Our Ford: *My Life and Work* and *Brave New World*." *South Atlantic Quarterly* 78 (1979): 448–459.

Meireles, Cecília. *Ilusões do mundo: Crônicas*. Rio de Janeiro: Nova Aguilar, 1976.

Miller, Daniel, ed. *Car Cultures*. Oxford: Berg, 2001.

Mirbeau, Octave. *La 628-E8*. Paris: Union Générale d'Éditions, 1977.

Monteiro Lobato, José Bento. *América*. São Paulo: Editora Brasiliense, 1957.

Moraes, Marcos Antonio de, comp. *Correspondência Mário de Andrade & Manuel Bandeira*. São Paulo: Editora da Universidade de São Paulo, 2000.

Morand, Paul. "De la vitesse." *Papiers d'Identité*. Paris: Grasset, 1931.

Morasso, Mario. *La nuova arma: La macchina*. Turin: Bocca, 1905.

Mowry, George, ed. *The Twenties: Fords, Flappers & Fanatics*. Englewood Cliffs: Prentice-Hall, 1965.

Mumford, Lewis, *Technics and Civilization*. New York: Harcourt, Brace & World, 1963. Originally published in 1934.

Nader, Ralph. *Unsafe at Any Speed: The Designed-in Dangers of the American Automobile*. New York: Grossman, 1965.

Navarro, Nicanor. *Margarita bajo ruedas*. Mérida: Universidad de los Andes, 1995.

Néret, Gilles. *Lempicka*. Cologne: Taschen, 1999.

Nevins, Allan, and Frank Ernest Hill. *Ford: Decline and Rebirth, 1933–1962*. New York: Charles Scribner's Sons, 1962.

———. *Ford: Expansion and Challenge, 1915–1933*. New York: Charles Scribner's Sons, 1957.

———. *Ford: The Times, the Man, the Company*. New York: Charles Scribner's Sons, 1954.

Novo, Salvador. "El joven." *La Novela Mexicana* 1, no. 2 (1928).

Nye, David. *American Technological Sublime*. Cambridge: MIT Press, 1999.

Okubaro, Jorge J. *O automóvel, um condenado?* São Paulo: Senac, 2001.

Orr, John. *Cinema and Modernity*. New York: Polity Press, 1993.

Ortega y Gasset, José. "La moral del automóvil en España." *Obras completas*. Vol. 4. Madrid: Alianza, 1987.

Ortiz, Renato. *Los artífices de una cultura mundializada*. Bogotá: Siglo del Hombre Editores, 1998.

———. *Mundialização e cultura*. São Paulo: Brasiliense, 1994.

Padilha, Márcia. *A cidade como espetáculo: Publicidade e vida urbana na San Pablo dos anos 20.* São Paulo: Annablume, 2001.

Pauls, Alan. "Arlt: La máquina literaria." In *Lectura crítica de la literatura Americana: Vanguardias y tomas de posesión,* compiled by Saúl Sosnowski, 241–253. Caracas: Ayacucho, 1997.

Payró, Julio. "Vlaminck, el pintor ciclista." In *Contra: La revista de los francotiradores,* edited by Sylvia Saítta, 49–52. Buenos Aires: Universidad Nacional de Quilmes, (1933) 2005.

Pellettieri, Osvaldo. "Discépolo, Armando." *Diccionario enciclopédico de las letras de América Latina.* Caracas: Biblioteca Ayacucho, 1995.

Pérez, Louis A. *On Becoming Cuban: Identity, Nationality, and Culture.* New York: Ecco Press, 1999.

Pessoa, Fernando. *Lisboa: What the Tourist Should See.* Lisbon: Horizonte, 1997.

———. *Obra poética.* Rio de Janeiro: Nova Aguilar, 1986.

Poulet, Georges. *O espaço proustiano.* Translated by Ana Luiza Costa. Rio de Janeiro: Imago, 1992.

Primeau, Ronald. *Romance of the Road: The Literature of the American Highway.* Bowling Green: Bowling Green State University Popular Press, 1997s.

Proust, Marcel. *Contre Sainte-Beuve.* Paris: Gallimard, 1994.

Quiroga, Horacio. *Todos los cuentos.* Madrid: Scipione Cultural, 1997.

Rae, John B. *El automóvil norteamericano: Historia, evolución y desarrollo.* Translated by J. Meza Nieto. Mexico City: Editorial Limusa, 1968.

———, ed. *Henry Ford.* Englewood Cliffs: Prentice-Hall, 1969.

Reyes, Aurelio. "El cine en México." In *Cine latinoamericano: 1896–1930,* coordinated by Héctor García Mesa. Caracas: Consejo Nacional de la Cultura, 1992.

Reynolds, John. *André Citroën: The Man and the Motor Cars.* New York: St. Martin's Press, 1997.

Roberts, Peter. *Automóveis da Época Áurea.* Translated by Francisco Azevedo. Rio de Janeiro: Livro Técnico, 1983.

Rocca, Pablo. "Alfredo Mario Ferreiro: Un poeta a toda máquina." *El País Cultural* (Montevideo) (November 21, 1997).

Roger, Philippe. *L'Ennemi américain: Généalogie de l'antiaméricanisme français.* Paris: Éditions du Seuil, 2002.

Rougemont, Denis de. *O amor e o Ocidente.* Translated by Paulo Brandi. Rio de Janeiro: Guanabara, 1988.

Rousell, Raymond. "La casa sobre ruedas de D. Raymond Roussel." From *Magazine of the Touring Club de France.* In *Impresiones de África,* by Raymond Roussel, translated by María Gallego. Madrid: Siruela, 1990.

Russell, C. P. "The Pneumatic Hegira." In *The Twenties: Fords, Flappers & Fanatics,* edited by George Mowry. Englewood Cliffs: Prentice-Hall, 1965.

Rybczynski, Witold. "The Ceaseless Machine." In *Our Times,* 76–80. Atlanta: Turner Publishing, 1995.

Sachs, Wolfgang. *For Love of the Automobile: Looking Back into the History of Our Desires*. Berkeley and Los Angeles: University of California Press, 1992.

Saliba, Elias Thomé. "A dimensão cômica da vida privada na república." In *História da vida privada no Brasil. República: Da Belle Époque à Era do Radio*. São Paulo: Companhia das Letras, 1998.

Sapin, Louis. "La course à la mort: Paris-Madrid Automobile." In *La Belle Époque*, by Gilbert Guilleminault. Paris: Denoël, 1958.

Sarlo, Beatriz. *La imaginación técnica: Sueños modernos de la cultura argentina*. Buenos Aires: Nueva Visión, 1997.

———. *Una modernidad periférica: Buenos Aires 1920 y 1930*. Buenos Aires: Nueva Visión, 1999.

Schael, Guillermo José. *Apuntes para la historia: El automóvil en Venezuela*. Caracas: Gráficas Edición de Arte, 1969.

Scharff, Virginia. *Taking the Wheel: Women and the Coming of the Motor Age*. New York: Free Press, 1991.

Schnapp, Jeffrey. "Crash: Uma antropologia da velocidade ou por que ocorrem acidentes ao longo da estrada de Damasco." *Lugar Comum* (Rio de Janeiro), no. 8 (1999): 21–61.

———. "Two Drivers." Unpublished, 1997.

Schneider, Luis Mario, ed. *El estridentismo: México, 1921–1927*. Mexico City: Universidad Nacional Autónoma de México, 1985.

———. *El estridentismo o una literatura de la estrategia*. Mexico City: Instituto Nacional de Bellas Artes, 1970.

Schwartz, Jorge. "Cansinos Assens y Borges: ¿Un vínculo (anti)vanguardista?" *Hispamérica*, no. 46–47 (1997): 167–177.

———. "Utopías del lenguaje: Nuestra ortografía bangwardista." In *Lectura crítica de la literatura Americana: Vanguardias y tomas de posesión*, compiled by Saúl Sosnowski, 122–146. Caracas: Ayacucho, 1997.

———. *Las vanguardias latinoamericanas: Textos programáticos y críticos*. Madrid: Cátedra, 1991.

Sebreli, Juan José. *Buenos Aires: Vida cotidiana y alienación*. Buenos Aires: Siglo XX, 1990.

Sevcenko, Nicolau. "A capital irradiante: Técnica, ritmos e ritos do Rio." *Historia da vida privada no Brasil, República: Da Belle Époque à Era do Rádio*. São Paulo: Companhia das Letras, 1998.

———. *Literatura como missão: Tensões sociais e criação cultural na Primeira República*. São Paulo: Brasiliense, 1983.

Silk, Gerald. *Automobile and Culture*. New York: Abrams, 1984.

Skirius, John. *El ensayo hispanoamericano del siglo XX*. Mexico City: Fondo de Cultura Económica, 1994.

Sloan, Alfred P. *Meus anos com a General Motors*. Translated by N. Montingelli. São Paulo: Negócio Editora, 2001.

———. *My Years with General Motors*. New York: Doubleday, 1990.

Sloterdijk, Peter. *Eurotaoismus: Zur Kritik der politischen Kinetik.* Frankfurt: Suhrkamp, 1989.

Smith, Julian. "A Runaway Match: The Automobile in the American Film, 1900–1920." In *The Automobile and American Culture,* edited by David Lewis and Laurence Goldstein. Ann Arbor: University of Michigan Press, 1983.

Smith, Sidonie. *Moving Lives: Twentieth-century Women's Travel Writing.* Minneapolis: University of Minnesota Press, 2001.

Sosnowski, Saúl, comp. *Lectura crítica de la literatura Americana: Vanguardias y tomas de posesión.* Caracas: Ayacucho, 1997.

Sprague, Jesse Rainsford. "Confessions of a Ford Dealer." In *The Twenties: Fords, Flappers & Fanatics,* edited by George Mowry. Englewood Cliffs: Prentice-Hall, 1965.

Stein, Gertrude. *Everybody's Autobiography.* New York: Random House, 1937.

Stidger, William L. *Henry Ford: The Man and His Motives.* New York: George H. Doran, [ca. 1923].

Stinnes, Clara. *En auto a través de los continentes.* Barcelona: Juventud, 1930.

Stites, Richard. *Revolutionary Dreams: Utopian Vision and Experimental Life in the Russian Revolution.* New York: Oxford University Press, 1989.

Süssekind, Flora. "O cronista & o secreta amador." In *A profissão de Jacques Pedreira,* by João do Rio. São Paulo: Scipione, 1992.

Sward, Keith. *The Legend of Henry Ford.* New York: Atheneum, 1972.

Tarkington, Booth. *The Magnificent Ambersons.* Garden City: Doubleday, 1918.

Teles, Gilberto Mendonça. *Vanguarda européia e modernismo brasileiro.* Petrópolis: Vozes, 1983.

Thévenin, Leopoldo. "Automóviles." In *De la Patria Vieja al Centenario: La vida social y las costumbres,* compiled by Pablo Rocca. Montevideo: Ediciones de la Banda Oriental, 1992.

Urry, John. "Inhabiting the Car." In *Collective Imagination: Limits and Beyond.* Rio de Janeiro: UNESCO, 2001.

———. *O olhar do turista: Lazer e viagens nas sociedades contemporâneas.* Translated by Carlos Eugênio Marcondes de Moura. São Paulo: Studio Nobel, 1996.

———. *Sociology beyond Societies: Mobilities for the Twenty-first Century.* London: Routledge, 2000.

Vallejo, César. *Crónicas. Tomo I: 1915–1926.* Mexico City: Universidad Nacional Autónoma de México, 1984.

Vásquez Benítez, Edgar. *Historia de Cali en el siglo 20: Sociedad, economía, cultura y espacio.* Cali: Universidad del Valle, 2001.

Veríssimo, Érico. *Solo de clarineta: Memórias.* Vol. 1. Porto Alegre: Editora Globo, 1973.

Videla de Rivero, Gloria. *Direcciones del vanguardismo hispanoamericano.* Pittsburgh: Instituto Internacional de Literatura Iberoamericana, 1994.

Villiers de L'isle Adam, Philippe-Auguste. *La Eva futura.* Translated by Mauricio Bacarisse. Madrid: Valdemar, 1998.

Viñas, Moisés. *Historia del cine mexicano.* Mexico City: Universidad Nacional Autónoma de México, 1987.

Virilio, Paul. *The Aesthetics of Disappearance.* Translated by Philip Beitchman. Los Angeles: Semiotext, 2009.

———. *Estética de la desaparición.* Translated by Noni Benegas. Barcelona: Anagrama, 1988.

———. *Un paisaje de acontecimientos.* Translated by Marcos Mayer. Buenos Aires: Paidós, 1997.

Volti, Rudi. "A Century of Automobility." *Society for the History of Technology* 37, no. 4 (1996): 663–685.

Wain, John. *Motopolis: Les ouvriers de la MG. Oxford 1919–1939: Un creuset intellectuel ou les métamorphoses d'une generation.* Paris: Autrement, 1991.

West, Nancy. *Kodak and the Lens of Nostalgia.* Charlottesville: University Press of Virginia, 2000.

White, Elwyn Brooks. "Farewell, My Lovely." *New Yorker* (May 5, 1936).

Wik, Reynold M. *Henry Ford and Grass-roots America.* Ann Arbor: University of Michigan Press, 1973.

Wilson, Edmund. *The American Jitters: A Year of the Slump.* New York: Charles Scribner's Sons, 1932.

Young, Diana. "The Life and Death of Cars: Private Vehicles on the Pitjantjatara Lands, South Australia." In *Car Cultures,* edited by Daniel Miller. Oxford: Berg, 2001.

Zapiola, Guillermo. "El cine mudo en Uruguay." In *Cine latinoamericano: 1896–1930,* coordinated by Héctor García Mesa. Caracas: Consejo Nacional de la Cultura, 1992.

ILLUSTRATION CREDITS

Aerial view of the River Rouge Ford factory, 1930. From David Hounshell, *From the American System to Mass Production, 1800–1932*, 269.

Automobile and sexuality. From Walter Hönscheidt and Uwe Scheid, *Wheels and Curves*, 91.

Margaret Bourke-White, *At the Time of the Louisville Flood*, 1937. From Gerald Silk, *Automobile and Culture*, 113.

J. Carlos, 1935. From *O Rio de J. Carlos*, org. Cássio Loredano, text Zuenir Ventura, Rio de Janeiro, Lacerda, 1998, 357.

Salvador Dalí, Phantoms of Two Automobiles, 1925. From Gerald Silk, *Automobile and Culture*, 116.

Tamara de Lempicka, Self-portrait (Tamara in a Green Bugatti), 1925. From *Tamara de Lempicka, 1898–1980*, Cologne, Taschen, 1999, 6.

Marcello Dudovich, Fiat Balilla, 1934. From Gerald Silk, *Automobile and Culture*, 114.

Erotic photographs of the Twenties. From Walter Hönscheidt and Uwe Scheid, *Wheels and Curves*, 67.

Walker Evans, Joe's Auto Graveyard, Pennsylvania, 1936. From Gerald Silk, *Automobile and Culture*, 112. The first cross-country automobile trip in South America, Rio de Janeiro–Lima, 1926. From M. Roger Courteville, *La Première Traversée de l'Amérique du Sud en Automobile*, 131.

INDEX

acceleration, xiv, 15, 18, 60, 66, 111, 115, 118, 122–123, 124, 132, 140. *See also* speed
Adler car, 6, 55, 56, 57
Adorno, Theodor, 41
adventure, 7, 51–75, 89, 104, 126, 128, 160, 171. *See also* road trips/expeditions
advertising, xviii, 13, 17, 29, 62, 76, 77, 80, 86, 101, 115, 143, 145, 189; and the assembly line, 23; and competition, 60; and the factory, 60–61; and forcing demand, 145; and imagination, 150; and merchandise, 142, 143; and the Model T, 100; in Portugal, 90; and propaganda, 133
Africa, xvi, 12, 57; Citroën expeditions to, 62–66, 67
Aguilar, Gonzalo, 78
airplane, xix, 65, 72, 109, 129, 135, 178; and modernization, 137
"Al volante" (Torre), 129–130
Álbum Sud-americano, 75
Alcântara Machado, Antonio de, 149
Alfa Romeo, 89
"All'Automobile da corsa" (Marinetti), 51, 177
Almeida, Renato, 118, 130
Alzaga Unzué, Martín "Macoco," 78; and the San Sebastián Race, 187
Amar, verbo intransitivo, (M. Andrade), 88–89
América (Monteiro Lobato), 26, 118
Americanism, 6, 21, 84, 181, 190; and Fordism, 35; and speed, 130
Americanization, 6, 20, 25
"Los amores monstruosos" 173, 174
Amorim, Enrique, 185–186

Andrade, Mário de, 8, 23, 84–85, 90, 138, 172
Andrade, Oswald de, 84, 191
anti-Semitism, 25; of Ford, 58
anxiety, 130, 146, 151
Anzola, Édgar, 26
Apollinaire, Guillaume, 94, 128
Aranha, Luís, 138
Arciniegas, Germán, 23, 147–148, 149
Argentina, 22, 56–57, 76, 77 78, 89, 91, 101
Arlt, Roberto, 78, 79, 138
Arnold, H. L., 21
Arocena, Felipe, 202n4
Arteaga, Cristina de, 98
Ascari, Alberto, 87
Ashdown, William, 113, 145
Asia, 68. *See also specific countries*
assembly line, xii, 3, 8, 14, 26, 27, 28, 38, 42, 49, 59, 60, 84; and Americanization, 6; critique of, 48; and cultural values, 47; description of, 23–24; and human cost, 48; and Hoover, 20; and Huxley, 40; and the Model T, 6; and semi-immobility of workers, 33; as spiritual, 29; as tourist attraction, 23; transformation of, 2. *See also* kinetic modernity; mass production
Asturias, Miguel Ángel, xviii, 58, 150, 168, 169; on luxury, 149
Audibert & Lavirotte, 142
Audouin-Dubreuil, Louis, 63, 65, 66
Augé, Marc, 195n13
Australia, 22, 58, 61, 76
auto industry, xvii, 3, 9, 13–14, 16, 35, 157; crisis in, 49; evolution of, 141–142; Ford on, 17; and Latin America,

22, 75–76; and progress, 22; transformations in, 9–10
Automobile Girls, 170
Automobile Salon (Montevideo), 92
Automobile Salon (Portugal), 90
automobile: accessibility of, 3, 17, 111; advertising of, 76–77, 143, 144, 145; aesthetic evolution of, 89, 142; age of the, 82; as anarchist, 123; as animal, 132, 139; and art, xviii; and black men, 190; blessing of, 186; and civilization, 102; and the clergy, 157; compared to the Parthenon, 44; contributions of, 72; as cult object, xiii, 41; and culture, xiii, xix, 67; and death, 185, 187; and debt, 146, 148; as destructive, 117, 122, 123; devaluation of purpose of, 43; early versions of, xiii; effects of, xi, xii, xvi, 102, 112, 127–128; and ego, xii; electric, 43; as emblem of modernization, 137, 190; and eroticism in photography, 171; external costs of, 19; fascination for, 192; and fashion, 144, 193; and freedom, 90, 102, 126, 170, 189; and gender, 160, 170; and globalization, xvii; as global figure, 61; glorification of, 122; as hero, 45; humanity of, xvii; image of, 42; and immorality, xiii, 97, 102, 128, 147, 158, 190; and individual self-representation, 101; as luxury good, 17, 104, 110, 145, 147, 157, 163, 189; as main character, 57; meaning of, 58, 182; as merchandise, 89; and national identity, 101; and nature, 82, 89, 175, 177; as necessity, 102, 145; and nostalgia, xii; as object of consumption, 2; as object of desire, 146; and obsession, 151, 192; as part of the family, 192; pop songs about, 159; and power, 183, 189; Proustian, 134; purpose of, 106; and rape, 160; and religion, 186, 190; and seduction, 162, 163, 164, 168; and sexuality, xiii, xviii, 158–160, 171–172; and smell, 134, 146; and social status, xix, 44, 89, 146, 147, 162, 169, 183; as symbol of progress and modernity,

101, 185; as symbol of wealth, 156, 162; and transformations in life, 97, 112; and uniformity, xv; and utility, xiv. *See also* literature; nature
automobilism, 20, 42, 175; Brazilian, 69, 83; diffusion of, 100; encouragement of, 89; and the press, 178; in Puerto Rico, 103
automobility, xiii, xiv, xv, xvii, xix; and the chauffeur, 161; and fashion, 144; lexicon of, 131–140; in Portugal, 89; reactions to, 192; and travel, 176, 177
automobilization, xiii, xiv
automóvil gris, El (film), 104, 105, 106, 144
"El automóvil nos reivindica," (Robreño), 102
"El automóvil," (Lasplaces), 150–154
"Automóviles" (Thévenin), 183–184
avant-garde, 78, 84, 85, 93, 122, 123, 126, 136, 175; in Colombia, 99; identity, 138; language, 172; and parody, 94; and the past, 128; poetry, 137; and technological imagery, 92; tone of, 132; in Uruguay, 95

Bacon, Francis, 91
Bailey, Beth, 158
Baker, Josephine, 59, 111
Balla, Giacomo, 123
Ballard, James G., xi, 51, 160, 177
Ballent, Anahí, 77
Balzac, Honoré de, 47
Bandeira, Manuel, 23, 85
Barbosa da Silva, Luiz, 69
Barbosa, Agenor, 88
Baron of Rio Branco, xvi, 80, 81
Barreiros, Dulce, 87
Barreto, Lima, xviii, 163, 164
Barros Rodrigues, J. C., 90
Barthes, Roland, 178, 193
Bastos Barros, Benedito (Belmonte), 169
Battles of the Flowers, 175
Baudelaire, Charles, xviii
Baudrillard, Jean, 43, 154
Bayart, Jean-François, 50

Bébéli (car builder), 143
Belasco, Warren J., 202n1
Benjamin, Walter, 47, 133
Bennett, Harry, 34
Bentham, Jeremy, 32, 38
Benz Victoria, 75
Benz, Karl, xv, 11, 16, 120, 175, 189
Bernard, Tristan, 161
bicycle, xix, 110, 111
Bierbaum, Otto Julius, 189
Bilac, Olavo, 178
Black Journey: Across Central Africa with the Citroën Expedition, 63
Bloy, Leon, 183
Boccioni, Umberto, 123
Borges, Jorge Luis, 78, 94
Bourke-White, Margaret, 144
Bradbury, Ray, 44
Brasier, 68
Brave New World, 36, 38, 39–41
Brazil, 68, 69–71, 80, 88, 89, 163; automobiles in, 101, 141; and changes in language, 136; and driver-pedestrian rivalry, 113; and emerging bourgeois class, 22; Ford company in, 22, 23; and official vehicles, 149. *See also specific cities*
Brilli, Attilio, 162
British Red Flag Act, 178
Brouhot (car builder), 142
Buck-Morss, Susan, 197n15
Budd Company, 111
Buenos Aires, 7, 79, 83, 116, 131, 138, 181–182
Bugatti automobile, 87, 92, 170, 171
Buick, xii, 75, 102, 115
Buick, David, 120
Burkett, Walter, 196n2
buses, 78, 92, 97, 118, 121, 130

cabeza de Goliat, La (Martínez Estrada), 131, 182–183
Cabriolet B14, 59
Cadillac, xii, 86, 95, 102, 191; "aristo-cratic" ads for, 144; as luxury vehicle, 110; Model A, 97; in poetry, 93
Calvino, Italo, 49, 50

Camus, Albert, 178
Canada, 15, 22, 127
Candido, Antonio, 85, 86
Cansinos Assens, Rafael, 135, 136
capitalism, xiv, 15, 36, 61, 191; and *Brave New World*, 41; Henry Ford on, 12; and work ethic, 10
car excursions, 127, 128, 189
car racing, 53–54, 77, 78, 80, 81, 83, 87, 90, 92, 96, 120, 132, 186–187. *See also* road trips/expeditions
car salesmen, 52–53
Caracas, Venezuela, 26, 99
Carrà, Carlo, 123
Carreño, Manuel Antonio, 157
cartoons, 184–185
Carvalho, Ronald de, 20
Casal Tatlock, Álvaro, 75
Casey, Roger, 50
Castañeda Aragón, G., 98
Castellanos, Pintín, 96
Castro Vicente, Miguel de, 42
Cavalheiro, Edgar, 198n7
Céline, Louis-Ferdinand, xviii, 36–38
Cendrars, Blaise, 89, 133
Centro Automovilista del Uruguay, 92
Chanel, Coco, 59
Chaplin, Charles, 10, 48, 58
Charron, Fernand, 189
chauffeurs, 92, 96, 116, 118, 126, 130, 142, 149, 156, 157, 162, 189, 190, 192; and automobility, 161; egoism of, 185; in literature, 164, 167, 168; prestige of, 101, 111; and super-chauffeur, 184; two types of, 161
Chevrolet, Louis, 120
Chevrolet cars, xii, 90, 91; ad for, 144; interest in, 22; in literature, 139; in Uruguay, 92; in Venezuela, 100, 101
China, xv, 22, 53
Churión, Juan José, 185
"Las cinco partes de la aventura," (González Tuñón), 7–8
Citroën 10 HP, 59, 61, 62
Citroën Trans-African Company, 63

Citroën cars, 22, 61, 62, 63, 193; half-tracks, 65, 67, 68
Citroën, André, 27, 57–58, 61, 62, 120; generosity of, 59; and publicity, 150; and visit to Ford factory, 110–111
civilization, 2, 18, 19, 36, 47, 101, 102, 164; American, 115; and the car, 124; and culture, 66; and destruction, 82; Ford's model of, 12–13; and speed, 130; and technology, 65. *See also* modernity; progress
Clair, René, 48
Clifford, James, 67
Colombia, 96–97
Columbia (car builder), 143
Communism, xiv, 7, 46
Communist Manifesto, 180
computers, xi, xvii, 130, 136
consumerism, 10, 12, 15, 44, 79, 146, 157, 181, 190; criticism of, 45; and demand for variety, 8
consumption, xviii, 2, 4, 12, 13, 61, 110, 115, 149, 155, 157; and the assembly line, 38; as based on novelty and difference, 18; cycle of, 78; and happiness, 150; and production, 25; technological, 147
Cortázar, Julio, 193
Coss, Joaquín, 104
Count Lesdain, 68, 69
Count Matarazzo Suplicy, 87
Coupé, 76
Courteville, Roger, 69–75
Cowan, Ruth Schwartz, 195n1
Cowley, Malcolm, 109
La croisère noire, 64
"Croisière Jaune" (Yellow Journey), 68
"Croisière Noire" (Black Journey), 63–66, 68
Cronenberg, David, 155
Crowther, Samuel, 8
Crystal Palace, 178
Cuba, 101–102
cultural production, xviii, 190
Cummings, E. E., xviii, 172
Curie, Pierre, 178

Daimler automobiles, 79, 89
Daimler, Gottlieb, xv
Dalí, Salvador, 193
Darío, Rubén, 93–95, 122, 184, 187
Davidson, Francisco, 83
Davis, Donald F., 196n22
De Diétrich (car builder), 143
De Dion Bouton, 96–97, 101
"De la vitesse" (Morand), 125
Dean, James, 178
Del pingo al volante (From the saddle to the steering wheel) (Kourí film), 95–96, 145
Delahaye, 143
Delaunay-Belleville automobile, 52
Delaunay, Sonia, 150
Deleuze, Gilles, 135
Delgado, José María, 27–28, 29
democracy, 4, 46, 191
Depression, 46, 101. *See also* Great Depression
Detering, Henry, 59
Detroit (Motor City), 3, 14, 18, 22, 26, 33; as city of hate and fear, 34; factory in, 27, 50; visit to, by Diego Rivera and Frida Kahlo, 30; visit to, by Edmund Wilson, 45
Dettelbach, Cynthia G., 192
Discépolo, Armando, 116
"Disorder and Early Sorrow," 111
Doctorow, E. L., 50
documentation, 64; cinematic, 68, 69, 83
Dodge factory, 33
"El dolor de ser Ford," (The pain of being a Ford) (Ferreiro), 93–94
Dos Passos, John, 46, 47, 48, 50
Downs, Linda, 31
driver, 190; arrogance of, 150; in art, 175–176; as enemy of walkers, 113; as king, 175; and relationship to object, 170; woman, 100, 161
driving, 26, 92, 140, 179–180
Duchamp, Marcel, 128
Duesenberg automobile, 110, 144
Duhamel, Georges, 180, 181
Durant, William, xv, 9
Dymaxion, 44

E. J. Brierre (car builder), 142
Edison, Thomas, xv, 1, 46
Edwards, Blake, 53
efficiency, 25, 27, 109; and the assembly line, 38
Ehrenburg, Ilya, 59, 61–62
electric motorcars, 103, 119
Elias, Norbert, xv, 195n13
Eliot, T. S., 8
Emperor Franz Joseph, 110
Engels, Friedrich, 15
England, xii, 15, 22, 76, 111–112, 119, 159, 175, 179
environment, xvii, 19, 41, 42
"A era do automóvel," (Rio), 136, 179
Eroica, 21
eroticism, xviii, 150, 171, 172
"Esthétique de la machine" (Léger), 142
Eugene O'Neill, 8
Europe, 16, 22, 35, 108, 109, 147, 148; Aldous Huxley in, 38; versus Americanism, 130; car factories in, 13; culture of, 72; and horses, 114; and Latin America, 79, 83. *See also specific countries*
Exhibition of Decorative and Industrial Arts (1925), 150
Exile's Return, 109

factory, 28, 29, 59, 60; in literature, 36–38. *See also* Ford factories
Fangio, Juan Manuel, 78, 87
Far East, 22. *See also specific countries*; Asia
Fascism, xiv, 191
Faurote, F. L., 21
Faurote, Ray L., 27
Fawcett, P. H., 72
Fernández Flórez, Wenceslao, 154, 156
Ferreiro, Alfredo Mario, 92–93, 94, 95, 173, 191
Fiat, 22, 60, 61, 111, 122
Fischer, Claude, xi, 145
Fisher, Harriet White, 189
500 Miles of Rafaela, 77
flappers, 102, 127, 143

Flivver King: The Story of Ford-America, The, (Sinclair) 48–49
flivver, 35, 48. *See also* Model T
Flusser, Vilém, 178
Folgore, Luciano, 52
Fon-Fon!, 149, 184
"Fon-Fon," 87–88, 139–140
Ford Bigode. *See* Ford Model T Moustache
Ford cars, 61, 65, 89, 95; in American Midwest, 112; in Batman, 158; in Cuba, 101, 102; in literature, 85, 90, 93, 139, 161, 191; in Venezuela, 100, 101
Ford factories, xii, 16, 17, 20–21, 23, 29, 45, 92; Citroën visit to, 110–111; description of, 27, 48; Foucault on, 33; as hell on earth, 34; in Latin America, 22, 23, 83; in literature, 36–37; as place of learning, 11–12. *See also* Highland Park factory; River Rouge factory
Ford Fiesta, 15
Ford Methods and the Ford Shops, 21
Ford Model A, 29
Ford Model T Moustache, 23, 44
Ford Motor Company, 2, 3, 4, 9, 14, 22, 26; account of employee's experience in, 33–34; agents of, 26; competing with General Motors, 35; and Diego Rivera, 30; and documentation, 29; expansion of, in Europe, 22; Ford Service Department of, 34; and interference in employees' lives, 33; in Latin America, 22, 76, 83, 104; as model society, 20; and the panoptical society, 39; and publicity, 5; seventy-fifth anniversary of, 31; Sociology Department of, 33, 34
Ford V-8, 31
Ford-Freud complex, 40
Ford-osis, 5
Ford, Edsel, 26, 30, 31, 48
Ford, Henry, xv, 1, 2, 3, 6, 24–25, 26, 27, 38, 41, 42, 45, 60, 120, 141, 145, 148, 190; and adaptation of colonial

roads, 100; Aldous Huxley on, 38–39; and American history, 5, 6; on the auto industry, 17; books on, 45–46; as Businessman of the Century, 2; and capitalism, 12, 15; as collector, 47; compared to Citroën, 58; and comparison to famous men, 45; contradictions of, 50; and the creation of a totalitarian ministate, 33; and cultural values, 47; as dangerous utopist, 38; depiction of, by Dos Passos, 46 47; depiction of, by González Tuñón, 7–8; and education, 11–12; and the Eiffel tower, 150; as hero of mobility, 4; and hygiene, 15, 16; and the "impure," 19; interests of, 5, 19; as legend, 2; on mass production, 4; negative attritubes of, 5; persona of, 49; personality of, 5, 49; in Peruvian indigenist poetry, 7; physical attributes of, 5; on progress and jobs, 18; and service, 13, 26; Sinclair's fictional biography of, 49; on social problems, 19; on thinking, 12; and time, 33; and the universal car, 16–17; on value of use, 13; viewpoints of, 9, 10, 12, 14; on work, 10–11

Fordism, xii, xvii, 3, 4, 6, 9, 10, 15, 19, 20, 44, 47, 60, 84; and Aldous Huxley, 39; and Americanism, 35; formula of, 6; global spread of, 23; and literary production, 93; and nationalism, 26; and Superman, 158; and Taylorism, 36; victory of, 190. *See also* post-Fordism

Fordlândia project, 26

Forest, Malcolm, 140, 175

Formula 1, 87

"Fornication of Automobiles," 160

Fortune magazine, xv, 2

Foucault, Michel, 32, 33

France, xii, xv, 15, 22, 119, 147, 175; and popularizing the car, 110. *See also* Paris

freedom, 90, 102, 109, 180; and the horse, 114; and movement, 137; and speed, 126, 169

French car builders, 142–143

Freud, Sigmund, 38, 177

Freyre, Gilberto, 113, 114–115, 121

Fuchs, Eduard, 47

Fuller, Buckminster, 44

futurism, 122, 123, 169, 177; Italian, 122, 160, 189; in Río de la Plata, 173

futurists, 28, 52, 85, 86, 91, 94

Gadda, Carlo Emilio, 161

Galíndez, Bartolomé, xviii

Galli, Gino, 123

Galsworthy, John, 8

García Heras, Raúl, 76

Gardel, Carlos, 144

Gartman, David, 205n15

Garvey, Pauline, xvi

General Motors Company, xv, 9, 26; in Latin America, 76, 83, 104; and yearly model change, 35, 146

Georges Richard (car builder), 142

Germany, xii, xv, 6, 15, 22, 57, 76, 100, 102, 147, 191; and fascination with New World, 6

Ghiano, Juan Carlos, 203n13

Giedion, Siegfried, 3

Gilroy, Paul, 207n1

Giovanni, Ramón, 96

Girondo, Oliverio, 8, 78

Gleizes, Albert, 128

Glidden, Charles L., 52

globalization, xvii, 15, 18, 65, 68, 78; of Ford company, 22

Gobron-Brillié (car builder), 143

Goldstein, Laurence, 21

Gómez de la Serna, Ramón, 135, 204n41

Gomez, Nick, 190

Gonçalves, Vergniaud, 68

Góngora, Luis de, 94

González Casanova, Manuel, 105

González Tuñón, Raúl, 7–8

Gorelik, Adrián, 77

Gramsci, Antonio, 35, 36

Great Depression, xiii, 45. *See also* Depression

Great Race, The, 53–54

Great Trans-Andean Highway, 100
Grunow, Hans, 54, 55
Guatemala, 149, 169
Gumbrecht, Hans Ulrich, 202n6, 204n36
Gutenberg, Johannes, 3

Haardt, Georges-Marie, 62, 65, 66, 68
Hall, Edward, 42
Hardy, Oliver, 144
Harlow, Jean, 144
Harvey, David, 3–4, 43
Haskell, Barbara, 29
Heard, Gerald, 38
Hearst, William Randolph, 47
Heidegger, Martin, 132–133
Heidtlinger, Victor, 54, 55
Helvetius, {Claude Adrien?}, 38
Hesse, Hermann, 8
Heterington, Kevin, 201n29
Hidalgo, Alberto, 123–124
Highland Park factory, 3, 20, 21; employee's experience in, 33–34; as model for Latin American factories, 22; visit to, by Chaplin, 48
Hill, Frank E., 22, 49
Hitler, Adolf, 77
Hobsbawm, Eric, xiii
Holzer, Marie, 123
El hombre que compró un automóvil, (Fernández Flórez), 154–156, 169–170
El hombre que se comió un autobús (poemas con olor a nafta), (The man who ate a bus [poems that smell of naphtha]) (Ferreiro), 92–93, 94, 173
Homer, 94
Hoover, Herbert, 20, 76
horse, 114, 115, 131, 182; and the car, 142; and the train, 189
"Hôtel Notre-Dame," 133–134
Hounshell, David, 197n7, 199n43
Hudson, W. H., 110
Hughes, Thomas, 6
Huidobro, Vicente, 128
humanism, 39, 181
Hupmobile, 83
Hutcheon, Linda, 94

Huxley, Aldous, xviii, 36, 38, 39
Huyke, Emilio, 103, 202n59
hygiene, 15, 17, 19, 149
hyperstimulation, 178

Iacovleff, Alexandre, 64
idealism, 33, 58, 69
Im Auto durch zwei Welten (Stinnes), 54, 57
imagination, 91, 165, 171
immobility, xiv, 84
Indianapolis 500, 77
individualism, xiii, 17, 34, 39, 41, 122, 123, 148; and the car, 190; economic, 35; and individual success, 4
individualization, 192, 196n13
industrialism, 29; of Detroit, 30
inhumanity, 33, 34, 37, 110
Italy, xii, 15, 22, 42

Jacob, Mary Jane, 198n21
James, Henry, 189
Jameson, Fredric, 196n17
Japan, xv, 13, 53, 61
Jenatzy, Camille, 119
Jordan car, 143
Jordan, Ned, 143–144
Jornal do Brasil, 1, 23, 69
Joyce, James, 8, 94
"Joyriding," 127

Kahlo, Frida, 30, 31
Kahn, Albert, 21
Kelly, Grace, 178
Kern, Stephen, 122, 203n22
Kettenman, Andrea, 31
Kienholz, Edward, 160
kinetic modernity, xiv, xviii, xix, 6, 19, 41, 54, 109, 131, 141, 169, 171, 193; and accidents, 177; and the chauffeur, 161; and the factory, 12; and idols, 2; definition of, xi; evolution of, 32; example of, 69; and kinetic vocation, 10; and shrinking the earth, 66; and speed, 119; and tradition, 107; trans-national trend of, 15; triumph of, 28, 75, 190

kinetic utopia, 15, 60, 73, 118
King João VI, 163
King, Stephen, 160
Klee, Paul, 133
Kline, R. 195n3
Koch-Grünberg, Theodor, 139
Konody, Paul, 189
Kopytoff, Igor, xvi–xvii, 196n15
Kotzent, Julio, 74
Kourí, Roberto, 95

La Salle automobiles, 148
Lagrée, Michel, 186
Landi, Francisco (Chico), 87
Lange, Dorothea, 144
language, xi, 84, 85, 93, 115, 129, 132,
    133, 135–136, 137, 168, 172, 175; and
    automotive jargon, 140; and cultural
    transformations, 135–137; industrial,
    138, 139; and religious terminology,
    140
Lartigue, Jacques-Henri, 176
Lasplaces, Alberto, 150–154
Latin America, xvi, 29, 44, 80, 113, 149,
    162; automobiles in, 75, 83, 91–92,
    191; cinematographic presence of car
    in, 144–145; and Ford market, 22;
    and linguistic loan words, 132. See
    also specific countries
Laurel, Stan, 144
Laurencin, Marie, 128
Law, Clara, 193
Lawrence, D. H., 38
Le Corbusier, 21, 44
Leblanc, Georgett, 120
Lefebvre, Henri, 43
Léger, Fernand, 142
Lempicka, Tamara de, 170, 171
Lenin, Vladimir, 7
León, Alfonso Ponce de, 178
Leone, Mario de, 160
Leuchsenring, Emilio Roig de, 102
Levassor, Émile, 53
Lévi-Strauss, Claude, 2
Levin, Orna Messer, 205n27
Lewis, David, 159
Lewis, Sinclair, 8, 45, 112

Lewis, Wyndham, 123
license plates, 80, 101, 183
Lima, Herman, 184–185
Lincoln cars, 86, 93, 95, 110, 148
Lindbergh, Charles, 58
Lindsay, Vachel, 20, 108
literary Fordism, 23, 93
literature, 7, 8, 23, 40, 93, 94, 154,
    172–173; and the automobile, xvii,
    xviii, 52, 84, 90, 102, 111, 117, 128,
    129–130, 182; on infidelity, 102; and
    social inequalities, 191; and technical
    vocabulary, 137; and technology, xiv,
    78, 84. See also specific authors and
    works; avant-garde; language; poetry
"Lo fatal," (Darío), 93, 94
"Loa en acción de gracias para mi
    voiturette 'Buick,' 13-331, Modelo
    1927" (Ferreiro), 173–174
Lobo, Mara, 191
Locomobile, 103
London, 102, 113, 147, 163, 178
loneliness, 39, 150
Lorraine Dietrich cars, 86
Lost Generation writers, 46, 109
"Louvação da tarde" (Andrade), 84–85
Ludwig, Emil, 110
Lynd, Helen, 112
Lynd, Robert, 112

Machado de Assis, Joachim Maria, 163
machines, 130, 138, 139; as destructive,
    181; linked to women, 172; per-
    sonified, 173; sexualized, 173. See also
    mechanization
Macunaíma (M. de Andrade), 13, 138
Madison, Charles, 33–34
Maeterlinck, Maurice, 120, 132, 176
"Manifesto of Futurism" (Marinetti),
    122, 124, 177, 189
Mann, Thomas, 111
Maples Arce, Manuel, 8, 104
Margarita Island, Venezuela, 100–101
Maria-Gasolina, xix
Mariátegui, José Carlos, 113
Marinetti, F. T., 51, 85, 94, 104, 122–123,
    125, 144, 177

Marot-Gardon (car builder), 143
Martin, John, 75
Martínez Estrada, Ezequiel, 44, 131,
    149, 163, 181–183
Martínez Villena, Rubén, 102
Marx, Karl, 7, 15
mass production, xii, 4, 6, 29, 39, 42,
    62; as beginning of modern history,
    40; and contradictions, 109; of Ford
    car, 47; and human cost, 48; in lit-
    erature, 84. *See also* assembly line;
    Fordism;
Massey, Beatrice, 189
Mateo (Discépolo), 116–118
materialism, xiii, xvii, 6, 11, 12, 46, 180
Mattarazzo, Francisco, 80
Matteoti, Giacomo, 59
Mayakovsky, Vladimir, 20, 191
McLuhan, Marshall, 42, 43, 169
mechanics, 11, 53, 54, 64, 69, 72, 74, 79,
    81, 83, 97, 103, 135, 156, 161–162, 167,
    168, 176; female, 171–172
mechanization, 10, 14, 25, 28, 104;
    Aldous Huxley's opinion of, 39; of
    daily life, 15, 138; in film, 48; Fordist,
    36; and resulting transformations,
    110; of society, 36, 38; of transporta-
    tion, 114. *See also* assembly line;
    mass production
Meckier, Jerome, 38
Meireles, Cecília, 191–192
memory, xix, 14, 91, 109, 115, 128, 134,
    196n23
Mercedes, 42, 61, 132; in poetry, 124, 125
Mexico, 30, 105, 127; automobiles in,
    101, 103–104; Ford company expan-
    sion to, 22, 104
MG, 111
Michelin Guide, 142, 176, 179
Michelin, 62, 81, 119, 143
Middle East, 22, 52, 55
Middletown (Lynd and Lynd), 112
Miller, Daniel, xvii
Milord, 76
Miranda, Carmen, 87, 144
Mirbeau, Octave, 120–121, 126, 161, 162,
    189

Miró Quesada, César Alfredo, 7
Miró, Joan, 162
Mistral, Gabriela, 8
mobility, xiv, xvii, 3, 4, 7, 8, 14, 42, 82,
    86, 110, 116, 128, 132, 143, 169, 176;
    aristocratic, 108; automotive, 127;
    celebration of, 51; and consumption,
    155; contradictions of, 111; demo-
    cratic, 108; glorified, 122; of goods,
    xvi; and idols, 2; importance of, 100;
    and love, 172; and modernity, 155;
    nature of, 116; principle of, 32; as a
    social function, 43; and tradition,
    xvii; and youth, 158
mobilization, xiv, 6, 10, 15, 32, 132; and
    civilization, 181; and economic and
    social conflicts, xv; planetary, 34;
    resulting problems of, 122; and tech-
    nology, 41
Model T, 2, 3, 6, 7, 14, 16, 17, 29, 42, 45,
    140, 145; announcement of, 8; and
    children, 58; in comics, 157; end of,
    35; as example of kinetic utopia, 15;
    exportation of, 4; as failure, 13; and
    foreign operations, 22; French ver-
    sion of, 111; and inhibiting sexuality,
    160; and interchangeability of parts,
    3, 4; introduction of, 39; in Latin
    America, 22, 26, 83, 92, 100, 191; as
    reference point, 20; tribute of, by E.
    B. White, 44–45; as universal car,
    17–18
modern era, 14, 16, 24, 25. *See also*
    modernity
"Modern Girls" (Rio), 163–164
modern subjectivity, 15, 32
Modern Times (Chaplin film), 10, 48
Modernism, 85, 94; Brazilian, 85, 86,
    139, 178
modernity, xix, 15, 34, 108, 115, 119,
    137; in Africa, 67; automobile as
    indicator of, xviii; and "Celtiberian
    backwardness," 147; and the chauf-
    feur, 161; and consumption, 155; in
    Cuba, 101; as defined by velocity,
    60; and Edison, 1; and language, 137;
    and mobility, 155; as process, xiv;

technological, 145. *See also* kinetic
modernity
modernization, 43, 72, 77, 88, 101; crisis
of, 42; emblems of, 137, 138; experience of, 137; of images, 111; industrial,
44; and poetic resistance, 98; of the
senses, 159; technological, 95; and
time and space, 98, 120
Monteiro Lobato, José Bento Renato,
24–25, 118
Montevideo, 95, 113, 115
Moog, Otto, 21
morality, 12, 15, 36, 123, 147, 148
Morand, Paul, 20, 110, 125, 126, 130; on
love and cars, 159
Morasso, Mario, 51, 131, 161
Moreira de Paula, Luiz, 74
Morris, William Richard, 111–112
motor shows, 149–150
motorcycle, xix, 80, 110, 124, 177
motorization, xv, xix, 6, 20, 33, 44, 49,
54, 67, 83, 101, 147–148; in Brazil, 136;
and culture, 102; fans of, 86; and
fiction, 111, 153; and Ford agents, 26;
and gender, 170; importance of, 65;
mark of, on literature, 174; versus
sedentary life, 126; and sexuality, 158;
trust in, 191; in Uruguay, 92; victory
of, 190
movement, xi, xiv, 4, 7, 29, 83, 111; and
art, xix; auto, as creator of, 104; cinematographic element of, 86; emotion of, 104; and eroticism, 172; and
freedom, 137; in gangster films, 145;
and kinetic modernity, 131; motorized, 91; power of, 35; in literature,
52; progress of, xv; and seduction,
171; triumph of, 3, 166; utopia of, 33.
See also mobility
movimiento V. P., El (The V. P. movement) (Cansinos Assens), 135–136
Mowry, George, 198n1
Mumford, Lewis, 15, 187
Mundo Ford magazine, 76
Musil, Robert, 111
Mussolini, Benito, 34 {"Mussolini of
Detroit" is all it says}

My Life and Work (Ford), 7, 8–9, 14–15,
18, 25, 39–40, 118, 145; and Aldous
Huxley, 38

Naòu, Liu, xviii
Nader, Ralph, 42
Naef, Ernest, 150, 168
Napoleon, 58
National Exposition in Rio de Janeiro
(1908), 80
nationalism, 26, 58, 135
nature, xviii, 85, 177, 193; and the auto-
mobile, 72; contemplation of, 86;
and culture, 73; and the horse, 114;
lack of awareness of, 115; loss of con-
tact of, 110; versus machine, 88; sub-
ordination of, 82; and technology,
181; as tourist attraction, 108
Navarro, Nicanor, 202n52
Nazareth, Ernesto, 144
Nazism, xiv
Néret, Gilles, 170
Netto, Américo R., 83, 86–87
Nevins, Allan, 22, 49
New Deal, 77
New York Times, 34, 109, 170
New York, 23, 25, 29, 31, 55, 102
New York–Paris race, 53, 54, 81
Nice, Hellé, 87
Nicholas II, 52
1950s, xvi, 49
1926 Frankfurt Automobile Exhibi-
tion, 55
Nizhny Novgorod, 53
nostalgia, xii, 66, 114, 115
Novo, Salvador, 104, 162, 190
Nye, David, 27

obsolecence, 10, 17, 35, 146, 157
"Oda al automóvil," 124–125
Okubaro, Jorge, 196n18
Oldsmobile automobiles, 75, 86, 143
omnibus, 130, 131
O'Neill, Eugene, 8
Orberg, Kristian, 26–27
Ortega y Gasset, José, 147, 148
Ortiz, Renato, 15, 196n23

Orwell, George, 36
Overland automobile, 100–101
overmodernity, 195n13

Packard automobile, 52, 93, 95, 173
Panhard & Levassor, 53, 89, 143
Panhard, 132
Panoplia lírica (Hidalgo), 123, 124
panopticism, 32, 36, 41
Paraguay, 91
Paris-Madrid race (1903), 187
Paris, xii, xiv, 42, 52, 59, 61, 67, 102, 126, 128, 133, 149, 163; as global automotive capital, 119; Latin American writers in, 168; in literature, 161
"Passe-Partout," 53
Patrocínio, José do, 178, 179
Pauls, Alan, 204n45
Pavlov, Ivan, 38
Payró, Julio, 135
pedestrians, xiii, xv, 113, 184; and accidents, 182. *See also* walking
Pérez, Louis, 101
Peru, 7, 22, 74
Pessoa, Fernando (Álvaro de Campos), 90–91
Peugeot, 22, 60, 79, 142, 143
photography, and eroticism of the car, 171–172
Picabia, Francis, 128
Picasso, Pablo, 135
Pierce-Arrow cars, 110, 144
Pierrot, George, 31
Pinch, T., 195n3
Piquero, José, 75
Pirandello, Luigi, 116
Placci, Carlo, 189
Poe, Edgar Allan, 193
"Poema del caminante," 98–99
Poirier, Léon, 64
Pollock, Jackson, 178
pornography, 112, 171
Portugal, 89, 90
post-Fordism, xvii, 20
Poulet, Georges, 134
poverty, 14, 19, 25, 105, 157, 168
Prado, Paulo, 89

pragmatism, 11, 190
Primeau, Ronald, 196n22
Prince of Wales, the, 59, 64
Princess Diana, 178
privacy, 16, 32, 33, 158–159, 165, 182
progress, xv, 22, 47, 72, 116, 150; automobile as symbol of, 101, 185; and criminality, 185; inevitability of, 82; and nature, 73
Prohibition, 127
proletariat, xvi, 7, 49, 191; erotic desire of, 174–175; and language, 137
Protestant work ethic, 10
Protos car, xvi, 80, 81, 82
Proust, Marcel, xviii, 134, 162
Puerto Rico, 102–103

Queen Mary of England, 59
Quiroga, Horacio, 167, 168

Racine car, 142
Radiguet, Raymond, 121 {first name per websearch, not on list}
radio, xiii, 20, 39, 62, 76, 108, 112, 125, 137, 138
railroads, xv, 24. *See also* trains
rationalization, 2, 3, 35, 36
Raymond, Roussel, 107, 108
realism, 29, 30, 116, 168
Reed, John, 5
Renault car, 22, 61, 69, 80, 93, 95, 143, 150, 170, 171
Renault-Ford car, 74
Renault, Louis, 63
Reyes, {Aurelio de los? per list?}, 105
Reynolds, John, 57–58, 62
Rio de Janeiro, 71, 72, 83, 122, 127, 162, 178, 183; and speed, 121
Rio, João do (Paulo Barreto), 82, 127–128, 136, 163, 164, 179
River Rouge factory, 20, 29, 30; description of, 21–22, 27, 28; as embodying the American Dream, 21; foundry of, 27, 29; working conditions in, 34–35
Rivera, Diego, 30, 31, 32
road trips/expeditions, 52, 53, 108; in

Africa, 62–66; in Asia, 68; Fawcett's, 72; in South America, 68–75, 83; Stinnes's, 54–57 roads/highways, xv, 76, 77, 110, 170; adaptation of, in Venezuela, 100; building of, 82; in Canada, 127; in Colombia, 97, 98; improvement of, in Brazil, 26; in Latin America, 127; opening of, 80, 83; in Puerto Rico, 102–103

Robinson Crusoe, 13

Robreño, Gustavo, 102

Rochet & Schneider (car builder), 143

Rockefeller family, 31

Roger, Philippe, 181

Rolls-Royce, 52, 148

Rosas, Enrique, 104, 105, 145

Rothschild firm, 81

Royal Dutch, 61

Russell, C. P., 20

Russia, 7, 53, 54

Russolo, Luigi, 123

Rybczynski, Witold, 3

safety, 13, 115, 142, 179, 180

"Sage of Dearborn," xv, 1, 2, 5. *See also* Ford, Henry

Saliba, Elias Thomé, 206n36

San Sebastián race, 187

Sandburg, Carl, 172

Santos Dumont car, 145

Santos Dumont, Henrique, 79, 80, 179

São Paulo, 23, 26, 70, 79, 83, 87, 138, 169, 175

Sarlo, Beatriz, 204n45

Sartre, Jean-Paul, 193

Schael, Guillermo José, 100

Scharff, Virginia, 161, 205n23

Sebald, W. G., 178

Sebreli, Juan José, 44

Séche, Alphonse, 39

Second Industrial Revolution, xi, 6

secularism, 28, 29, 41

Sedes, Héctor Suppici, 96

Seedorf, Marta-Emma, 74

semi-immobility, 33, 119

Senna, Ayrton, 178

Serpollet, 132

Severini, Gino, 123

sexuality, xi, xiii, xviii, 13, 36, 39, 138, 158–160, 162, 165, 166, 171, 172, 174, 190, 193

Sheeler, Charles, 29, 31, 32

Shershenevich, Vadim, 123

Siemen–Schucket Werke, 81

Silk, Gerald, 196n22, 223

Silva Brito, Mário da, 178

Simmel, Georg, 137

Sinclair, J. G., 112

Sinclair, Upton, 49, 50

Singapore, 12

Sironi, Mario, 123

Six twenty eight*628-E8, La* (Mirbeau), 161–162, 189

Skirius, John, 149, 198n5

Sloan, Alfred P., xv, 9

Sloterdijk, Peter, xiii–xiv

Smith, Julian, 204n2

social justice, 46, 150

Söderström, Carl Axel, 55, 57

Sonata interrumpida (Rodríguez Acosta), 101

Sorenson, Charles, 34

South America, xviii, 12, 68. *See also* Latin America

Soviet Union, 6, 7, 11, 22

Spain, 15, 22, 136, 147

speed (velocity), xviii, 4, 60, 65, 85, 94, 114, 115, 125, 176; and Americanism, 130; celebration of, in the arts, 122; and the city, 131; and civilization, 130, 131; as contradictory to progress, 119; and danger, 179; exhibitions of, 150; in films, 145; as foundation of modern civilization, 120; and freedom, 126, 169; and kinetic modernity, 119; limit, 137; and love, 169; and masculinity, 192; Morand on, 110; negative aspects of, 130; in poetry, 99, 125; philosophy of, 86; and pleasure, 179; preference for, 117, 119; satisfaction of, 148; sensation of, 102; symbol of, 113; viewed as mental illness, 121

Spengler, Oswald, 125

standardization, 3, 43, 44, 109, 181
steam engine, 3
steam-combustion automobiles, 103
Stein, Gertrude, 161, 181
Steinbeck, John, 160
Stevens, Wallace, 101
Stidger, William, 27
Stinnes, Clärenore (Clara), 27, 54–57
Stites, Richard, 7
stock market crash, 83, 92
streetcar, 96, 110, 117, 118, 124, 130, 137, 138, 148, 159, 165, 191
Stridentists, 104
Stuart, Aubrey, 24
Studebaker factory, 33
"Su chauffeur" (Quiroga), 167–168
Sward, Keith, 5
"Sybarites," 107

Talbot automobiles, 86
Tarkington, Booth, 141
taxis, 18, 59, 60, 61, 80, 97, 101, 113, 117, 130, 161, 164, 186
Taylor, Frederick, 33
Taylorism, 4, 6, 7, 15, 46, 48, 57, 122; and Fordism, 36
technology, xi, xii, xvii, 128, 130, 177; aesthetics of, 142; American, 26; and art, 133; and civilization, 64; democratizing element of, 192; era of, 31; and gender, 170; and homogenization, 67; and history, 6; influence of, on workers, 36; and inhumanity, 110; in literature, 84; and mobilization, 41; and nature, 88, 181; progress of, 38, 67; and social change, xi; of transportation, xix, 67; and violence, xiv; of war, 133. *See also* computers; literature, and technology
technosis, 130
telephone, xii, 1, 11, 136, 137, 193
10-HP, 101
Thévenin, Leopoldo (Monsieur Perrichon), 183–184
time and space, 11, 19, 28, 65, 66, 86, 98, 114, 119, 120, 122, 126, 136, 142, 148, 176, 184, 189

Tin Lizzie, 46, 48; in poetry, 93
Tin Pan Alley, 159
Torre, Guillermo de, 129
Toulouse-Lautrec, 175–176
Tourand (car builder), 143
tourism, 64, 98, 108, 126, 127; in Puerto Rico, 103; and roads, 182
Toyotaism, xv
traffic, xiii, 98; and accidents, xviii, xix, 19, 42, 92, 101, 177, 178, 182, 185, 186; jams, xiv, 19, 42; regulation of, 179; as school of learning, 181
trains, xvii, xix, 46, 108, 109, 121, 128, 145, 189, 190. *See also* railroads
transportation, xix, 159, 173, 176, 177–178; dependency on, 130; mechanization of, 114; modern, 83, 109; and the technological revolution, 122. *See also specific forms of transportation*
24-HP Napier, 52

"Um e outro" (Barreto), 164–167
United Kingdom, 111, 136. *See also* England
United States, xii, xiii, xv, xvi, 20, 76, 108, 147, 148, 157, 159; car purchasing in, 16; and car, as symbol of progress, 141; and car-related fatalities, 187; compared to Europe, 35, 130; and consumption, 110, 157; factories in, 13; and fascination with Japan, 6; and Fordist industrialization, 35; and horses and mules, 114; and the Model T in 1927, 3; and practical ideas, 10; traffic accidents in, 178
universal automobile, 15, 16, 17–18
Universal Exposition in Paris, 54
Urry, John, xvii
Uruguay, 22, 91, 95
utilitarianism, 12, 33
utopia, 40, 41

Valentino, Rudolph, 111, 144
Valle-Inclán, Ramón del, 135–136
Vallejo, César, 8, 149, 150, 168
Van Deventer, John H., 27
Vasconcelos, José, 114

Veblen, Thorstein, 13, 44
Vega, Garcilaso de la, 94
Velocidade (Almeida), 118, 130
Venezuela, 22, 99–101
Venice, 42, 108
Veríssimo, Érico, 191
Vermorel, 142
Verne, Jules, xiv, 17, 51, 53, 107
Vidales, Luis, 99
Vienna, 102
Villiers de l'Isle-Adam, Phillipe de, xv, 1
Viñas, Moisés, 105
Virilio, Paul, 126–127, 177
Voisin automobile, 59, 111
Voisin, Gabriel, 111
Voiture maximum, 44
voiturette, 95, 143, 173, 174
Volkswagen, 44
Vollrath, Ernesto, 104–105
Voyage au bout de la nuit, 36, 37–38

walking: art of, 113; in Brazil, 121; in Europe, 110, 122, 132 stigma of, 155. *See also* pedestrians
Watson, John, 38
Watt, James, 3
Weber, Max, 10
Welles, Orson, 47, 141
Wells, H. G., 31, 111

West, Nathanael, 178
Wharton, Edith, 189
Wheeler, Charles, 6
White, E. B., 44–45
Wilkins, Mira, 22
Wilson, Edmund, 45
Winged Victory of Samothrace, 51, 189
Wood, Grant, 178
Wood, Natalie, 53
Woolf, Virginia, 111
workers, 18, 36, 60; as terrorized, 33; in factory, 21, 33–34, 45
World War I, 6, 7, 36, 45, 58, 89, 92, 108, 109, 128, 161, 180; and American car sales in Latin America, 22; and the decadence of Europe, 72; and displacement of horse, 113–114; and trade relations with the Old World, 83
World War II, xvi, 157
Wright brothers, 46
Wright, Frank Lloyd, 46

Young, Diana, 58

Zamiatin, Yevgeni, 36
Zapiola, Guillermo, 95
Zayas, Marius de, 128
Zola, Émile, 59